25 JOBS
That Have It All

SECOND EDITION

Checkmark Books®

An imprint of Facts On File, Inc.

Checkmark Books
An imprint of Facts On File, Inc.
132 West 31st Street
New York NY 10001

25 Jobs that have it all.—2nd ed.
    p. cm.
  Includes bibliographical references and index.
  ISBN 0-8160-5478-9 (pbk.)
    1. Vocational guidance. 2. Occupations—Forecasting. 3. Employment forecasting.
  I. Title: Twenty-five jobs that have it all.

HF5382.A15
331.7'02—dc21   2003055061

Checkmark Books are available at special discounts when purchased in bulk quantities for businesses, associations, institutions, or sales promotions. Please call our Special Sales Department in New York at (212) 967-8800 or (800) 322-8755.

You can find Facts On File on the World Wide Web at http://www.factsonfile.com

Text design by David Strelecky

Cover design by Cathy Rincon

Printed in the United States of America

MP FOF 10 9 8 7 6 5 4 3 2 1

This book is printed on acid-free paper.

CONTENTS

INTRODUCTION

What does "a job that has it all" mean to you? If you think of a job with high pay, fast growth, and the most new positions available, then you're on the right track. With the help of data from the U.S. Department of Labor (DOL), we have assembled in this book a group of careers that offer all of these things. In *25 Jobs That Have It All, 2nd Edition* you'll find descriptions of the top careers in the fastest growing industries, such as computers, health care, education, design, business, and protective services. From typical salary ranges to advancement opportunities, this book outlines today's most promising careers and the skills and experience you will need to pursue them.

UNDERSTANDING THE "JOBS THAT HAVE IT ALL" CRITERIA

High pay. When you choose a career, compensation is always an important consideration. The careers in *25 Jobs That Have It All* offer salaries that are higher than the 2001 national average of $34,020 a year. A good example of a high-paying job profiled in this book is physician assistants, who earn a median income of $69,567 annually—more than double the national average.

Fast growth. According to the DOL, fast growing occupations "usually have better employment prospects and conditions more favorable for mobility and advancement." The careers in this book will grow faster than the average (an increase of 21 to 35 percent) or much faster than the average (an increase of 36 percent or more) over the next several years, according to the DOL. The average growth rate for all occupations is 15 percent, according to the *Occupational Outlook Quarterly*. Software engineer is an example of a career with "much faster than average" growth: The DOL predicts that this career will grow by a whopping 95 percent through 2010.

Two careers in this book are predicted to have only "about as fast as the average" growth: business managers and secondary school teachers. Although average growth is predicted for all types of business managers, faster than average growth is predicted for business managers in a number of industry sectors, including the service and information technology industries. Business managers earn some of the highest average salaries in the United States ($61,160 annually). Finally, a large number of jobs—464,000—are expected to be available for business managers through 2010.

Secondary school teachers are predicted to have employment growth of almost 17 percent through 2010—a percentage that is actually slightly higher than the average of 15 percent for all occupations. Over the next few years, secondary school teachers will be in greater demand for several reasons: a large proportion of current teachers will become eligible for retirement; enrollments are increasing, thus teacher–student ratios will need to be lowered; and certain states (for example, California, Texas, Arizona, and Georgia) are experiencing rapid population growth and will need more teachers. Secondary school teachers are also included in this book because they earn median salaries that are higher than the national average, and the field will offer more than 200,000 new positions through 2010.

Most new jobs. Many careers are fast-growing but do not offer a large number of openings to new job applicants. The career of desktop publishing specialist is a good example of this. Although much faster than average growth is predicted for this career, there will only be 25,000 new positions available to workers, which makes finding this type of job a real challenge. But the careers listed in this book offer fast growth in addition to the most new positions available to job seekers. These openings result from both employment growth and replacement needs (workers who retire, transfer to other occupations, or return to school). Registered nurses are included in the "most new jobs" category. The Department of Labor predicts that over 561,000 new positions will be available for registered nurses by 2010.

CHANGES TO THE SECOND EDITION

This edition of *25 Jobs That Have It All* offers a number of new features. Eight new careers have been added, including business managers, dental hygienists, medical record technicians, occupational therapists, pharmacy technicians, physician assistants, public relations specialists, and speech–language pathologists and audiologists. Seventy-five percent of these positions are in the health services industry. Employment in the health services industry is projected to increase 25 percent through 2010, adding about 2.8 million new jobs over the 2000–2010 period.

Each career article features a **Quick Facts** section that contains an overview of important facts for the career, such as suggested school subjects, minimum educational requirements, and salary ranges. Also new to this edition is a **History** section, which traces the career from its beginnings to its place in the modern work world. For more information on these new sections, see "How to Use This Book."

Throughout the book you will also find interviews with workers in these top fields. These interviews provide a personal glimpse into these careers as workers discuss the education or training they received for their jobs, how they got their jobs, typical job duties, recommended personal skills, and the future of their careers.

WHAT YOU WON'T SEE IN THE SECOND EDITION

The world of work is always changing, and some careers that were included in the first edition of *25 Jobs That Have It All* no longer meet all three criteria for inclusion: high pay, fast growth, and most new jobs. For example, growth has slowed considerably for computer programmers for several reasons: new technologies have eliminated some routine programming; there is now an increased availability of packaged software programs; and many computer users have become more sophisticated and are able to write and implement their own programs. Other careers that have been removed from this edition because they do not currently meet the "jobs that have it all" criteria are commodities brokers, electrical and electronics engineers, financial services brokers, hardware engineers, illustrators, physicians, and social workers.

HOW TO USE THIS BOOK

The **Quick Facts** section provides a brief summary of the career, including recommended school subjects, personal skills, work environment, minimum educational requirements, salary range, certification or licensing requirements, and employment outlook. This section also provides acronyms and identification numbers for the following government classification indexes: the Dictionary of Occupational Titles (DOT), the Guide to Occupational Exploration (GOE), the National Occupational Classification (NOC) Index, and the Occupational Information Network (O*NET)-Standard Occupational Classification System (SOC) index. The DOT, GOE, and O*NET-SOC indexes were created by the U.S. government; the NOC index is Canada's career classification system. Readers can use the identification numbers listed in the Quick Facts section to access further information on a career. Print editions of the DOT (*Dictionary of Occupational Titles*. Indianapolis, Ind.: JIST Works, 1991) and GOE

(*The Complete Guide for Occupational Exploration*. Indianapolis, Ind.: JIST Works, 1993) are available at libraries, and electronic versions of the NOC (http://www23.hrdc-drhc.gc.ca/2001/e/generic/welcome.shtml) and O*NET-SOC (http://online.onetcenter.org) are available on the World Wide Web.

The **Overview** section is an introductory description of the duties and responsibilities of this career. Also, if a career uses a variety of job titles, alternate career titles are presented in this section.

The Job section describes the primary and secondary duties of the job, the types of tools, machinery, or equipment used to perform this job, and other types of workers in this environment. Growing subfields or subspecialties of this career are also described in this section.

The **Requirements** section outlines the formal educational requirements—from high school diploma to advanced college degree—that are needed to work and advance in a field. This section provides information on how to learn new skills, for example, via on-the-job training, apprenticeships, the armed forces, or other activities, if a college degree is not required for a career. Certification, licensing, and continuing education requirements are also covered. Finally, the "Requirements" section recommends personal qualities that will give you an advantage in this field.

In the **Exploring** section, you will find a variety of ways to explore the field further before you invest time and money in education and training. Examples of how to do this include reviewing periodicals, working at summer jobs and programs, volunteering, joining associations and clubs, and pursuing hobbies related to the career.

The **Employers** section lists major employers of workers in the field and, when available, employment statistics for the career.

The **Starting Out** section offers tips on how to land your first job, be it through newspaper ads, the Internet, college placement offices, or through personal contacts. This section explains how the average job hunter finds employment in this field.

The **Advancement** section describes possible career paths and the experience you will need, such as advanced training or outside education, to move up in this field.

The **Earnings** section lists salary ranges for beginning, mid-range, and experienced workers in this field. Fringe benefits, such as paid vacation and sick days, health insurance, pensions, and profit-sharing plans, are also covered.

Work Environment describes a typical day on the job and the many work-environment factors you should consider when looking into a career. For example, is indoor or outdoor work required? Are safety measures and equipment such as protective clothing necessary? Is the job in a quiet office or on a noisy assembly line? What are the standard hours of work? Are overtime and weekend work required? Is travel frequent, and if so, to where and for how long?

The **Outlook** section predicts the potential long-term employment outlook for the field. Job growth terms follow those used in the *Occupational Outlook Handbook*.

In the last section, **For More Information**, you'll find the names, street addresses, phone numbers, email addresses, and websites of a variety of associations, government agencies, and unions. These organizations can provide further information regarding educational requirements, accreditation and certification, and other general information about the career you've just read about.

We hope that *25 Jobs That Have It All* will increase your knowledge of careers and help you make informed choices regarding your future. The world of work is always changing, and this book will help you see how your experience, skills, and interests might translate into one of today's most promising careers. To stay current on the latest information in a career field, be sure to contact the associations listed at the end of each article, talk with workers in these fields, and continue to research these careers and others via the Internet or your school or local library. Remember that the most informed and best educated workers will stay ahead in today's—and tomorrow's—job market.

Good luck with your career exploration!

ADVERTISING ACCOUNT EXECUTIVES

QUICK FACTS

School Subjects
Business
English
Speech

Personal Skills
Communication/ideas
Helping/teaching

Work Environment
Primarily indoors
Primarily one location

Minimum Education Level
Bachelor's degree

Salary Range
$20,000 to $55,940 to
$150,000+

Certification or Licensing
None available

Outlook
Faster than the
average

DOT
164

GOE
08.01.02

NOC
1122

O*NET-SOC
11-2011.00

OVERVIEW

The *advertising account executive* coordinates and oversees everything related to a client's advertising account and acts as the primary liaison between the agency and the client. Account executives are also responsible for building and maintaining professional relationships among clients and coworkers to ensure the successful completion of major ad campaigns and the assurance of continued business with clients. Advertising account executives and related workers hold 707,000 jobs in the United States.

HISTORY

When the advertising industry formally developed in the late 1800s, advertisers themselves were usually the ones who handled the promotion of their products and services, placing ads in newspapers and magazines in order to reach their customers. As the number of newspapers increased and print advertising became more widespread, however, these advertisers called on specialists who knew how to create and coordinate effective advertisements. One such specialist, the advertising account executive, emerged to produce and handle the ad campaigns for businesses.

Advertising agencies were commonly used by companies by the 1920s, and account executives worked for such agencies. Together with a staff of creative professionals, the account executive was able to develop an advertising "package," including slogans, jingles, and images, as well as a general campaign strategy. In addition, account executives did basic market research, oversaw the elements that went into a campaign, and worked hand-in-hand with writers and artists to develop effective ads for their client companies.

Today, account executives handle all aspects of their clients' ad campaigns. As a result, they bring to the job a broad base of knowledge, including account management, marketing, sales promotion, merchandising, client accounting, print production, public relations, and the creative arts.

THE JOB

Account executives track the day-to-day progress of the overall advertising campaigns of their clients. Together with a staff commonly consisting of a creative director, an art director, a copywriter, researchers, and production specialists, the account executive monitors all client accounts from beginning to end.

Before an advertising campaign is actually launched, a lot of preparatory work is needed. Account executives must familiarize themselves with their clients' products and services, target markets, goals, competitors, and preferred media. Together with the agency team, the account executive conducts research and holds initial meetings with clients. Then the team, coordinated by the account executive, uses this information to analyze market potential and presents recommendations to the client.

After an advertising strategy has been determined and all terms have been agreed upon, the agency's creative staff goes to work, developing ideas and producing various ads to present to the client. During this time, the account executive works with *media buyers* (who purchase radio and television time and publication space for advertising) in order to develop a schedule for the project and make sure that the costs involved are within the client's budget.

When the ad campaign has been approved by the client, production can begin. In addition to supervising and coordinating the work of copywriters, editors, graphic artists, production specialists, and other employees on the agency team, the account executive must also write reports and draft business correspondence, follow up on all client meetings, interact with outside vendors, and ensure that all pieces of the advertising campaign clearly communicate the desired message. In sum, the account executive is responsible for making sure that the client is satisfied. This may require making modifications to the campaign, revising cost estimates and events schedules, and redirecting the efforts of the creative staff.

In addition to their daily responsibilities of tracking and handling clients' advertising campaigns, account executives must also develop and bring in new business, keep up to date on current advertising trends, evaluate the effectiveness of advertising programs, and track sales figures.

REQUIREMENTS
High School

You can prepare for a career as an advertising account executive by taking a variety of courses at the high school level. Basic courses in English, journalism, communication, economics, psychology, business, social science, and mathematics are important for aspiring advertising account executives.

Postsecondary Training

Most advertising agencies hire college graduates whose degrees can vary widely, from English, journalism, or marketing to business administration, speech communications, or fine arts. Courses in psychology, sociology, business, economics, and any art medium are helpful. Some positions require a graduate degree in advertising, art, or marketing. Others may call for experience in a particular field, such as health care, insurance, or retail.

While most employers prefer a broad liberal arts background with courses in marketing, market research, sales, consumer behavior, communication, and technology, many also seek employees who already have some work experience. Those candidates who have completed on-the-job internships at agencies or have developed portfolios will have a competitive edge.

Other Requirements

While account executives do not need to have the same degree of artistic skill or knowledge as art directors or graphic designers, they must be imaginative and understand the communication of art and photography in order to direct the overall progress of an ad campaign. They should also be able to work under pressure, motivate employees, solve problems, and demonstrate flexibility, good judgment, decisiveness, and patience.

Account executives must be aware of trends and be interested in the business climate and the psychology of making purchases. In addition, they should be able to write clearly, make effective presentations, and communicate persuasively. It is also helpful to stay abreast of the various computer programs used in advertising design and management.

EXPLORING

Read publications like *Advertising Age* (http://www.adage.com), *Adweek* (http://www.adweek.com), and *Brandweek* (http://www.brandweek.com) to become familiar with advertising issues, trends, successes, and failures. Visit the Clio Awards website (http://www.clioawards.com). Clios are awards for advertising excellence and given each year in the categories of TV, print, outdoor, radio, integrated media, design, Internet, and student work. The site also has information about advertising and art schools, trade associations, and links to some of the trade magazines of the industry.

To gain practical business experience, become involved with advertising or promotion activities at your school for social events, sports events, political issues, or fund-raising events. If your school newspaper or yearbook has paid advertising, offer to work in ad sales.

EMPLOYERS

More than 700,000 advertising, marketing, promotions, public relations, and sales managers work in the United States. Advertising agencies all across the country and abroad employ advertising account executives. Of the 22,000 agencies in the United States, the large firms located in New York, Chicago, and Los Angeles tend to dominate the advertising industry. However, four out of five organizations employ fewer than 10 people. These "small shops" offer employment opportunities for account executives with experience, talent, and flexibility.

STARTING OUT

Many people aspiring to the job of account executive participate in internships or begin as assistant executives, allowing them to work with clients, study the market, and follow up on client service. This work gives students a good sense of the rhythm of the job and the type of work required of account executives.

College graduates with or without experience can start their job searches in their schools' career placement offices. Staff there can set up interviews and help polish resumes.

The advertising arena is rich with opportunities. When looking for employment, you don't have to target agencies. Instead, search for jobs with large businesses that may employ advertising staff. If you want to work at an agency, you'll find the competition for jobs intense. Once hired, account executives often participate in special training programs that both initiate them and help them to succeed.

ADVANCEMENT

Since practical experience and a broad base of knowledge are often required of advertising account executives, many employees work their way up through the company, from assistant to account executive to account manager and finally to department head. In smaller agencies, where promotions depend on experience and leadership, advancement may occur slowly. In larger firms, management-training programs are often required for advancement. Continuing education is occasionally offered to account executives in these firms, often through local colleges or special seminars provided by professional societies.

EARNINGS

According to the U.S. Department of Labor, advertising account executives earned between $29,210 to $125,880 annually in 2001, with median annual earnings of approximately $55,940. In smaller agencies, the salary may be much lower ($20,000 or less), and in larger firms, it is often much higher (over $150,000). Salary bonuses are common for account executives. Benefits typically include vacation and sick leave, health and life insurance, and a retirement plan.

WORK ENVIRONMENT

It is not uncommon for advertising account executives to work long hours, including evenings and weekends. Informal meetings with clients, for example, frequently take place after normal business hours. In addition, some travel may be required when clients are based in other cities or states or when account executives must attend industry conferences.

Advertising agencies are usually highly charged with energy and are both physically and psychologically exciting places to work.

The account executive works with others as a team in a creative environment where a lot of ideas are exchanged among colleagues.

As deadlines are critical in advertising, it is important that account executives possess the ability to handle pressure and stress effectively. Patience and flexibility are also essential, as are organization and time-management skills.

OUTLOOK

The growth of the advertising industry depends on the health of the economy. In a thriving economy in which many new products and services are developed and consumer spending is up, advertising budgets are large. Although the economy has been weaker as of late, the U.S. Department of Labor still predicts that employment for advertising account executives will grow faster than the average for all occupations through the next decade.

Most opportunities for advertising account executives will be in larger cities such as Chicago, New York, and Los Angeles, which enjoy a high concentration of business. Competition for these jobs, however, will be intense. The successful candidate will be a college graduate with a lot of creativity, strong communications skills, and extensive experience in the advertising industry. Those able to speak another language will have an edge because of the increasing supply of products and services offered in foreign markets.

FOR MORE INFORMATION

The AAF combines the mutual interests of corporate advertisers, agencies, media companies, suppliers, and academia. Visit its website to learn more about internships, scholarships, and awards.

American Advertising Federation (AAF)
1101 Vermont Avenue, NW, Suite 500
Washington, DC 20005-6306
Tel: 202-898-0089
Email: aaf@aaf.org
http://www.aaf.org

For industry information, contact:
American Association of Advertising Agencies
405 Lexington Avenue, 18th Floor
New York, NY 10174-1801
Tel: 212-682-2500
http://www.aaaa.org

BUSINESS MANAGERS

QUICK FACTS

School Subjects Business Computer science	**Certification or Licensing** None available
Personal Skills Helping/teaching Leadership/management	**Outlook** About as fast as the average
Work Environment Primarily indoors One location with some travel	**DOT** 189 **GOE** 11.05.01
Minimum Education Level Bachelor's degree	**NOC** 0611
Salary Range $38,710 to $61,160 to $136,760+	**O*NET-SOC** 11-1011.00, 11-1011.02, 11-1021.00, 11-3031.01

OVERVIEW

Business managers plan, organize, direct, and coordinate the operations of firms in business and industry. They may oversee an entire company, a geographical territory of a company's operations, or a specific department within a company. Of the approximately three million managerial jobs in the United States, about 60 percent are found in retail, services, and manufacturing industries.

HISTORY

Everyone has some experience in management. For example, if you schedule your day so that you can get up, get to school on time, go to soccer practice after school, have time to do your homework, and get to bed at a reasonable hour, you are practicing management skills. Running a household, paying bills, balancing a checkbook, and keeping track of appointments, meetings, and social activities are also examples of managerial activities. Essentially, the term "manage" means to handle, direct, or control.

Management is a necessary part of any enterprise in which a person or group of people are trying to accomplish a specific goal. In fact, civilization could not have grown to its present level of complexity without the planning and organizing involved in effective management. Some of the earliest examples of written documents had to do with the management of business and commerce. As societies and individuals accumulated property and wealth, they needed effective record-keeping of taxes, trade agreements, laws, and rights of ownership.

The technological advances of the Industrial Revolution brought about the need for a distinct class of managers. As complex factory systems developed, skilled and trained managers were required to organize and operate them. Workers specialized in a limited number of tasks that required managers to coordinate and oversee production.

As businesses began to diversify their production, industries became so complex that management tasks had to be divided among several different managers, as opposed to one central, authoritarian figure. With the expanded scope of managers and the trend toward decentralized management, the transition to the professional manager took place. In the 1920s, large corporations began to organize with decentralized administration and centralized policy control.

Managers provided a forum for the exchange and evaluation of creative ideas and technical innovations. Eventually these management concepts spread from manufacturing and production to office, personnel, marketing, and financial functions. Today, management is more concerned with results than activities, taking into account individual differences in work styles.

THE JOB

Management is found in every industry, including food, clothing, banking, education, health care, and business services. All types of businesses have managers to formulate policies and administer the firm's operations. Managers may oversee the operations of an entire company, a geographical territory of a company's operations, or a specific department, such as sales and marketing.

Business managers direct a company's or a department's daily activities within the context of the organization's overall plan. They implement organizational policies and goals. This may involve developing sales or promotional materials, analyzing the department's budgetary requirements, and hiring, training, and supervising staff. Business managers are often responsible for long-range planning for their company or department. This involves setting goals for the organization and developing a workable plan for meeting those goals.

A manager responsible for a single department might work to coordinate his or her department's activities with other departments. A manager responsible for an entire company or organization might work with the managers of various departments or locations to oversee and coordinate the activities of all departments. If the business is privately owned, the owner may be the manager. In a large corporation, however, there will be a management structure above the business manager.

Jeff Bowe is the Midwest General Manager for Disc Graphics, a large printing company headquartered in New York. Bowe oversees all aspects of the company's Indianapolis plant, which employs about 50 people. When asked what he is responsible for, Bowe answers, "Everything that happens in this facility." Specifically, that includes sales, production, customer service, capital expenditure planning, hiring and training employees, firing or downsizing, and personnel management.

The hierarchy of managers includes top executives such as the *president*, who establishes an organization's goals and policies along with others, such as the chief executive officer, chief financial officer, chief information officer, executive vice president, and the board of directors. Top executives plan business objectives and develop policies to coordinate operations between divisions and departments and establish procedures for attaining objectives. Activity reports and financial statements are reviewed to determine progress and revise operations as needed. The president also directs and formulates funding for new and existing programs within the organization. Public relations plays a big part in the lives of executives as they deal with executives and leaders from other countries or organizations and with customers, employees, and various special interest groups.

The top-level managers for Bowe's company are located in the company's New York headquarters. Bowe is responsible for reporting certain information about the Indianapolis facility to them. He may also have to work collaboratively with them on certain projects or plans. "I have a conversation with people at headquarters about every two to three days," he says. "I get corporate input on very large projects. I would also work closely with them if we had some type of corporate-wide program we were working on—something where I would be the contact person for this facility."

Although the president or chief executive officer retains ultimate authority and responsibility, Bowe is responsible for overseeing the day-to-day operations of the Indianapolis location. A manager in this position is sometimes called a *chief operating officer* or *COO*. Other duties of a COO may include serving as chairman of committees, such as management, executive, engineering, or sales.

Some companies have an *executive vice president,* who directs and coordinates the activities of one or more departments, depending on the size of the organization. In very large organizations, the duties of executive vice presidents may be highly specialized. For example, they may oversee the activities of business managers of marketing, sales promotion, purchasing, finance, personnel training, industrial relations, administrative services, data processing, property management, transportation, or legal services. In smaller organizations, an executive vice president might be responsible for a number of these departments. Executive vice presidents also assist the chief executive officer in formulating and administering the organization's policies and developing its long-range goals. Executive vice presidents may serve as members of management committees on special studies.

Companies may also have a *chief financial officer* or *CFO.* In small firms, the CFO is usually responsible for all financial management tasks, such as budgeting, capital expenditure planning, cash flow, and various financial reviews and reports. In larger companies, the CFO may oversee financial management departments, to help other managers develop financial and economic policy and oversee the implementation of these policies.

Chief information officers, or *CIOs,* are responsible for all aspects of their company's information technology. They use their knowledge of technology and business to determine how information technology can best be used to meet company goals. This may include researching, purchasing, and overseeing the setup and use of technology systems, such as Intranet, Internet, and computer networks. These managers sometimes take a role in implementing a company's website.

In companies that have several different locations, managers may be assigned to oversee specific geographic areas. For example, a large retailer with facilities all across the nation is likely to have a number of managers in charge of various territories. There might be a Midwest manager, a Southwest manager, a Southeast manager, a Northeast manager, and a Northwest manager. These managers are often called *regional* or *area managers*. Some companies break their management territories up into even smaller sections, such as a single state or a part of a state. Managers overseeing these smaller segments are often called *district managers* and typically report directly to an area or regional manager.

INTERVIEW: Business Manager

Julie LaFore is a Territory Manager for Weight Watchers, International. She spoke with the editors of 25 Jobs That Have It All *about her career.*

Q. Please briefly describe your primary and secondary job duties.

A. My primary job duties include managing day-to-day operations of a territory consisting of 28 locations and 150 employees in the North Chicagoland area, as well as developing business plans and strategies to grow our business going forward. Secondary job duties support our growth and development. These include interviewing and hiring talented staff and scouting for new, as well as improved, real estate opportunities. I also coach and help develop current staff and assist in creating communication networks so staff teams can work well together as well as communicate their needs to me and each other. Managing the flow of new hire paperwork, payroll, and business reports to pinpoint opportunities also fall into my secondary job duties.

I travel throughout the North Chicagoland area about 60–70% of my workweek. We also travel out of state three to four times a year for regional and national meetings.

Q. What was your college major? How did you train for this job?

A. I attended the University of Wisconsin-Madison and majored in journalism with an emphasis on public relations and broadcast news. I trained for my job at Weight Watchers in the exact same manner as I trained for my previous job with the company I started with fresh out of college. I interviewed for a part-time position with a company I found interesting, and the entry-level opportunities at both companies turned into full-time positions with much higher levels of responsibility.

Q. Did you participate in any internships while you were in college?

A. Although I did not participate in any internships during college, I interviewed and was chosen as a House Fellow for the Division of University Housing at UW-Madison my sophomore year. House Fellows were not permitted to participate in outside internships at that time. These positions offered intensive training for supervising co-ed floors of 80 residents in the undergraduate residence halls and provided a wealth of experience in working with diverse communities and managing challenging situations. As well as paying our room, board, and tuition, the Division of University Housing gave us unique opportunities to represent Housing on University committees. I was selected as a member of one of Chancellor Donna Shalala's Steering Committees.

Q. How/where did you get your first job in this field? What did you do?

A. After graduating from college in a tight job market with no internship experience in my field, I took a part-time job in the rental car industry booking reservations on the phone, figuring I would have plenty of time to interview for my "real" job. After a week, I was working full time with an offer for placement in operations management within a few months. Over the course of the next 10 years I was promoted several times and eventually became a revenue manager. In this position, I controlled pricing and assisted Hawaii and Florida in developing and achieving their business plans at our corporate headquarters. At the same time, I joined Weight Watchers to lose a few pounds and was recruited to work with them part time as a receptionist. I assisted members at the front desk and at the scale, which was a lot fun and quite rewarding. As time progressed, I had a desire to get out from behind a desk 100% of my workweek and then the territory manager position at Weight Watchers became available.

Q. What kind of sources were/are available to someone looking to get into business management?

A. I think the best sources of getting into management, or any ideal job you're aiming for after college, is to get into the company you're interested in on the ground floor and give your best effort—especially when it comes to teamwork and flexibility.

Q. What are the most important personal and professional qualities for people in your career?

A. The most important personal qualities for people in management are creativity, flexibility, a sense of humor, and your own personal commitment and dedication to your job and the company. If your staff knows you enjoy your job and will go the extra mile when things get tough, they will be there for you when you need them and together you will achieve your goals. The most important professional qualities in management are communication and leading by example. Being comfortable with written and verbal communication, whether for a big or small audience, really helps make the job much easier. Keeping a large group of employees informed and comfortable approaching each other and you are valuable skills to master. If you aren't living the standards you set for your group, it's tough for anyone to grow and advance. Your group won't reach their goals and neither will you.

Q. What are some of the pros and cons of being a business manager?

A. The pros of my job include the opportunity to work with such a wonderfully diverse and dedicated staff and colleagues. We have everyone from teachers and actors to journalists and marketing directors among our part-time staff, and all of them are working to help others change their lives. It doesn't matter what kind of stress could be going on during any given day, you just can't leave a Weight Watchers meeting without being inspired by the dedication of the staff and the fact that they change lives on a daily basis. The cons are small in comparison. There are, of course, less exciting tasks that go along with management. These include a good amount of paperwork and the occasional disciplinary action that needs to be taken care of in a timely manner.

Q. What is the most important piece of advice that you have to offer college students as they graduate and look for jobs in business management?

A. My advice to anyone interested in management is to pick a field you're passionate about! Plan on investing a lot of hours early on and work all levels of the positions you'll be managing. Then you should spend even more hours getting to know your staff and set your expectations by getting in there and leading by example. In time, you will find a comfort level in your position, start to develop your staff, and delegate tasks to them so they are able to grow and strengthen their skills as well as help you keep your job manageable. Then you get to stand back and really appreciate your team and what they do each day to help your team's customers. You can take pride in their work as well as your accomplishments.

REQUIREMENTS
High School

The educational background of business managers varies as widely as the nature of their diverse responsibilities. Many have a bachelor's degree in liberal arts or business administration. If you are interested in a business managerial career, you should start preparing in high school by taking college preparatory classes. According to Jeff Bowe, your best bet academically is to get a well-rounded education. Because communication is important, take as many English classes as possible. Speech classes are another way to improve your communication skills. Courses in mathematics, business, and computer science are also excellent choices to help you prepare for this career. Finally, Bowe recommends taking a foreign language. "Today speaking a foreign language is more and more important," he says. "Which language is not so important. Any of the global languages are something you could very well use, depending upon where you end up."

Postsecondary Training

Business managers often have a college degree in a subject that pertains to the department they direct or the organization they administer, for example, accounting for a business manager of finance, computer science for a business manager of data processing, engineering or science for a director of research and development. As computer usage grows, many managers are expected to have experience with the information technology that applies to their field.

Graduate and professional degrees are common. Bowe, along with many managers in administrative, marketing, financial, and manufacturing activities, has a master's degree in business administration. Managers in highly technical manufacturing and research activities often have a master's degree or doctorate in a technical or scientific discipline. A law degree is mandatory for business managers of corporate legal departments, and hospital managers generally have a master's degree in health services administration or business administration. In some industries, such as retail trade or the food and beverage industry, competent individuals without a college degree may become business managers.

Other Requirements

There are a number of personal characteristics that can help one be a successful business manager, depending upon the specific responsibilities of the position. A manager who oversees other employees should have good communication and interpersonal skills. The ability to delegate work is another important personality trait of a good manager. The ability to think on your feet is often key in business management, according to Bowe. "You have to be able to think extremely quickly and not in a reactionary manner," he says. Bowe also says that a certain degree of organization is important, since managers are often managing several different things simultaneously. Other traits considered important for top executives are intelligence, decisiveness, intuition, creativity, honesty, loyalty, a sense of responsibility, and planning abilities. Finally, the successful manager should be flexible and interested in staying abreast of new developments in his or her industry. "In general, you need to be open to change because your customers change, your market changes, your technology changes," he says. "If you won't try something new, you really have no business being in management."

EXPLORING

To get experience as a manager, start with your own interests. Whether you're involved in drama, sports, school publications, or a part-time job, there are managerial duties associated with any organized activity. These can involve planning, scheduling, managing other workers or volunteers, fund-raising, or budgeting. Local businesses also have job opportunities through which you can get firsthand knowledge and experience of management structure. If you can't get an actual job, at least try to schedule a meeting with a business manager to talk with him or her about the career. Some schools or community organizations arrange job shadowing, where you can spend part of a day observing a selected employee to see what his or her job is like. Joining Junior Achievement (http://www.ja.org) is another excellent way to get involved with local businesses and learn about how they work. Finally, take every opportunity to work with computers, since computer skills are vital to today's business world.

EMPLOYERS

There are approximately 3 million general managers and executives employed in the United States. These jobs exist in every industry. However, approximately 60 percent are in the manufacturing, retail, and service industries. In a 1998 survey of members of the American Management Association, 42.6 percent of the 4,585 participants worked in manufacturing. Approximately 32 percent worked in the for-profit services industry.

Virtually every business in the United States has some form of managerial positions. Obviously, the larger the company is, the more managerial positions it is likely to have. Another factor is the geographical territory covered by the business. Companies doing business in larger geographical territories are likely to have more managerial positions than those with smaller territories.

STARTING OUT

Generally you will need a college degree, although many retail stores, grocery stores, and restaurants hire promising applicants who have only a high school diploma. Job seekers usually apply directly to the manager of such places. Your college placement office is often the best place to start looking for these positions. A number of listings can also be found in newspaper help wanted ads.

Many organizations have management-trainee programs that college graduates can enter. Such programs are advertised at college career fairs or through college job placement services. However, these management-trainee positions in business and government are often filled by employees who already work for the organization and who have demonstrated management potential. Jeff Bowe suggests researching the industry you are interested in to find out what might be the best point of entry for that field. "I came into the printing company through customer service, which is a good point of entry because it's one of the easiest things to learn," he says. "Although it requires more technical know-how now than it did then, customer service is still not a bad entry point for this industry."

ADVANCEMENT

Most business management and top executive positions are filled by experienced lower level managers and executives who display valuable managerial traits, such as leadership, self-confidence, creativity, motivation, decisiveness, and flexibility. In small firms advancement to a higher management position may come slowly, while promotions may occur more quickly in larger firms.

An employee can accelerate his or her advancement by participating in different kinds of educational programs available for managers. These are often paid for by the organization. Company training programs broaden knowledge of company policy and operations. Training programs sponsored by industry and trade associations and continuing education courses in colleges and universities can familiarize managers with the latest developments in management techniques. In recent years, large numbers of middle managers were laid off as companies streamlined operations. Competition for jobs is keen, and business managers committed to improving their knowledge of the field and of related disciplines—especially computer information systems—will have the best opportunities for advancement.

Business managers may advance to executive or administrative vice president. Vice presidents may advance to peak corporate positions such as president or chief executive officer. Presidents and chief executive officers, upon retirement, may become members of the board of directors of one or more firms. Sometimes business managers establish their own firms.

EARNINGS

Salary levels for business managers vary substantially, depending upon the level of responsibility, length of service, and type, size, and location of the organization. Top-level managers in large firms can earn much more than their counterparts in small firms. Also, salaries in large metropolitan areas, such as New York City, are higher than those in smaller cities.

According to the U.S. Department of Labor, general managers had a median yearly income of $61,160 in 2000. To show the range of earnings for general managers, however, the Department notes that those in the computer and data processing industry had an annual median of $101,340; those in public relations, $84,610; and those at eating and drinking establishments, $38,710.

Chief executives earned a median of $113,810 annually in 2000. And again, salaries varied by industry. For example, the median yearly salary for those in management and public relations was $136,760, while those at commercial banks earned a median of $120,840. A survey by Abbott, Langer, & Associates found that chief executives working for nonprofits had a median yearly salary of $75,000 in 2000. Some executives, however, earn hundreds of thousands of dollars more than this annually.

Benefit and compensation packages for business managers are usually excellent and may even include such things as bonuses, stock awards, company-paid insurance premiums, use of company cars, paid country club memberships, expense accounts, and generous retirement benefits.

WORK ENVIRONMENT

Business managers are provided with comfortable offices near the departments they direct. Top executives may have spacious, lavish offices and may enjoy such privileges as executive dining rooms, company cars, country club memberships, and liberal expense accounts.

Managers often travel between national, regional, and local offices. Top executives may travel to meet with executives in other corporations, both within the United States and abroad. Meetings and conferences sponsored by industries and associations occur regularly and provide invaluable opportunities to meet with peers and keep up with the latest developments. In large corporations, job transfers between the parent company and its local offices or subsidiaries are common.

Business managers often work long hours under intense pressure to meet, for example, production and marketing goals. Jeff Bowe's average workweek consists of 55 to 60 hours at the office. This is not uncommon—in fact, some executive spend up to 80 hours working each week. These long hours limit time available for family and leisure activities.

OUTLOOK

Overall, employment of business managers and executives is expected to grow about as fast as the average, according to the U.S. Bureau of Labor Statistics. Many job openings will be the result of managers being promoted to better positions, retiring, or leaving their positions to start their own businesses. Even so, the compensation and prestige of these positions make them highly sought-after, and competition to fill openings will be intense.

Projected employment growth varies by industry. For example, employment in the service industry, particularly business services, should increase faster than the average, while employment in some manufacturing industries is expected to decline.

The outlook for business managers is closely tied to the overall economy. When the economy is good, businesses expand both in terms of their output and the number of people they employ, which creates a need for more managers. In economic downturns, businesses often lay off employees and cut back on production, which lessens the need for managers.

FOR MORE INFORMATION

For news about management trends, resources on career information and finding a job, and an online job bank, contact:

American Management Association
1601 Broadway
New York, NY 10019-7420
Tel: 800-262-9699
http://www.amanet.org

For brochures on careers in management for women, contact:

Association for Women in Management
927 15th Street, NW, Suite 1000
Washington, D.C. 20005
Tel: 202-659-6364
Email: awm@benefits.net
http://www.womens.org

For information about programs for students in kindergarten through high school, and information on local chapters, contact:

Junior Achievement
One Education Way
Colorado Springs, CO 80906
Tel: 719-540-8000
Email: newmedia@ja.org
http://www.ja.org

For a brochure on management as a career, contact:

National Management Association
2210 Arbor Boulevard
Dayton, OH 45439
Tel: 937-294-0421
Email: nma@nma1.org
http://nma1.org

COLLEGE PROFESSORS

QUICK FACTS

School Subjects
English
History
Speech

Personal Skills
Communication/ideas
Helping/teaching

Work Environment
Primarily indoors
Primarily one location

Minimum Education Level
Master's degree

Salary Range
$35,790 to $60,000 to $108,000+

Certification or Licensing
None available

Outlook
Faster than the average

DOT
090

GOE
11.02.01

NOC
4121

O*NET-SOC
25-1011.00, 25-1021.00,
25-1022.00, 25.1031.00,
25-1032.00, 25-1041.00,
25-1042.00, 25-1043.00,
25-1051.00, 25-1052.00,
25-1053.00, 25-1054.00,
25-1061.00, 25-1062.00,
25-1063.00, 25-1064.00,
25-1065.00, 25-1066.00,
25-1067.00, 25-1071.00,
25-1072.00, 25-1081.00,
25-1082.00, 25-1111.00,
25-1112.00, 25-1113.00,
25-1121.00, 25-1122.00,
25-1123.00, 25-1124.00,
25-1125.00, 25-1126.00,
25-1191.00, 25-1192.00,
25-1193.00, 25-1194.00

OVERVIEW

College professors instruct undergraduate and graduate students in specific subjects at colleges and universities. They are responsible for lecturing classes, leading small seminar groups, and creating and grading examinations. They also may conduct research, write for publication, and aid in administration. Approximately 1.3 million postsecondary teachers are employed in the United States.

HISTORY

The concept of colleges and universities goes back many centuries. These institutions evolved slowly from monastery schools, which trained a select few for certain professions, notably theology. Outside of academia, the terms *college* and *university* have become virtually interchangeable in America, although originally they designated two very different kinds of institutions.

Two of the most notable early European universities were the University of Bologna in Italy, thought to have been established in the 12th century, and the University of Paris, which was chartered in 1201. These universities were considered to be the models after which other European universities were patterned. Oxford University in England was probably established during the 12th century. Oxford served as a model for early American colleges and universities and today is still considered one of the world's leading institutions.

Harvard, the first U.S. college, was established in 1636. Its stated purpose was to train men for the ministry; the early colleges were all established for religious training. With the growth of state-supported institutions in the early 18th century, the process of freeing the curriculum from ties with the church began. The University of Virginia established the first liberal arts curriculum in 1825, and these innovations were later adopted by many other colleges and universities.

Although the original colleges in the United States were patterned after Oxford University, they later came under the influence of German universities. During the 19th century, more than 9,000 Americans went to Germany to study. The emphasis in German universities was on the scientific method. Most of the people who had studied in Germany returned to the United States to teach in universities, bringing this objective, factual approach to education and to other fields of learning.

In 1833, Oberlin College in Oberlin, Ohio became the first college founded as a coeducational institution. In 1836, the first women-only college, Wesleyan Female College, was founded in Macon, Georgia.

The junior college movement in the United States has been one of the most rapidly growing educational developments. Junior colleges first came into being just after the turn of the 20th century.

THE JOB

College and university faculty members teach at junior colleges or at four-year colleges and universities. At four-year institutions, most faculty members are *assistant professors, associate professors,* or *full professors.* These three types of professorships differ in status, job responsibilities, and salary. Assistant professors are new faculty members who are working to get tenure (status as a permanent professor); they seek to advance to associate and then to full professorships.

College professors perform three main functions: teaching, advising, and research. Their most important responsibility is to teach students. Their role within a college department will determine the level of courses they teach and the number of courses per semester. Most professors work with students at all levels, from college freshmen to graduate students. They may head several classes a semester or only a few a year. Some of their classes will have large enrollment, while graduate seminars may consist of only 12 or fewer students. Though college professors may spend fewer than 10 hours a week in the actual classroom, they spend many hours preparing lectures and lesson plans, grading papers and exams, and preparing grade reports. They also schedule office hours during the week to be available to students outside of the lecture hall, and they meet with students individually throughout the semester. In the classroom, professors lecture, lead discussions, administer exams, and assign textbook reading and other research. In some courses, they rely heavily on laboratories to transmit course material.

Another important professorial responsibility is advising students. Not all faculty members serve as advisers, but those who do must set aside large blocks of time to guide students through the program. College professors who serve as advisers may have any number of students assigned to them, from fewer than 10 to more than 100, depending on the administrative policies of the college. Their responsibility may involve looking over a planned program of studies to make sure the students meet requirements for graduation, or it may involve working intensively with each student on many aspects of college life.

The third responsibility of college and university faculty members is research and publication. Faculty members who are heavily involved in research programs sometimes are assigned a smaller teaching load. College professors publish their research findings in various scholarly journals. They also write books based on their research or on their own knowledge and experience in the field. Most textbooks are written by college and university teachers. In arts-based programs, such as master's of fine arts programs in painting, writing, and theater, professors practice their craft and exhibit their art work in various ways. For example, a painter or photographer will have gallery showings, while a poet will publish in literary journals.

Publishing a significant amount of work has been the traditional standard by which assistant professors prove themselves worthy of becoming permanent, tenured faculty. Typically, pressure to publish is greatest for assistant professors. Pressure to publish increases again if an associate professor wishes to be considered for a promotion to full professorship.

In recent years, some liberal arts colleges have recognized that the pressure to publish is taking faculty away from their primary duties to the students, and these institutions have begun to place a decreasing emphasis on publishing and more on performance in the classroom. Professors in junior colleges face less pressure to publish than those in four-year institutions.

Some faculty members eventually rise to the position of *department chair,* where they govern the affairs of an entire department, such as English, mathematics, or biological sciences. Department chairs, faculty, and other professional staff members are aided in their myriad duties by *graduate assistants,* who may help develop teaching materials, conduct research, give examinations, teach lower level courses, and carry out other activities.

Some college professors may also conduct classes in an extension program. In such a program, they teach evening and weekend courses for the benefit of people who otherwise would not be able to take advantage of the institution's resources. They may travel away from the campus and meet with a group of students at another location. They may work full time for the extension division or may divide their time between on-campus and off-campus teaching.

Distance learning programs, an increasingly popular option for students, give professors the opportunity to use today's technologies to remain in one place while teaching students who are at a variety of locations simultaneously. The professor's duties, like those when teaching correspondence courses conducted by mail, include grading work that students send in at periodic intervals and advising students of their progress. Computers, the Internet, email, and video conferencing, however, are some of the technology tools that allow professors and students to communicate in "real time" in a virtual classroom setting. Meetings may be scheduled during the same time as traditional classes or during evenings and weekends. Professors who do this work are sometimes known as *extension work, correspondence,* or *distance learning instructors.* They may teach online courses in addition to other classes or may have distance learning as their major teaching responsibility.

The *junior college instructor* has many of the same kinds of responsibilities as the teacher in a four-year college or university. Because junior colleges offer only a two-year program, they teach only undergraduates.

INTERVIEW: College Professor

Dr. Wendy Cotter, Ph.D., C.S.J., is an Associate Professor of Scripture in the Theology Department of Loyola University in Chicago, Illinois. Her specialties include the Synoptic Gospels, Greco-Roman Antiquity, First Generation Christianity, and Miracle Narratives. Dr. Cotter spoke with the editors of 25 Jobs That Have It All *about her career as a theology professor.*

Q. Please briefly describe your work.

A. I have primary duties as a teaching professor; as a publishing scholar, with my own associations in the larger world of the biblical guild; and I have duties to my University colleagues to sit on committees to facilitate the programs of the University and the Department. Then, there are the jobs that go with this, such as directing student papers, giving lectures to various groups, and being on ad hoc committees at various levels of the University.

Q. As a theology teacher, do students sometimes have preconceptions about what majoring in theology entails? If so, what are their expectations and how would you describe the study of theology?

A. Many students are under the impression that only priests, nuns, ministers, and people with religious life plans become theology majors. This is because they think that theology will turn out to be like Sunday school. That is, they think that the professor will be presuming faith, praying with the class, asking them to state their love for Jesus, and their belief in the infallibility of the pope.

The study of theology is done professionally, which means that the professor has knowledge to impart on whatever the course topic is, and what faith the students embrace, if any at all, is not something that needs ever to be mentioned by any student in the class. Each course features knowledge. Of course, should the student volunteer some statement about what he or she believes, or what larger religious tradition it is to which he or she belongs, then no one is going to fall over in surprise. But theology has to do with knowledge. If a student wants to become a Theology/Religious Studies/World Religions Major or Minor, I advise that he or she be ready to jump into a great deal of serious learning.

Q. How did you train for this job? What did you study in college?

A. My undergraduate degree was in General Arts. I majored in religious studies because I found it so interesting, especially scripture.

I received top-notch preparation to be a professor from the University of St. Michael's College in Toronto, one of Canada's most prestigious graduate university programs in theology. The University of St. Michael's College is also part of a consortium with six other graduate colleges in the area; together these seven make up the Toronto School of Theology. The biblical section, for example, had 21 professors. I could not think of any other place that could boast so many. And students were free to take courses from whomever they wished. Usually, students study their for their master's degree at one university and then take their Ph.D. at another. But in my case, since I had such a huge choice, I didn't move. I just kept learning.

Q. Did this major prepare you for your career or, in retrospect, would you pursue another major? If so, what major?

A. While I do not regret the major I took, I wish I had gone for counseling while I was chipping away at my undergraduate degree. Then, someone could have advised me that, if I was so interested in New Testament writings, I should take courses in the first century Classics and also archaeology. That would have proved to be very helpful. I also wish someone had suggested that I study Koine (Greek spoken in the first century C.E.) on the side with a tutor. That would have helped me so much.

Q. What are the most important personal and professional qualities for theology professors?

A. People in New Testament studies have to be very strict about learning the most meticulous method in studying a text, and then they need a combination of discipline in applying that method, together with courage to accept what the method reveals. They need to keep learning about the first century and about better and better method.

A good theology professor should remain a curious student. They should want to be involved in fresh research and share it with scholars all over the world by publishing their findings and giving papers at meetings of their colleagues. In this way, they remain intellectually alive and imaginatively active for their students. Like every good professor, the theology professor should show respect for the students by coming to his or her lectures very well prepared and organized, so that their teaching is clear and more easily understood by the student. A theology professor, like every professor, should try a number of ways to reach students—through lecture, discussion groups, audio-visuals, and student presentations. They should also know how to listen to the questions and comments of the students, for each student is unique.

Q. What advice would you give students as they attend college and prepare for the work world?

A. Find a professor who inspires you, and let them mentor you, counsel you, and help you.

Q. Many of your students who major in theology will pursue religious careers including teaching, youth and parish ministry, missionary work, religious consulting, and as directors of vocations. What non-religious careers do theology majors pursue upon graduation or with additional education?

A. Theology/religious studies/world religions majors don't have a special market like chemistry or pharmacy majors. They are open to a variety of very challenging and interesting careers. Depending on the student's own particular gifts, theology/religious studies majors can become journalists, editors/publishers, public relation directors, personnel managers, teachers, professors, educational workshop specialists, doctors, nurses, lawyers, counselors, social workers, administrators, or day care workers and organizers.

REQUIREMENTS
High School

Your high school's college preparatory program likely includes courses in English, science, foreign language, history, math, and government. In addition, you should take courses in speech to get a sense of what it will be like to lecture to a group of students. Your school's debate team can also help you develop public speaking skills, along with research skills.

Postsecondary Training

At least one advanced degree in your field of study is required to be a professor in a college or university. The master's degree is considered the minimum standard, and graduate work beyond the master's is usually desirable. If you hope to advance in academic rank above instructor, most institutions require a doctorate.

In the last year of your undergraduate program, you'll apply to graduate programs in your area of study. Standards for admission to a graduate program can be high and the competition heavy, depending on the school. Once accepted into a program, your responsibilities will be similar to those of your professors—in addition to attending seminars, you'll research, prepare articles for publication, and teach some undergraduate courses.

You may find employment in a junior college with only a master's degree. Advancement in responsibility and in salary, however, is more likely to come if you have earned a doctorate.

Other Requirements

You should enjoy reading, writing, and researching. Not only will you spend many years studying in school, but your whole career will be based on communicating your thoughts and ideas. People skills are important because you'll be dealing directly with students, administrators, and other faculty members on a daily basis. You should feel comfortable in a role of authority and possess self-confidence.

EXPLORING

Your high school teachers use many of the same skills as college professors, so talk to your teachers about their careers and their college experiences. You can develop your own teaching experience by volunteering at a community center, working at a day care center, or working at a summer camp. Also, spend some time on a college campus to get a sense of the environment. Write to colleges for their admissions brochures and course catalogs (or check them out online); read about the faculty members and the courses they teach. Before visiting college campuses, make arrangements to speak to professors who teach courses that interest you. These professors may allow you to sit in on their classes and observe. Also, make appointments with college advisers and with people in the admissions and recruitment offices. If your grades are good enough, you might be able to serve as a teaching assistant during your undergraduate years, which can give you experience leading discussions and grading papers.

EMPLOYERS

Employment opportunities vary based on area of study and education. Most universities have many different departments that hire faculty. With a doctorate, a number of publications, and a record of good teaching, professors should find opportunities in universities all across the country. There are more than 3,800 colleges and universities in the United States. Professors teach in undergraduate and graduate programs. The teaching jobs at doctoral institutions are usually better paying and more prestigious. The most sought-after positions are those that offer tenure. Teachers that have only a master's degree will be limited to opportunities with junior colleges, community colleges, and some small private institutions. There are approximately 1.3 million postsecondary teachers employed in the United States.

STARTING OUT

You should start the process of finding a teaching position while you are in graduate school. The process includes developing a curriculum vitae (a detailed, academic resume), writing for publication, assisting with research, attending conferences, and gaining teaching experience and recommendations. Many students begin applying for teaching positions while finishing their graduate program. For most positions at four-year institutions, you must travel to large conferences where interviews can be arranged with representatives from the universities to which you have applied.

Because of the competition for tenure-track positions, you may have to work for a few years in temporary positions, visiting various schools as an *adjunct professor*. Some professional associations maintain lists of teaching opportunities in their areas. They may also make lists of applicants available to college administrators looking to fill an available position.

ADVANCEMENT

The normal pattern of advancement is from instructor to assistant professor, to associate professor, to full professor. All four academic ranks are concerned primarily with teaching and research. College faculty members who have an interest in and a talent for administration may be advanced to chair of a department or to dean of their college. A few become college or university presidents or other types of administrators.

The instructor is usually an inexperienced college teacher. He or she may hold a doctorate or may have completed all the Ph.D. requirements except for the dissertation. Most colleges look upon the rank of instructor as the period during which the college is trying out the teacher. Instructors usually are advanced to the position of assistant professors within three to four years. Assistant professors are given up to about six years to prove themselves worthy of tenure, and if they do so, they become associate professors. Some professors choose to remain at the associate level. Others strive to become full professors and receive greater status, salary, and responsibilities.

Most colleges have clearly defined promotion policies from rank to rank for faculty members, and many have written statements about the number of years in which instructors and assistant professors may remain in grade. Administrators in many colleges hope to encourage younger faculty members to increase their skills and competencies and thus to qualify for the more responsible positions of associate professor and full professor.

EARNINGS

Earnings vary depending on the departments professors work in, the size of the school, the type of school (for example, public, private, or women's only), and by the level of position the professor holds. In its 2000–2001 salary survey, the American Association of University Professors (AAUP) reported the average yearly income for all full-time faculty was $60,000. It also reports that professors averaged the following salaries by rank: full professors, $78,912; associate professors, $57,380; assistant professors, $47,358; and instructors, $35,790. Full professors working in disciplines such as law, business, health professions, computer and information sciences, and engineering have the highest salaries. Lower paying disciplines include visual and performing arts, agricultural studies, education, and communications. The American Association for the Advancement of Science reports that, according to findings from its member salary survey, the median earnings for full professors in the life science fields were approximately $108,000 in 2001. Associate professors in life sciences earned a median of $72,000 that same year.

According to a study by the College and University Professional Association for Human Resources, the average salary in all fields at public institutions was $60,893 for 2001–2002. At private colleges, the average was $60,289. Law professors earned top salaries of $107,696 at private colleges, and library science faculty members were near the bottom of the salary scale, earning $44,206 per year.

Many professors try to increase their earnings by completing research, publishing in their field, or teaching additional courses. Professors working on the west coast and the east coast of the United States and those working at doctorate-granting institutions tend to have the highest salaries.

Benefits for full-time faculty typically include health insurance and retirement funds and, in some cases, stipends for travel related to research, housing allowances, and tuition waivers for dependents.

WORK ENVIRONMENT

A college or university is usually a pleasant place in which to work. Campuses bustle with all types of activities and events, stimulating ideas, and a young, energetic population. Much prestige comes with success as a professor and scholar; professors have the respect of students, colleagues, and others in their community.

Depending on the size of the department, college professors may have their own office, or they may have to share an office with one or more colleagues. Their department may provide them with a computer, Internet access, and research assistants. College professors are also able to do much of their office work at home. They can arrange their schedule around class hours, academic meetings, and the established office hours when they meet with students. Most college teachers work more than 40 hours each week. Although college professors may teach only two or three classes a semester, they spend many hours preparing for lectures, examining student work, and conducting research.

OUTLOOK

The U.S. Department of Labor predicts faster than average employment growth for college and university professors over the next several years. College enrollment is projected to grow due to an increased number of 18- to 24-year-olds, an increased number of adults returning to college, and an increased number of foreign-born students. Additionally, opportunities for college teachers will be good in areas such as engineering, business, computer science, and health science, which offer strong career prospects in the world of work. Retirement of current faculty members will also provide job openings. However, competition for full-time, tenure-track positions at four-year schools will be very strong.

A number of factors threaten to change the way colleges and universities hire faculty. Some university leaders are developing more business-based methods of running their schools, focusing on profits and budgets. This can affect college professors in a number of ways. One of the biggest effects is in the replacement of tenure-track faculty positions with part-time instructors. These part-time instructors include adjunct faculty, visiting professors, and graduate students. Organizations such as the AAUP and the American Federation of Teachers are working to prevent the loss of these full-time jobs, as well as to help part-time instructors receive better pay and benefits. Other issues involve the development of long-distance education departments in many schools. Though these correspondence courses have become very popular in recent years, many professionals believe that students in long-distance education programs receive only a second-rate education. A related concern is about the proliferation of computers in the classroom. Some courses consist only of instruction by computer software and the Internet. The effects of these alternative methods on the teaching profession will be offset somewhat by the expected increases in college enrollment in coming years.

FOR MORE INFORMATION

To read about the issues affecting college professors, contact the following organizations:

American Association of University Professors
1012 14th Street, NW, Suite 500
Washington, DC 20005
Tel: 202-737-5900
Email: aaup@aaup.org
http://www.aaup.org

American Federation of Teachers
555 New Jersey Avenue, NW
Washington, DC 20001
Tel: 202-879-4400
Email: online@aft.org
http://www.aft.org

COMPUTER NETWORK ADMINISTRATORS

QUICK FACTS

School Subjects Computer science Mathematics	**Certification or Licensing** Recommended
Personal Skills Helping/teaching Leadership/management Technical/scientific	**Outlook** Much faster than the average
	DOT 031
Work Environment Primarily indoors Primarily one location	**GOE** 07.06.01
Minimum Education Level Bachelor's degree	**NOC** 0213
Salary Range $33,820 to $53,770 to $90,000+	**O*NET-SOC** 15-1071.00, 15-1081.00

OVERVIEW

Computer network administrators, or *network specialists,* design, install, and support an organization's local area network (LAN), wide area network (WAN), network segment, or Internet system. They maintain network hardware and software, analyze problems, and monitor the network to ensure availability to system users. Administrators also might plan, coordinate, and implement network security measures, including firewalls. Approximately 229,000 computer network and systems administrators work in the United States.

HISTORY

The first substantial developments in modern computer technology took place in the early and mid-twentieth century. After World War II, plans for computer use were limited to large government projects, such as the census, because computers at this time were enormous in size (they easily took up the space of entire warehouses).

Smaller and less expensive computers came about after the introduction of semiconductors. Businesses began using computers in their operations as early as 1954. Within 30 years, computers revolutionized the way people worked, played, and shopped. Today, computers are everywhere, from businesses of all kinds to government agencies, charitable organizations, and private homes. Over the years, technology has continued to shrink the size of computers and increase computer speed at an unprecedented rate.

The first commercially used computers were composed of a system of several big mainframe computers. These computers were located in special rooms and several independent terminals around the office. Though efficient and effective, the mainframe had several problems. One was the update delay, or the time lapse, between when an employee input information into a computer and when that information became available to other employees. Although advances in hardware technology have begun addressing this and other problems of mainframes, many computer companies and businesses have now turned to networking instead.

Rather than relying on a mainframe system, computer networks use a network server to centralize the processing capacity of several different computers and other related equipment, known as peripherals. In a network, terminals and other computers are linked directly to the server. This direct link provides other computer users with instantaneous access to the information. The increased need for qualified computer network administrators to oversee network operations has paralleled the growth of computer networking.

The use of networks has grown rapidly as more companies move from mainframe computers to client–server networks or from paper-based systems to automated record-keeping using networked databases. The rapid growth of Internet technology has created a new area that also is in need of networking professionals.

THE JOB

Businesses use computer networks for several reasons. One important reason is that networks make it easy for many employees to share hardware and software as well as printers, faxes, and modems. For example, it would be very expensive to buy individual copies of word-processing programs for each employee in a company. By investing in a network version of the software that all employees can access, companies can often save a lot of money. Also, businesses that rely on databases for daily operations use networks to allow authorized personnel quick and easy access to the most updated version of the database.

Networks vary greatly in size: they can be as small as two computers connected together or as large and complex as hundreds of computer terminals linked across locations around the world. A good example of a large network is the Internet, which is a system that allows people from every corner of the globe to access millions of pieces of information about almost any subject. Besides varying in size, networks are all at least slightly different in terms of configuration, or what the network is designed to do; businesses customize networks to meet their specific needs. All networks, regardless of size or configuration, experience problems. For example, communications with certain equipment can break down, users might need extra training or forget their passwords, backup files may be lost, or new software might need to be installed and configured. Whatever the crisis, computer network administrators must know the network system well enough to diagnose and fix the problem.

Computer network administrators or specialists may have one or several networking responsibilities. A person's specific job duties depend on the nature and scope of the employer. For example, in a medium-size company that uses computers only minimally, a computer network specialist might be expected to do everything associated with the office computer system. In larger companies with more sophisticated computing systems, computer network administrators are likely to hold more narrow and better defined responsibilities.

In the narrowest sense, computer network administrators are responsible for adding and deleting files to the network server, which is a centralized computer. Among other things, the server stores the software applications used by network users on a daily basis. Administrators update files from the database, electronic mail, and word-processing applications. They also ensure that printing jobs run properly. This task entails telling the server where the printer is and establishing a printing queue, or line, designating which print jobs have priority.

Some network administrators set up user access. Since businesses store confidential information on the server, users typically have access to only a limited number of applications. Network administrators tell the computer who can use which programs and when they can use them. They create a series of passwords to secure the system against internal and external spying. They also troubleshoot problems and questions encountered by staff members.

In companies with large computer systems, *network security specialists* concentrate solely on system security. They set up and monitor user access and update security files as needed. In universities, for example, only certain administrative personnel are allowed to change student grades on the database. Network security specialists must protect the system from unauthorized grade changes. Network security specialists grant new passwords to users who forget them, record all nonauthorized entries, report unauthorized users to appropriate management, and change any files that have been tampered with. They also maintain security files with information about each employee.

Network control operators are in charge of all network communications, most of which operate over telephone lines or fiber optic cables. When users encounter communications problems, they call the network control operator. A typical communications problem is when a user cannot send or receive files from other computers. Since users seldom have a high level of technical expertise on the network, the network control operator knows how to ask appropriate questions in user-friendly language to determine the source of the problem. If it is not a user error, the network control operator checks the accuracy of computer files, verifies that modems are functioning properly, and runs noise tests on the communications lines using special equipment. As with all network specialists, if the problem proves to be too difficult for the network control operator to resolve, he or she seeks help directly from the manufacturer or warranty company.

Network control operators also keep detailed records of the number of communications transactions made, the number and nature of network errors, and the methods used to resolve them. These records help them address problems as they arise in the future.

Network systems administrators that specialize in Internet technology are essential to its success. One of their responsibilities is to prepare servers for use and link them together so others can place things on them. Under the supervision of the *Webmaster*, the systems administrator might set aside areas on a server for particular types of information, such as documents, graphics, or audio. At sites that are set up to handle secure credit card transactions, administrators are responsible for setting up the secure server that handles this job. They also monitor site traffic and take the necessary steps to ensure uninterrupted operation. In some cases the solution is to provide additional space on the server. In others, the only solution might be to increase bandwidth by upgrading the telephone line linking the site to the Internet.

REQUIREMENTS
High School

In high school, take as many courses as possible in computer science, mathematics, and science, which provide a solid foundation in computer basics and analytical-thinking skills. You should also practice your verbal and written communications skills in English and speech classes. Business courses are valuable in that they can give you an understanding of how important business decisions, especially those concerning investment in computer equipment, are made.

Postsecondary Training

Most network jobs require at least a bachelor's degree in computer science or computer engineering. More specialized positions require an advanced degree. Workers with a college education are more likely to deal with the theoretical aspects of computer networking and are more likely to be promoted to management positions. Opportunities in computer design, systems analysis, and computer programming, for example, are open only to college graduates. If you are interested in this field, you should also pursue postsecondary training in network administration or network engineering.

"I believe that you cannot have enough education and that it should be an ongoing thing," says Nancy Nelson, a network administrator at Baxter Healthcare Corporation in Deerfield, Illinois. "You can learn a lot on your own, but I think you miss out on a lot if you don't get the formal education. Most companies don't even look at a resume that doesn't have a degree. Keeping up with technology can be very rewarding."

Certification or Licensing

Besides the technical/vocational schools that offer courses related to computer networking, several major companies offer professionally taught courses and nationally recognized certification; chief among them are Novell and Microsoft. The Certified Network Professional program supports and complements the aforementioned vendor product certifications. Offered by The Network Professional Association, the program covers fundamental knowledge in client operating systems, microcomputer hardware platforms, network operating system fundamentals, protocols, and topologies. This program requires that you receive certification in two specialty areas.

Commercial postsecondary training programs are flexible. You can complete courses at your own pace, but you must take all parts of the certification test within one year. You may attend classes at any one of many educational sites around the country or you can study on your own. Many students find certification exams difficult.

Other Requirements

Continuing education for any computer profession is crucial to success. Many companies will require you to keep up to date on new technological advances by attending classes, workshops, and seminars throughout the year. Also, many companies and professional associations update network specialists through newsletters, other periodicals, and online bulletin boards.

Computer work is complex, detailed, and often very frustrating. In order to succeed in this field, you must be well organized and patient. You should enjoy challenges and problem solving, and you should be a logical thinker. You must also be able to communicate complex ideas in simple terms, as well as be able to work well under pressure and deadlines. As a network specialist, you should be naturally curious about the computing field; you must always be willing to learn more about new and different technologies.

EXPLORING

"One of the greatest learning experiences in this field is just unpacking a new computer, setting it up, and getting connected to the Internet, continually asking yourself how and why as you go," says Dan Creedon, a network administrator at Nesbitt Burns Securities in Chicago.

If you are interested in computer networking you should join computer clubs at school and community centers and surf the Internet or other online services. Ask your school administration about the possibility of working with the school system's network specialists for a day or longer. Parents' or friends' employers might also be a good place to find this type of opportunity.

If seeking part-time jobs, apply for those that include computer work. Though you will not find networking positions, any experience on computers will increase your general computing knowledge. In addition, once employed, you can actively seek exposure to the other computer functions in the business.

You might also try volunteering at local-area charities that use computer networks in their office. Because many charities have small budgets, they may offer more opportunities to gain experience with some of the simpler networking tasks. In addition, experiment by creating networks with your own computer, those of your friends, and with any printers, modems, and faxes.

In general, you should play around on computers as much as possible. Read and learn from any computer-related resource you can, such as magazines, newsletters, and online bulletin boards.

EMPLOYERS

The U.S. Department of Labor reports that approximately 229,000 computer network and systems administrators are employed today. Any company or organization that uses computer networks in its business employs network administrators. These include insurance companies, banks, financial institutions, health care organizations, federal and state governments, universities, and other corporations that rely on networking. Also, since smaller companies are moving to client–server models, more opportunities at almost any kind of business are becoming available.

STARTING OUT

There are several ways to obtain a position as a computer network specialist. If you are a student in a technical school or university, take advantage of your campus placement office. Check regularly for internship postings, job listings, and notices of on-campus recruitment. Placement offices are also valuable resources for resume tips and interviewing techniques. Internships and summer jobs with corporations are always beneficial and provide experience that will give you the edge over your competition. General computer job fairs are also held throughout the year in larger cities.

There are many online career sites listed on the Web that post job openings, salary surveys, and current employment trends. The Web also has online publications that deal specifically with computer jobs. You can also obtain information from computer organizations, such as the IEEE Computer Society and the Network Professional Association (see contact information at the end of this article).

When a job opportunity arises, you should send a cover letter and resume to the company promptly. Follow up with a phone call about one week later. If interested, the company recruiter will call you to ask questions and possibly arrange an interview. The commercial sponsors of network certification, such as Novell and Microsoft, also publish newsletters that list current job openings in the field. The same information is distributed through online bulletin boards and on the Internet, as well. Otherwise, you can scan the classified ads in local newspapers and computer magazines or work with an employment agency to find such a position.

Individuals already employed but wishing to move into computer networking should investigate the possibility of tuition reimbursement from their employer for network certification. Many large companies have this type of program, which allows employees to train in a field that would benefit company operations. After successfully completing classes or certification, individuals are better qualified for related job openings in their own company and more likely to be hired for them.

ADVANCEMENT

"I would say that as much as a person is willing to learn is really the amount of advancement opportunities that are open to them," notes Dan Creedon. Among the professional options available are promotion to network manager or movement into network engineering. *Network engineers* design, test, and evaluate network systems, such as LAN, WAN, Internet, and other data communications systems. They also perform modeling, analysis, and planning. Network engineers might also research related products and make hardware and software recommendations.

Network specialists also have the option of going into a different area of computing. They can become computer programmers, systems analysts, software engineers, or multimedia professionals. All of these promotions require additional education and solid computer experience.

EARNINGS

Factors such as the size and type of employer, the administrator's experience, and specific job duties influence the earnings of network administrators. Robert Half Technology's *2002 Salary Guide* found that salaries of network managers ranged from $66,750 to $90,000. Also according to this survey, LAN/WAN administrators had earnings ranging from $47,000 to $68,250. According to the U.S. Department of Labor, the median yearly income for computer network and systems administrators was $53,770 in 2001. The lowest paid 10 percent made less than $33,820 per year, and the highest paid 10 percent earned more than $85,910 annually that same year.

Most computer network administrators are employed by companies that offer the full range of benefits, including health insurance, paid vacation, and sick leave. In addition, many companies have tuition reimbursement programs for employees seeking to pursue education or professional certification.

WORK ENVIRONMENT

Computer network administrators work indoors in a comfortable office environment. Their work is generally fast paced and can be frustrating. Some tasks, however, are routine and might get a little boring after a while. But network specialists are often required to work under a lot of pressure. If the network goes down, for example, the company is losing money, and it is the network specialist's job to get it up and running as fast as possible. The specialist must be able to remember complicated relationships and many details accurately and quickly. Specialists are also called on to deal effectively with the many complaints from network users.

When working on the installation of a new system, many network specialists are required to work overtime until it is fully operational. This usually includes long and frequent meetings. During initial operations of the system, some network specialists may be on call during other shifts for when problems arise, or they may have to train network users during off hours.

One other potential source of frustration is communications with other employees. Network specialists deal every day with people who usually don't understand the system as well as they do. Network administrators must be able to communicate at different levels of understanding.

OUTLOOK

The U.S. Department of Labor projects the job of computer network and systems administrator will be one of the fastest growing occupations over the next several years, and employment is expected to grow at a rate that is much faster than the average. Network administrators are in high demand, particularly those with Internet experience. "Technology is constantly changing," Nancy Nelson says. "It is hard to tell where it will lead in the future. I think that the Internet and all of its pieces will be the place to focus on." As more and more companies and organizations discover the economic and convenience advantages linked to using computer networks at all levels of operations, the demand for well-trained network specialists will increase. Job opportunities should be best for those with certification and up-to-date training.

FOR MORE INFORMATION

For information on internships, student membership, and the student magazine, Crossroads, *contact:*

Association for Computing Machinery
1515 Broadway
New York, NY 10036
Tel: 800-342-6626
Email: sigs@acm.org
http://www.acm.org

For information on scholarships, student membership, and the student newsletter, looking.forward, *contact:*

IEEE Computer Society
1730 Massachusetts Avenue, NW
Washington, DC 20036-1992
Tel: 202-371-0101
Email: membership@computer.org
http://www.computer.org

For industry information, contact:

Network Professional Association
195 South C Street, Suite 250
Tustin, CA 92780
Tel: 714-573-4780
Email: npa@npa.org
http://www.npa.org

COMPUTER SYSTEMS PROGRAMMER/ ANALYSTS

QUICK FACTS

School Subjects Computer science Mathematics	**Certification or Licensing** Voluntary
	Outlook Much faster than the average
Personal Skills Mechanical/manipulative Technical/scientific	
	DOT 033
Work Environment Primarily indoors Primarily one location	**GOE** 05.01.03
Minimum Education Level Bachelor's degree	**NOC** 2162
Salary Range $38,870 to $61,990 to $93,200	**O*NET-SOC** 15-1051.00

OVERVIEW

Computer systems programmer/analysts analyze the computing needs of a business and then design a new system or upgrade an old system to meet those needs. The position can be split between two people, the *systems programmer* and the *systems analyst,* but it is frequently held by just one person who oversees the work from beginning to end.

HISTORY

The need for systems programmer/analysts grew out of the proliferation of hardware and software products on the market in the past several decades. Although many offices have an unofficial "computer expert," whose main job may be in accounting, word processing, or office administration, most medium-size to larger companies that have invested in expensive computer systems employ a systems analyst or programmer analyst either full-time or on a consulting basis.

In addition, the computer revolution brought with it awareness that choosing the appropriate system from the start is crucial to business success. Purchasing decisions are based on many complicated scientific and mathematical models as well as on practical business sense. Therefore, systems analysts have become essential to business decision making.

Businesses and organizations also discovered that, like all new technology, computer systems break down a lot. It has become more cost effective for many organizations to have full-time systems analysts on site instead of calling computer repairers to fix every little glitch.

THE JOB

Businesses invest hundreds of thousands of dollars in computer systems to make their operations more efficient and thus, more profitable. As older systems become obsolete, businesses are also faced with the task of replacing them or upgrading them with new technology. Computer systems programmer/analysts plan and develop new computer systems or upgrade existing systems to meet changing business needs. They also install, modify, and maintain functioning computer systems. The process of choosing and implementing a computer system is similar for programmer/analysts who work for very different employers. However, specific decisions in terms of hardware and software differ depending on the industry.

The first stage of the process involves meeting with management and users in order to discuss the problem at hand. For example, a company's accounting system might be slow, unreliable, and generally outdated. During many hours of meetings, systems programmer/analysts and management discuss various options, including commercial software, hardware upgrades, and customizing possibilities that may solve the problems. At the end of the discussions, which may last as long as several weeks or months, the programmer analyst defines the specific system goals as agreed upon by participants.

Next, systems programmer/analysts engage in highly analytic and logical activities. They use tools such as structural analysis, data modeling, mathematics, and cost accounting to determine which computers, including hardware and software and peripherals, will be required to meet the goals of the project. They must consider the tradeoffs between extra efficiency and speed and increased costs. Weighing the pros and cons of each additional system feature is an important factor in system planning. Whatever preliminary decisions are made must be supported by mathematical and financial evidence.

As the final stage of the planning process, systems programmer/analysts prepare reports and formal presentations to be delivered to management. Reports must be written in clear, concise language that business professionals, who are not necessarily technical experts, can understand thoroughly. Formal presentations in front of groups of various sizes are often required as part of the system proposal.

If the system or the system upgrades are approved, equipment is purchased and installed. Then, the programmer/analysts get down to the real technical work so that all the different computers and peripherals function well together. They prepare specifications, diagrams, and other programming structures and, often using computer-aided systems engineering (CASE) technology, they write the new or upgraded programming code. If they work solely as systems analysts, it is at this point that they hand over all of their information to the systems programmer so that he or she can begin to write the programming code.

Systems design and programming involves defining the files and records to be accessed by the system, outlining the processing steps, and suggesting formats for output that meet the needs of the company. User-friendliness of the front-end applications is extremely important for user productivity. Therefore, programmer/analysts must be able to envision how nontechnical system users view their on-screen work. Systems programmer/analysts might also specify security programs that allow only authorized personnel access to certain files or groups of files.

As the programming is written, programmer/analysts set up test runs of various parts of the system, making sure each step of the way that major goals are reached. Once the system is up and running, problems, or "bugs" begin to pop up. Programmer/analysts are responsible for fixing these last-minute problems. They must isolate the problem and review the hundreds of lines of programming commands to determine where the mistake is located. Then they must enter the correct command or code and recheck the program.

Depending on the employer, some systems programmer/analysts might be involved with computer networking. Network communication programs tell two or more computers or peripherals how to work with each other. When a system is composed of equipment from various manufacturers, networking is essential for smooth system functioning. For example, shared printers have to know how to order print jobs as they come in from various terminals. Some programmer/analysts write the code that establishes printing queues. Others might be involved in user training, since they know the software applications well. They might also customize commercial software programs to meet the needs of their company.

Many programmer/analysts become specialized in an area of business, science, or engineering. They seek education and further on-the-job training in these areas to develop expertise. They may therefore attend special seminars, workshops, and classes designed for their needs. This extra knowledge allows them to develop a deeper understanding of the computing problems specific to the business or industry.

REQUIREMENTS
High School
Take a college preparatory program with advanced classes in math, science, and computer science to prepare you for this work. This will provide a foundation of basic concepts and encourage the development of analytic and logical thinking skills. Since programmer/analysts do a lot of proposal writing that may or may not be technical in nature, English classes are valuable as well. Speech classes will help prepare you for making formal presentations to management and clients.

Postsecondary Training
A bachelor's degree in computer science is a minimum requirement for systems programmer/analysts. Course work in preparation for this field includes math, computer programming, science, and logic. Several years of related work experience, including knowledge of programming languages, are often necessary as well. For some very high-level positions, an advanced degree in a specific computer subfield may be required. Also, depending on the employer, proficiency in business, science, or engineering may be necessary.

Certification or Licensing
Some programmer/analysts pursue certification through the Institute for Certification of Computing Professionals. In particular,

they take classes and exams to become certified computing professionals (CCPs). Certification is voluntary and is an added credential for job hunters. CCPs have achieved a recognized level of knowledge and experience in principles and practices related to systems.

Other Requirements

Successful systems programmer/analysts demonstrate strong analytic skills and enjoy the challenges of problem solving. They are able to understand problems that exist on many levels, from technical to practical to business-oriented. They can visualize complicated and abstract relationships between computer hardware and software and are good at matching needs to equipment.

Systems programmer/analysts have to be flexible as well. They routinely deal with many different kinds of people, from management to data entry clerks. Therefore, they must be knowledgeable in a lot of functional areas of the company. They should be able to talk to management about cost-effective solutions, to programmers about detailed coding, and to clerks about user-friendliness of the applications.

As is true for all computer professionals, systems programmer/analysts must be able to learn about new technology quickly. They should be naturally curious about keeping up on cutting-edge developments, which can be time consuming. Furthermore, they are often so busy at their jobs that staying in the know is done largely on their own time.

EXPLORING

If you are interested in this career, you have several options to learn more about what it is like to be a computer systems programmer/analyst. You can spend a day with a working professional in this field in order to experience firsthand a typical day. Career days of this type can usually be arranged through school guidance counselors or the public relations manager of local corporations.

Strategy games, such as chess, played with friends or school clubs are a good way to put your analytic thinking skills to use while having fun. Commercial games range in themes from war simulations to world historical development. When choosing a game, the key is to make sure it relies on qualities similar to those used by programmer/analysts.

Lastly, you should become a computer hobbyist and learn everything you can about computers by working and playing with them on a daily basis. Surfing the Internet regularly, as well as reading trade magazines, will also be helpful. You might also want to try hooking up a mini-system at home or school, configuring terminals, printers, modems, and other peripherals into a coherent system. This activity requires a fair amount of knowledge and should be supervised by a professional.

EMPLOYERS

Computer systems programmer/analysts work for all types of firms and organizations that do their work on computers. Such companies may include manufacturing companies, data processing service firms, hardware and software companies, banks, insurance companies, credit companies, publishing houses, government agencies, and colleges and universities. Many programmer/analysts are employed by businesses as consultants on a temporary or contractual basis.

STARTING OUT

Since systems programmer/analysts typically have at least some experience in a computer-related job, most are hired into these jobs from lower level positions within the same company. For example, programmers, software engineering technicians, and network and database administrators all gain valuable computing experience that can be put to good use at a systems job. Alternatively, individuals who acquire expertise in systems programming and analysis while in other jobs may want to work with a headhunter to find the right systems positions for them. Also, trade magazines, newspapers, and employment agencies regularly feature job openings in this field.

Students in four-year degree programs should work closely with their schools' placement offices. Companies regularly work through such offices in order to find the most qualified graduates. Since it may be difficult to find a job as a programmer analyst to begin with, it is important for students to consider their long-term potential within a certain company. The chance for promotion into a systems job can make lower level jobs more appealing, at least in the short run.

For those individuals already employed in a computer-related job but wanting to get into systems programming and analysis, additional formal education is a good idea. Some employers have educational reimbursement policies that allow employees to take courses inexpensively. If the employee's training could directly benefit the business, companies are more willing to pay for the expense.

ADVANCEMENT

Systems programmer/analysts already occupy a relatively high-level technical job. Promotion, therefore, usually occurs in one of two directions. First, programmer/analysts can be put in charge of increasingly larger and more complex systems. Instead of concentrating on a company's local system, for example, an analyst can oversee all company systems and networks. This kind of technically based promotion can also put systems programmer/analysts into other areas of computing. With the proper experience and additional training, they can get into database or network management and design, software engineering, or even quality assurance.

The other direction in which programmer/analysts can go is managerial. Depending on the position sought, formal education (either a bachelor's degree in business or a master's in business administration) may be required. As more administrative duties are added, more technical ones are taken away. Therefore, programmer/analysts who enjoy the technical aspect of their work more than anything else may not want to pursue this advancement track. Excellent computing managers have both a solid background in various forms of computing and a good grasp of what it takes to run a department. Also, having the vision to see how technology will change in the short and long terms, and how those changes will affect the industry concerned, is a quality of a good manager.

EARNINGS

According to the U.S. Bureau of Labor Statistics, the median annual salary for computer systems analysts was $61,990 in 2001. At the low end of the pay range, 10 percent of systems analysts earned less than $38,870. The top 10 percent earned more than $93,200. Salaries are slightly higher in geographic areas where many computer companies are clustered, such as Silicon Valley in California and Seattle, Washington.

Level of education also affects analysts' earnings. The National Association of Colleges and Employers reports that starting salaries for those with master's degrees in computer science averaged $61,453 in 2001. Those with bachelor's degrees in computer science, however, had starting salaries averaging $52,723, and those with bachelor's degrees in computer systems analysis averaged $45,643, also in 2001.

Those in senior positions can earn much higher salaries. *Computerworld* reports that senior systems programmers earned a national average of $68,900 in 2001, while senior systems analysts earned $72,300.

Most programmer/analysts receive health insurance, paid vacation, and sick leave. Some employers offer tuition reimbursement programs and in-house computer training workshops.

WORK ENVIRONMENT

Computer systems programmer/analysts work in comfortable office environments. If they work as consultants, they may travel frequently. Otherwise, travel is limited to trade shows, seminars, and visitations to vendors for demonstrations. They might also visit other businesses to observe their systems in action.

Programmer/analysts usually work 40-hour weeks and enjoy the regular holiday schedule of days off. However, as deadlines for system installation, upgrades, and spot-checking approach, they are often required to work overtime. Extra compensation for overtime hours may come in the form of time-and-a-half pay or compensatory time off, depending on the precise nature of the employee's duties, company policy, and state law. If the employer operates off-shifts, programmer/analysts may be on-call to address any problems that might arise at any time of the day or night. This is relatively rare in the service sector but more common in manufacturing, heavy industry, and data processing firms.

Computer systems programming and analysis is very detailed work. The smallest error can cause major system disruptions, which can be a great source of frustration. Systems programmer/analysts must be prepared to deal with this frustration and be able to work well under pressure.

OUTLOOK

The U.S. Department of Labor predicts that the job of computer systems programmer/analyst will be one of the fastest growing over the next several years, with employment increasing much faster than the average. Increases are mainly a product of the growing number of businesses that rely extensively on computers. When businesses automate, their daily operations depend on the capacity of their computer systems to perform at desired levels. The continuous development of new technologies means that businesses must also update their old systems to remain competitive in the marketplace. Additionally, the need for businesses to network their information adds to the demand for qualified programmer/analysts. Businesses will rely increasingly on systems programmer/analysts to make the right purchasing decisions and to keep systems running smoothly.

Many computer manufacturers are beginning to expand the range of services they offer to business clients. In the years to come, they may hire many systems programmer/analysts to work as consultants on a per-project basis with a potential client. These workers would perform essentially the same duties, with the addition of extensive follow-up maintenance. They would analyze business needs and suggest proper systems to answer them. In addition, more and more independent consulting firms are hiring systems programmer/analysts to perform the same tasks.

Analysts with advanced degrees in computer science, management information systems, or computer engineering will be in great demand. Individuals with master's degrees in business administration with emphasis in information systems will also be highly desirable.

FOR MORE INFORMATION

For more information about systems programmer/analyst positions, contact:
Association of Information Technology Professionals
401 North Michigan Avenue, Suite 2200
Chicago, IL 60611-4267
Tel: 800-224-9371
Email: aitp_hq@aitp.org
http://www.aitp.org

For information on becoming an independent consultant, contact:
Independent Computer Consultants Association
11131 South Towne Square, Suite F
St. Louis, MO 63123
Tel: 800-774-4222
Email: info@icca.org
http://www.icca.org

For information on certification programs, contact:
Institute for Certification of Computing Professionals
2350 East Devon Avenue, Suite 115
Des Plaines, IL 60018-4610
Tel: 800-843-8227
Email: office@iccp.org
http://www.iccp.org

DATABASE SPECIALISTS

QUICK FACTS

School Subjects
Computer science
Mathematics

Personal Skills
Mechanical/manipulative
Technical/scientific

Work Environment
Primarily indoors
Primarily one location

Minimum Education Level
Bachelor's degree

Salary Range
$30,670 to $54,850 to
$102,750

Certification or Licensing
Voluntary

Outlook
Much faster than the
average

DOT
039

GOE
11.01.01

NOC
2172

O*NET-SOC
15-1061.00

OVERVIEW

Database specialists design, install, update, modify, maintain, and repair computer database systems to meet employers' needs. Database specialists must have strong math skills, the ability to work with many variables at once, and a solid understanding of the organization's objectives. They consult with other management officials to discuss computer equipment purchases, determine requirements for various computer programs, and allocate access to the computer system to users. They might also direct training of personnel who use company databases regularly. Database specialists may also be called *database designers, database analysts, database managers,* or *database administrators* in some businesses; while in other businesses the designations database designers, analysts, managers, and administrators represent separate jobs but all fall under the umbrella category of database specialist. There are approximately 106,000 database administrators working in the United States.

HISTORY

During the 1950s, computers were very large and were not considered practical for anything other than large government and research projects. However, by 1954, the introduction of semiconductors made computers smaller and more accessible to businesses. Within 30 years, computers had influenced nearly every aspect of life, such as work, entertainment, and even shopping. Today, computers are everywhere. Technology has continued to make computers smaller, more productive, and more efficient.

Technological advances have made database computing a promising subindustry. Businesses and other organizations use databases to replace existing paper-based procedures, but they also create new uses for them every day. For example, catalog companies use databases to organize inventory and sales systems, which before they did by hand. These same companies are pushing technology further by investigating ways to use databases to customize promotional materials. Instead of sending the same catalog out to everyone, some companies are looking to send each customer a special edition filled with items he or she might like, based on past purchases and a personal profile.

Database specialists are a crucial participant in database development. In fact, many companies who took an inexpensive route to database computing by constructing them haphazardly are now sorry they did not initially hire a specialist. Designing the database structure is important because it translates difficult, abstract relationships into concrete, logical structures. If the work is done well to begin with, the database will be better suited to handle changes in the future.

Most commercial computer systems make use of some kind of database. As computer speed and memory capacity continue to increase, databases will become increasingly complex and able to handle a variety of new uses. Therefore, the individuals and businesses that specialize in inputting, organizing, and enabling access to various types of information stand at the forefront of an ever-growing field.

THE JOB

Think of a database as the computer version of the old-fashioned file cabinet that contains folders full of important information. The database is the important information, and the database specialist is the person who designs or adjusts programs for the way the information is stored, how separate pieces of information relate and affect one another, and how the overall system should be organized. For example, a specialist may set up a retailer's customer database to have a separate "record" for each customer, in the same way that the retailer may have had a separate file folder in its file cabinet for each customer. In the retailer's sales database, each sale represented by an invoice will have a separate record. Each record contains many "fields" where specific pieces of information are entered. Examples of fields for the customer database include customer number, customer name, address, city, state, ZIP code, phone, and contact person. Examples of fields in the sales database include customer number, item purchased, quantity, price, date of purchase, and total. With information organized in separate fields, the retailer can easily sort customer records or invoices, just like filing folders in a file cabinet. In this way, the retailer could print a list of all its customers in Iowa, for example, or total sales for the month of April.

In the same way that records within a database can be sorted, databases themselves can be related to each other. The customer database can be related to the sales database by the common field: customer number. In this way, a business could print out a list of all purchases by a specific customer, for example, or a list of customers who purchased a specific product.

Database specialists are responsible for the flow of computer information within an organization. They make major decisions concerning computer purchases, system designs, and personnel training. Their duties combine general management ability with a detailed knowledge of computer programming and systems analysis.

A database specialist's specific responsibilities of a database depend on the size and type of his or her employer. For example, a database specialist working for a telephone company may develop a system for billing customers, while a database specialist for a large store may develop a system for keeping track of in-stock merchandise. To do this work accurately, database specialists need a thorough knowledge and understanding of the company's computer operations.

There are three main areas of the database specialist's work: planning what type of computer system a company needs; implementing and managing the system; and supervising computer room personnel.

To adequately plan a computer system, database specialists must have extensive knowledge of the latest computer technology and the specific needs of their company. They meet with high-ranking company officials, such as the president or vice president, and together they decide how to apply the available technology to the company's needs. Decisions include what type of hardware and software to order and how the data should be stored. Database specialists must be aware of the cost of the proposed computer system as well as the budget within which the company is operating. Long-term planning is also important. Specialists must ensure that the computer system can process not only the existing level of computer information received, but also the anticipated load and type of information the company could receive in the future. Such planning is vitally important since, even for small companies, computer systems can cost several hundred thousand dollars.

Implementing and managing a computer system involves a variety of technical and administrative tasks. Depending on the organization's needs, the specialist may modify a system already in place, develop a whole new system, or tailor a commercial system to meet these needs. To do this type of work the database specialist must be familiar with accounting principles and mathematical formulas. Scheduling access to the computer is also a key responsibility. Sometimes database specialists work with representatives from many different departments to create a schedule. The specialist prioritizes needs and monitors usage so that each department can do its work. All computer usage must be documented and stored for future reference.

Safeguarding computer operations is another important responsibility of database specialists. They must make contingency plans if a computer system fails or malfunctions so that the information stored in the computer is not lost. A duplication of computer files may be a part of this emergency planning. A backup system must also be employed so that the company can continue to process information. Database specialists also ensure that only authorized personnel have access to certain classified information in a system.

Database specialists may also supervise the work of computer-department personnel. They may train new computer personnel hires to use the company's database, in addition to current computer personnel when an existing database is modified. At some organizations, specialists are also required to train all employees in the use of an upgraded or a new system. Therefore, specialists need the ability to translate technical concepts into everyday language.

Database specialists may be known by a number of different titles and have a variety of responsibilities, depending on the size and the needs of the organizations that employ them. According to an article in *Computerworld,* the title *database designer* indicates someone who works on database programming. These workers usually have a math or engineering background. The title *database administrator* indicates someone who primarily focuses on the performance of the database, making sure everything is running smoothly. They may also do routine jobs, such as adding new users to the system. The title *database analyst* indicates someone who primarily focuses on the business, its goals, products, and customers. They work on improving the database so that the organization can meet its goals. In large businesses or organizations the many duties of the database specialist may be strictly divided among a number of specialists based on their titles. Smaller organizations may employ only one database specialist, designer, manager, administrator, or analyst who is responsible for carrying out all the tasks mentioned above. No matter what their title is, however, all database specialists work with an operation that processes millions of bits of information at a huge cost. This work demands accuracy and efficiency in decision-making and problem-solving abilities.

REQUIREMENTS
High School

While you are in high school, take as many math, science, and computer classes as you can. These courses will provide you with the basic technical and logical-thinking skills. Take electronics or other technical courses that will teach you about schematic drawing, working with electricity, and, again, logical thinking. Accounting English classes are also useful. To be able to do this work well, you will need strong communication skills, both written and verbal.

Postsecondary Training

A bachelor's degree in computer science, computer information systems, or another computer-related discipline is recommended as the minimum requirement for those wishing to work as database specialists. Some exceptions have been made for people without a degree but who have extensive experience in database administration. However, this route to becoming a database specialist is becoming increasingly rare. In the near future, most employers will expect you to have at least a four-year degree. Courses in a bachelor's degree program usually include data processing, systems analysis methods, more detailed software and hardware concepts, management principles, and information-systems planning. To advance in the field, you will probably need to complete further education. Many businesses, especially larger companies, prefer database managers to have a master's degree in computer science or business administration. Some companies offer to help with or pay for their employees' advanced education, so you may want to consider this possibility when looking for an entry-level job.

Certification or Licensing

Some database specialists become certified for jobs in the computer field by passing an examination given by the Institute for Certification of Computing Professionals (ICCP). For further information, contact the ICCP at the address given at the end of this article. Specialists who want to keep their skills current may also take training programs offered by database developers, such as Oracle. These programs may also lead to certifications.

Other Requirements

Database specialists are strong logical and analytical thinkers. They excel at analyzing massive amounts of information and organizing it into a coherent structure composed of complicated relationships. They are also good at weighing the importance of each element of a system and deciding which ones can be omitted without diminishing the quality of the final project.

Specialists also need strong communication skills. This work requires contact with employees from a wide variety of jobs. Specialists must be able to ask clear, concise, and technical questions of people who are not necessarily familiar with how a database works.

As is true for all computer professionals, specialists should be motivated to keep up with technological advances and able to learn new things quickly. Those who are interested in working almost exclusively in one industry (for example, banking) should be willing to gain as much knowledge as possible about that specific field in addition to their computer training. With an understanding of both fields of knowledge, individuals are more easily able to apply computer technology to the specific needs of the company.

EXPLORING

There are a number of ways to explore your interest in this field while you are still in high school. "Start by reading books on the subject," says Scott Sciaretta, an internal database consultant for Choicepoint in Atlanta, Georgia. "There are hundreds of them at most bookstores."

You can also join your high school's computer club to work on computer projects and meet others interested in the field. Learn everything you can about computers by working with them regularly. Online sources can be particularly good for keeping up to date with new developments and learning from people who are actively involved in this work. Learn to use a commercial database program, either by teaching yourself or taking a class in it. The Association for Computing Machinery has a Special Interest Group on Management of Data (SIGMOD). The Resources page of SIGMOD's website (http://www.acm.org/sigmod) provides an index of public domain database software that you may want to check out.

You may also want to ask your school guidance counselor or a computer teacher to arrange for a database specialist to speak to your class at school or to arrange for a field trip to a company to see database specialists at work. Another option is to ask your school administrators about databases used by the school and try to interview any database specialists working in or for the school system. Similar attempts could be made with charities in your area that make use of computer databases for membership and client records as well as mailing lists.

Look for direct-experience opportunities, such as part-time work, summer internships, and even summer camps that specialize in computers. "Try to get a job as an intern in a database shop and learn by watching, mentoring, and grunt work," Sciaretta recommends. If you can't find such a position, you can still put your skills to work by offering to set up small databases, such as address books, recipe databases, or videotape libraries for friends or family members.

EMPLOYERS

Approximately 106,000 database administrators are employed in the United States today. Any business or organization that uses databases as a part of its operations hires database professionals. Database specialists work for investment companies, telecommunications firms, banks, insurance companies, publishing houses, hospitals, school systems, universities, and a host of other large and midsize businesses and nonprofit organizations. There are also many opportunities with federal, state, and city governments.

STARTING OUT

Most graduating college students work closely with their school's placement office to obtain information about job openings and interviews. Local and national employers often recruit college graduates on campus, making it much easier for students to talk with many diverse companies. Another good source of information is through summer internships, which are completed typically between junior and senior year. Many major companies in the computer field, such as Intel (http://www.intel.com/education) and Oracle (http://education.oracle.com), have established undergraduate intern programs. This experience is valuable for two reasons. First, it gives students hands-on exposure to computer-related jobs. Second, it allows students to network with working computer professionals who may help them find full-time work after graduation. Interested individuals might also scan the classified ads or work with temporary agencies or headhunters to find entry-level and midlevel positions. Professional organizations, such as SIGMOD, and professional publications are other sources of information about job openings.

ADVANCEMENT

The job of database specialist is in itself a high-level position. Advancement will depend to some extent on the size of the business the specialist works for, with larger companies offering more opportunities for growth at the mid-level and senior levels of management. Scott Sciaretta explains his career path and advancement this way: "I got my first job in the field by internal promotion. Basically, I was doing some computer programming for my department on the side to automate a few of the menial tasks. My work got noticed, and I was given the job of running the company's computer department when the position opened. At my current level, the advancement opportunities are not easy. For me to advance I either need to expand my scope or work for a larger company, both of which are very feasible with hard work. However, salary advancements are easy and can be quite large. There are many opportunities for advancement from entry-level or junior positions."

Another factor influencing advancement is the interests of each individual. Generally, people fall into two categories: those who want to work on the business side and those who prefer to stay in a technical job. For individuals who want to get into the managerial side of the business, formal education in business administration is usually required, usually in the form of a master's degree in business administration. In upper-level management positions, specialists must work on cross-functional teams with professionals in finance, sales, personnel, purchasing, and operations. Superior database specialists at larger companies may also be promoted to executive positions.

Some database specialists prefer to stay on the technical side of the business. For them, the hands-on computer work is the best part of their job. Advancement for these workers will, again, involve further education in terms of learning about new database systems, gaining certification in a variety of database programs, or even moving into another technology area such as software design or networking.

As specialists acquire education and develop solid work experience, advancement will take the form of more responsibilities and higher wages. One way to achieve this is to move to a better paying, more challenging database position at a larger company. Some successful database specialists become highly paid consultants or start their own businesses. Teaching, whether as a consultant or at a university or community college, is another option for individuals with high levels of experience.

EARNINGS

A fairly wide range of salaries exists for database specialists. Earnings vary with the size, type, and location of the organization as well as a person's experience, education, and job responsibilities. According to the U.S. Bureau of Labor Statistics, median annual earnings for database administrators were $54,850 in 2001. The lowest paid 10 percent earned less than $30,670, while the highest paid 10 percent earned more than $92,280. Robert Half International reported that salaries for database administrators ranged from $71,500 to $102,750 in 2002.

Benefits for database professionals depend on the employer; however, they usually include such items as health insurance, retirement or 401-K plans, and paid vacation days.

WORK ENVIRONMENT

Database specialists work in modern offices, usually located next to the computer room. If they work as consultants, they may travel to client sites as little as once or twice per project or as often as every week. Most duties are performed at a computer at the individual's desk. Travel is occasionally required for conferences and visits to affiliated database locations. Travel requirements vary with employer, client, and level of position held. Database specialists may need to attend numerous meetings, especially during planning stages of a project. They work regular 40-hour weeks but may put in overtime as deadlines approach. During busy periods, the work can be quite stressful since accuracy is very important. Database specialists must therefore be able to work well under pressure and respond quickly to last-minute changes. Emergencies may also require specialists to work overtime or long hours without a break, sometimes through the night.

"I like what I do. It's kind of like playing," Scott Sciaretta says. "The hours are flexible. You get to work on and set up million-dollar systems. There also is a high degree of visibility from upper management. The downside is that I work lots of hours, including many weekends, and I have a never-ending list of work. The hardest part of the job is juggling the schedules and configurations for many projects at one time."

OUTLOOK

The use of computers and database systems in almost all business settings creates tremendous opportunities for well-qualified database personnel. Database specialists and computer support specialists are predicted by the U.S. Department of Labor to be among the fastest growing occupations over the next several years.

Employment opportunities for database specialists should be best in large urban areas because of the multitude of businesses and organizations located there that need employees to work with their databases. Since smaller communities are also rapidly developing job opportunities in this field, skilled workers can pick from a wide range of jobs throughout the country. Those with the best education and the most experience in computer systems and personnel management will find the best job prospects.

"The field of Unix systems and databases is wide open," notes Scott Sciaretta. "There is and will be greater demand for good talent than the industry can supply. Most companies are moving to larger databases, and the need for Oracle and Microsoft SQL Server database administrators in particular is a bottomless pit."

FOR MORE INFORMATION

For information on career opportunities or student chapters, contact:
Association of Information Technology Professionals
401 North Michigan Avenue, Suite 2200
Chicago, IL 60611-4267
Tel: 800-224-9371
Email: aitp_hq@aitp.org
http://www.aitp.org

The Data Management Association (DAMA) International is an organization for professionals involved in business intelligence and data management. Visit its website to read articles related to these issues in DM Review.

DAMA International
PO Box 5786
Bellevue, WA 98006-5786
Tel: 425-562-2636
Email: DAMA@DAMA.org
http://www.dama.org

For information about scholarships, student membership, and careers, contact:

IEEE Computer Society
1730 Massachusetts Avenue, NW
Washington, DC 20036-1992
Tel: 202-371-0101
Email: membership@computer.org
http://www.computer.org

For more information about computer certification, contact:

Institute for Certification of Computing Professionals
2350 East Devon Avenue, Suite 115
Des Plaines, IL 60018-4610
Tel: 800-843-8227
Email: office@iccp.org
http://www.iccp.org

To read articles from the quarterly bulletin Data Engineering, *produced by the IEEE Technical Committee on Data Engineering, visit:*

Data Engineering
http://research.microsoft.com/research/db/debull

For more information on the Association for Computing Machinery's special interest group on management of data, visit the website:

Special Interest Group on Management of Data
http://www.acm.org/sigmod

DENTAL HYGIENISTS

QUICK FACTS

School Subjects Biology Health	**Certification or Licensing** Required by all states
Personal Skills Helping/teaching Technical/scientific	**Outlook** Much faster than the average
Work Environment Primarily indoors Primarily one location	**DOT** 078 **GOE** 10.02.02
Minimum Education Level Associate's degree	**NOC** 3222
Salary Range $35,620 to $54,700 to $81,850+	**O*NET-SOC** 29-2021.00

OVERVIEW

Dental hygienists perform clinical tasks, serve as oral health educators in private dental offices, work in public health agencies, and promote good oral health by educating adults and children. Their main responsibility is to perform oral prophylaxis, a process of cleaning teeth by using sharp dental instruments, such as scalers and prophy angles. With these instruments, they remove stains and calcium deposits, polish teeth, and massage gums. There are approximately 147,000 dental hygienists employed in the United States.

HISTORY

The first dental hygienists were trained by dentists themselves. However, early in the 20th century, the first school for dental hygiene was organized, and in 1915 the practice of dental hygiene was first legalized on a state level.

Although the profession has existed since the beginning of the 20th century, dental hygienists were not particularly common before recent advances in the field. Discoveries in chemistry and the biomedical sciences have led to the development of dental radiography and improved dental instruments, materials, and treatment techniques. Using fluoride to prevent tooth decay has also created more work for dentists because fluoride treatments enable many more people to keep their teeth throughout their lives. In recent decades, with greater public awareness of the importance of dental care, more and more companies have begun providing dental insurance to employees.

These developments in the field of dental care have resulted in a greater workload for dentists. As they have taken on more patients and performed more dental services, they have had less time to complete routine cleanings and instruct patients on oral hygiene. Consequently, dental hygienists have become important members of many dentistry practices.

THE JOB

In clinical settings, hygienists help prevent gum diseases and cavities by removing deposits from teeth and applying sealants and fluoride to prevent tooth decay. They remove tartar, stains, and plaque from teeth, take X rays and perform other diagnostic tests, place and remove temporary fillings, take health histories, remove sutures, polish amalgam restorations, and examine head, neck, and oral regions for disease.

Their tools include hand and rotary instruments to clean teeth, syringes with needles to administer local anesthetic (such as Novocaine), teeth models to demonstrate home care procedures, and X-ray machines to take pictures of the oral cavity that the dentist uses to detect signs of decay or disease.

A hygienist also provides nutritional counseling and screens patients for oral cancer and high blood pressure. Dentists perform more extensive dental procedures. Other hygienist responsibilities depend on the employer.

Private dentists might require that the dental hygienist mix compounds for filling cavities, sterilize instruments, assist in surgical work, or even carry out clerical tasks such as making appointments and filling in insurance forms. The hygienist might well fill the duties of *receptionist* or *office manager*, functioning in many ways to assist the dentist in carrying out the day's schedule.

Although some of these tasks might also be done by a *dental assistant*, only the dental hygienist is licensed by the state to clean teeth. Licensed hygienists submit charts of each patient's teeth, noting possible decay or disease. The dentist studies these in making further diagnoses.

The *school hygienist* cleans and examines the teeth of students in a number of schools. The hygienist also gives classroom instruction on correct brushing and flossing of teeth, the importance of good dental care, and the effects of good nutrition. He or she keeps student dental records and notifies parents of any need for further treatment.

Dental hygienists may be employed by local, state, or federal public health agencies. These hygienists carry out an educational program for adults and children, in public health clinics, schools, and other public facilities. A few dental hygienists may assist in research projects. For those with further education, teaching in a dental hygiene school is another possibility.

Like all dental professionals, hygienists must be aware of federal, state, and local laws that govern hygiene practice. In particular, hygienists must know the types of infection control and protective gear that, by law, must be worn in the dental office to protect workers from infection. Dental hygienists, for example, must wear gloves, protective eyewear, and a mask during examinations. As with most health care workers, hygienists must be immunized against contagious diseases, such as hepatitis.

Dental hygienists are required by their state and encouraged by professional organizations to continue learning about trends in dental care, procedures, and regulations by taking continuing education courses. These may be held at large dental society meetings, colleges and universities, or in more intimate settings, such as a nearby dental office.

INTERVIEW: Dental Hygienist

Jane O'Donnell has worked as a dental hygienist for four years. She spoke with the editors of 25 Jobs That Have It All *about her career.*

Q. Can you describe your work?

A. My primary duties are to evaluate the oral state of the patient. This is done by a visual exam, reviewing previous records, updating medical histories, performing an oral cancer screening, taking and develop radiographs, and detecting cavities. I question the patient about any problem they might be having. I then remove plaque, tartar, and stain from above and below the gumline. I review good oral hygiene habits and demonstrate brushing and flossing techniques as needed. Secondary duties would be keeping my instruments and equipment in good working order.

Q. What is the educational path to become a dental hygienist?

A. To become a registered dental hygienist requires two years of classroom and clinical study in an accredited dental hygiene program. Before being accepted into the program, about two years of prerequisites are required. These classes are a mix of liberal arts and science classes.

Q. What kinds of licensing requirements exist for dental hygienists?

A. Hygienists are licensed by the state in which they work. The dental hygienist educational program prepares students for national and state boards. The national board is an eight-hour, multiple-choice test, with about 350–400 questions. The State Board of Illinois consists of a clinical portion, working on a patient, and another multiple choice test. After passing all three components, students may apply for a license.

Q. How can students locate schools that offer dental hygiene programs?

A. The library is always a good place to start. Check the reference desk for sources that list schools with dental hygiene programs in and out of state. Also, the American Dental Hygienists' Association has a website, http://www.adhA.org, with lots of information including phone numbers of local chapters.

Q. What are the top personal qualities for people working in this career?

A. Good communication skills are a must. A hygienist reviews a patient's oral hygiene and educates [them]. Being professional comes in handy when seeing what neglect can do to the oral cavity. Educating people with a mix of empathy and oral health information might help someone regain the interest in preserving their teeth and improving their overall health.

Q. What are the pros and cons of your job?

A. Pros: Dental hygienists are in demand. There are many job opportunities in almost every state. The hours are usually flexible, either part time or full time. The salary is good, and the working conditions are usually pleasant.

Cons: Many small offices do not offer benefits. This can be a problem for single people. Dental hygienists are at risk for repetitive stress injuries to the hand, wrist, elbow, shoulder, and back. Proper posture is a must.

Q. What is the most important piece of advice that you have to offer college students as they graduate and look for jobs in this field?

A. There is a job out there for everyone. Sometimes you have to be flexible and work a night or two and a few Saturdays. Most offices will not want to lose a good hygienist and compromises can be made, turning a so-so job into a great one!

Q. What is the future employment outlook for your career?

A. Every state varies. Ten years ago in Illinois there were only five or six dental hygiene education programs. Now there are 13, with plans for two more. Many of these programs were started in areas that were greatly underserved. It remains to be seen if these new programs create a tightening of the job market. Over the last few years, the state of Illinois has expanded the duties of the dental hygienist to include administering local anesthetic through injection. Hopefully more expanded duties will follow.

Right now in Illinois, a hygienist has to work under the direct supervision of a dentist, meaning the dentist has to be on the premises. In other states a hygienist can work under general supervision, meaning the dentist has authorized the procedure, but does not have to be present. This would allow working in settings other than an office, such as in a nursing home, and would create more job opportunities.

REQUIREMENTS
High School

The minimum requirement for admission to a dental hygiene school is graduation from high school. While in high school, you should follow a college preparatory program, which will include courses such as science, mathematics, history, English, and foreign language. Health courses will also be of much use to you in this career.

Postsecondary Training

Two types of postsecondary training are available in this field. One is a four-year college program offering a bachelor's degree. More common is a two-year program leading to a dental hygiene certification. The bachelor's degree is often preferred by employers, and more schools are likely to require completion of such a degree program in the future. There are about 235 accredited schools in the United States that offer one or both of these courses. Classroom work emphasizes general and dental sciences and liberal arts. Lectures are usually combined with laboratory work and clinical experience.

Certification or Licensing

After graduating from an accredited school, you must pass state licensing examinations, both written and clinical. The American Dental Association Joint Commission on National Dental Examinations administers the written part of the examination. This test is accepted by all states and the District of Columbia. The clinical part of the examination is administered by state or regional testing agencies.

Other Requirements

Dental hygiene schools frequently require that applicants complete aptitude tests sponsored by the American Dental Hygienists' Association; these tests help prospective students determine whether they will succeed in this field. Skill in handling delicate instruments, a sensitive touch, and depth perception are important attributes that are tested. To be a successful dental hygienist, you should be neat, clean, and personable.

EXPLORING

Work as a dental assistant can be a stepping-stone to a career as a dental hygienist. As a dental assistant, you could closely observe the work of a dental hygienist. You could then assess your personal aptitude for this work, discuss any questions with other hygienists, and enroll in a dental hygiene school where experience as a dental assistant would certainly be helpful.

You may be able to find part-time or summer work in high school as a dental assistant or clerical worker in a dentist's office. You also may be able to observe a dental hygienist working in a school or a dentist's office or visit an accredited dental hygiene school.

EMPLOYERS

Approximately 147,000 dental hygienists are employed in the United States. Dental hygienists can find work in private dentist's offices, school systems, or public health agencies. Hospitals, industrial plants, and the armed forces also employ a small number of dental hygienists.

STARTING OUT

Once you have passed the National Board exams and a licensing exam in a particular state, you must decide on an area of work. Most dental hygiene schools maintain placement services for the assistance of their graduates, and finding a satisfactory position is usually not too difficult.

ADVANCEMENT

Opportunities for advancement, other than increases in salary and benefits that accompany experience in the field, usually require additional study and training. Educational advancement may lead to a position as an administrator, teacher, or director in a dental health program or to a more advanced field of practice. With further education and training, some hygienists may choose to go on to become dentists.

EARNINGS

The dental hygienist's income is influenced by such factors as education, experience, locale, and type of employer. Most dental hygienists who work in private dental offices are salaried employees, although some are paid a commission for work performed or a combination of salary and commission.

According to the U.S. Department of Labor, full-time hygienists earned a median annual salary of $54,700 in 2001. The lowest paid 10 percent of hygienists earned $17.13 an hour (or $35,620 annually), and the highest 10 percent earned $39.35 an hour (or $81,850 annually). Salaries in large metropolitan areas are generally somewhat higher than in small cities and towns. In addition, dental hygienists in research, education, or administration may earn higher salaries.

A salaried dental hygienist in a private office typically receives a paid two- or three-week vacation. Part-time or commissioned dental hygienists in private offices usually have no paid vacation.

WORK ENVIRONMENT

Working conditions for dental hygienists are pleasant, with well-lighted, modern, and adequately equipped facilities. Hygienists usually sit while working. State and federal regulations require that hygienists wear masks, protective eyewear, and gloves. Most hygienists do not wear any jewelry. They are required by government infection control procedures to leave their work clothes at work, so many dentists' offices now have laundry facilities to properly launder work clothes. They must also follow proper sterilizing techniques on equipment and instruments to guard against passing infection or disease.

More than 50 percent of all hygienists work part time, or less than 35 hours a week. It is common practice among part-time and full-time hygienists to work in more than one office because many dentists schedule a hygienist to come in only two or three days a week. Hygienists frequently piece together part-time positions at several dental offices and substitute for other hygienists who take days off. About 88 percent of hygienists see eight or more patients daily, and 68 percent work in a single practice. Many private offices are open on Saturdays. Government employees' work hours are regulated by the particular agency.

OUTLOOK

The U.S. Department of Labor (DOL) projects that employment of dental hygienists will grow much faster than the average over the next several years. In fact, the DOL predicts that dental hygienists will be one of the 25 fastest growing occupations. The demand for dental hygienists is expected to grow as younger generations that grew up receiving better dental care keep their teeth longer.

Population growth, increased public awareness of proper oral home care, and the availability of dental insurance should result in the creation of more dental hygiene jobs. Moreover, as the population ages, there will be a special demand for hygienists to work with older people, especially those who live in nursing homes.

Because of increased awareness about caring for animals in captivity, hygienists are also among a small number of dental professionals who volunteer to help care for animals' teeth and perform annual examinations. Dental professionals are not licensed to treat animals, however, and must work under the supervision of veterinarians.

FOR MORE INFORMATION
For education information, contact:
American Dental Association
211 East Chicago Avenue
Chicago, IL 60611
Tel: 312-440-2500
http://www.ada.org

For publications, information on dental schools, and scholarship information, contact:
American Dental Education Association
1625 Massachusetts Avenue, NW, Suite 600
Washington, DC 20036-2212
Tel: 202-667-9433
Email: adea@adea.org
http://www.adea.org

For career information and tips for dental hygiene students on finding a job, contact:
American Dental Hygienists' Association
444 North Michigan Avenue, Suite 3400
Chicago, IL 60611
Tel: 312-440-8900
Email: mail@adha.net
http://www.adha.org

GRAPHIC DESIGNERS

QUICK FACTS

School Subjects Art Computer science	**Certification or Licensing** None available
	Outlook Faster than the average
Personal Skills Artistic Communication/ideas	
	DOT 141
Work Environment Primarily indoors Primarily one location	**GOE** 01.02.03
Minimum Education Level Some postsecondary training	**NOC** 5241
Salary Range $20,000 to $40,000 to $100,000+	**O*NET-SOC** 27-1024.00

OVERVIEW

Graphic designers are artists whose commercial creations are intended to express ideas, convey information, or draw attention to a product. They design a wide variety of materials including advertisements, displays, packaging, signs, computer graphics and games, book and magazine covers and interiors, animated characters, and company logos to fit the needs and preferences of their various clients. There are approximately 190,000 graphic designers employed in the United States.

HISTORY

The challenge of combining beauty, function, and technology in any form has preoccupied artisans throughout history. Graphic design work has been created products and promoted commerce for as long as people have used symbols, pictures, and typography to communicate ideas.

Graphic design has grown along with print media (newspapers, magazines, catalogs, and advertising). The graphic designer would typically sketch several rough drafts of the layout of pictures and words. After one of the drafts was approved, the designer would complete a final layout including detailed type and artwork specifications. The words were sent to a typesetter and the artwork assigned to an illustrator. When the final pieces were returned, the designer or a keyline and paste-up artist would adhere them to an illustration board with rubber cement or wax. Different colored items were placed on acetate overlays. This camera-ready art was then ready to be sent to a printer for photographing and reproduction.

Computer technology has revolutionized the way many graphic designers do their work: today it is possible to be a successful graphic designer even if you can't draw more than simple stick figures. Graphic designers are now able to draw, color, and revise the many different images they work with daily. They can choose typefaces, size type, and place it without having to align it on the page using a T-square and triangle. Computer graphics enable graphic designers to work more quickly, since details like size, shape, and color are easy to change.

Graphics programs for computers are continually being revised and improved, moving more and more design work from the artist's table to the computer mousepad and graphics tablet. This area of computer technology is booming and will continue to do so in the future, as computer graphics and multimedia move toward virtual reality applications. Many graphic designers with solid computer experience will be needed to work with these systems.

THE JOB

Graphic designers are not primarily fine artists, although they may be highly skilled at drawing or painting. Most designs commissioned to graphic designers involve both artwork and copy (that is, words). Thus, the designer must not only be familiar with the wide range of art media (photography, drawing, painting, collage, etc.) and styles, but he or she must also be familiar with a wide range of typefaces and know how to manipulate them for the right effect. Because design tends to change in a similar way as fashion, designers must keep up to date with the latest trends. At the same time, they must be well grounded in more traditional, classic designs.

Graphic designers can work as *in-house designers* for a particular company, as *staff designers* for a graphic design firm, or as *freelance designers* working for themselves. Some designers specialize in designing advertising materials or packaging. Others focus on corporate identity materials such as company stationery and logos. Some work mainly for publishers, designing book and magazine covers and page layouts. Some work in the area of computer graphics, creating still or animated graphics for computer software, videos, or motion pictures. A highly specialized type of graphic designer, the *environmental graphic designer,* designs large outdoor signs. Some graphic designers design exclusively on the computer, while others may use both the computer and traditional hand drawings or paintings, depending on the project's needs and requirements.

Whatever the specialty and whatever their medium, all graphic designers take a similar approach to a project, whether it is for an entirely new design or for a variation on an existing one. Graphic designers begin by determining as best they can the needs and preferences of the clients and the potential users, buyers, or viewers.

For example, a graphic designer working on a company logo will likely meet with company representatives to discuss how and where the company will use the logo and what size, color, and shape preferences company executives might have. Project budgets must be carefully respected: a design that may be perfect in every way but that is too costly to reproduce is useless. Graphic designers may need to compare their ideas with similar ones from other companies and analyze the image they project. Thus they must have a good knowledge of how various colors, shapes, and layouts affect the viewer psychologically.

After a plan has been conceived and the details worked out, the graphic designer does some preliminary designs (generally two or three) to present to the client for approval. The client may reject the preliminary design entirely and request a new one, or he or she may ask the designer to make alterations. The designer then goes back to the drawing board to attempt a new design or make the requested changes. This process continues until the client approves the design.

Once a design has been approved, the graphic designer prepares the design for professional reproduction, that is, printing. The printer may require a "mechanical," in which the artwork and copy are arranged on a white board just as it is to be photographed, or the designer may be asked to submit an electronic copy of the design. Either way, designers must have a good understanding of the printing process, including color separation, paper properties, and halftone (i.e., photograph) reproduction.

INTERVIEW: Graphic Designer

Sam Concialdi has been a graphic designer for 20 years and is the owner of Concialdi Design, a graphic design firm located in a Chicago suburb. He spoke with the editors of 25 Jobs That Have It All *about his career.*

Q. How did you train for this job? What was your college major?

A. I majored in graphic design at Northern Illinois University. I received the majority of my experience hands-on, working at a small, suburban newspaper where I was the head of the advertising department. I was in charge of designing and creating ads for the newspaper.

Q. How do you hire the graphic designers that work in your firm?

A. Seven of the eight designers in my office were hired by word of mouth; the other one was found through a newspaper ad.

Q. What are the most important personal and professional qualities for graphic designers?

A. The most important quality is to be flexible with your design work. You need to understand that a customer might like something you don't like at all. Also, you need good people skills to understand what will make your client happy.

Q. What are some of the pros and cons of your job?

A. Pros:

- The opportunity to exercise your creativity
- A feeling of accomplishment and satisfaction when a job is completed and it is well done

Cons:

- Rejections of ideas by clients
- Constant deadlines

Q. What is the most important piece of advice that you have to offer college students as they graduate and look for jobs in this field?

A. Computer skills are a key factor for aspiring graphic designers. Students should learn as much as they can and try to create their own design style.

REQUIREMENTS

High School

While in high school, take any art and design courses that are available. Computer classes are also helpful, particularly those that teach page layout programs or art and photography manipulation programs. Working on the school newspaper or yearbook can provide valuable design experience. You may also volunteer to design flyers or posters for school events.

Postsecondary Training

More graphic designers are recognizing the value of formal training, and at least two out of three people entering the field today have a college degree or some college education. Over 100 colleges and art schools offer graphic design programs that are accredited by the National Association of Schools of Art and Design. At many schools, graphic design students must take a year of basic art and design courses before being accepted into the bachelor's degree program. In addition, applicants to the bachelor's degree programs in graphic arts may be asked to submit samples of their work to prove artistic ability. Many schools and employers depend on samples, or portfolios, to evaluate the applicants' skills in graphic design.

Many programs increasingly emphasize the importance of computers in design work. Computer proficiency among graphic designers will be very important in the years to come. Interested individuals should select an academic program that incorporates computer training into the curriculum, or train themselves on their own.

A bachelor of fine arts program at a four-year college or university may include courses such as principles of design, art and art history, painting, sculpture, mechanical and architectural drawing, architecture, computerized design, basic engineering, fashion designing and sketching, garment construction, and textiles. Such degrees are desirable but not always necessary for obtaining a position as a graphic designer.

Other Requirements

As with all artists, graphic designers need a degree of artistic talent, creativity, and imagination. They must be sensitive to beauty and have an eye for detail and a strong sense of color, balance, and proportion. To a great extent, these qualities are natural, but they can be developed through training, both on the job and in professional schools, colleges, and universities.

It is increasingly important for graphic designers to have solid computer skills and a working knowledge of several of the common drawing, image editing, and page layout programs. Graphic design on the computer is done on both Macintosh systems and on PCs; many designers have both types of computers in their studios.

With or without specialized education, graphic designers seeking employment should have a good portfolio containing samples of their best work. The graphic designer's portfolio is extremely important and can make a difference when an employer must choose between two otherwise equally qualified candidates.

A period of on-the-job training is expected for all beginning designers. The length of time it takes to become fully qualified as a graphic designer may run from one to three years, depending on prior education and experience, as well as innate talent.

EXPLORING

If you are interested in a career in graphic design, there are a number of ways to find out whether you have the talent, ambition, and perseverance to succeed in the field. Take as many art and design courses as possible while still in high school and become proficient at working on computers. To get an insider's view of various design occupations, enlist the help of art teachers or school guidance counselors to arrange a tour of a design company and interviews with designers.

While in school, you can get practical experience by participating in school and community projects that call for design talents. These projects might include building sets for plays, setting up exhibits, planning seasonal and holiday displays, and preparing programs and other printed materials. If you are interested in publication design, work on the school newspaper or yearbook is invaluable.

Part-time and summer jobs are excellent ways to become familiar with the day-to-day requirements of a particular design occupation and gain some basic related experience. Possible places of employment include design studios, design departments in advertising agencies and manufacturing companies, department and furniture stores, flower shops, workshops that produce ornamental items, and museums. Museums also use a number of volunteer workers. Inexperienced people are often employed as sales, clerical, or general helpers; those with a little more education and experience may qualify for jobs in which they have a chance to develop actual design skills and build portfolios of completed design projects.

EMPLOYERS

Graphic designers hold approximately 190,000 jobs. They work in many different industries, including the wholesale and retail trade (department stores, furniture and home furnishings stores, apparel stores, florist shops), manufacturing industries (machinery, motor vehicles, aircraft, metal products, instruments, apparel, textiles, printing, and publishing), service industries (business services, engineering, architecture), construction firms, and government agencies. Public relations and publicity firms, advertising agencies, and mail-order houses all have graphic design departments. The publishing industry is a primary employer of graphic designers, including book publishers, magazines, newspapers, and newsletters.

About one-third of all graphic designers are self-employed, a higher proportion than is found in most other occupations. These freelance designers sell their services to multiple clients.

STARTING OUT

The best way to enter the field of graphic design is to have a strong portfolio. Potential employers rely on portfolios to evaluate talent and how that talent might be used to fit the company's special needs. Beginning graphic designers can assemble a portfolio from work completed at school, in art classes, and in part-time or freelance jobs. The portfolio should continually be updated to reflect the designer's growing skills, so it will always be ready for possible job changes.

Those just starting out can apply directly to companies that employ designers. Many colleges and professional schools have placement services to help graduates find positions, and sometimes it is possible to get a referral from a previous part-time employer or volunteer coordinator.

ADVANCEMENT

As part of their on-the-job training, beginning graphic designers generally are given simple tasks and work under direct supervision. As they gain experience, they move up to more complex work with increasingly less supervision. Experienced graphic designers, especially those with leadership capabilities, may be promoted to chief designer, design department head, or other supervisory positions.

Computer graphic designers can move into other computer-related positions with additional education. Some may pursue graphics programming to further improve their computer design capabilities. Others may become involved with multimedia and interactive graphics. Video games, touch-screen displays in stores, and even laser light shows are all products of multimedia graphic designers.

When designers develop personal styles that are in high demand in the marketplace, they sometimes go into business for themselves. Freelance design work can be erratic, however, so usually only the most experienced designers with an established client base can count on consistent full-time work.

EARNINGS

The range of salaries for graphic designers is quite broad. Many earn as little as $20,000, while others receive more than $100,000. Salaries depend primarily on the nature and scope of the employer, with computer graphic designers earning wages on the high end of the range. The Bureau of Labor Statistics reports that in 2001, graphic designers earned a median salary of $36,020; the highest 10 percent earned $61,050 or more, while the lowest 10 percent earned $21,700 or less.

Self-employed designers can earn a lot one year and substantially more or less the next. Their earnings depend on individual talent and business ability, but, in general, are higher than those of salaried designers, although like any self-employed individual, they must pay their own insurance costs and taxes and are not compensated for vacation or sick days.

The *American Institute of Graphic Arts/Aquent Salary Survey 2002* reports that designers earned a median salary of $40,000 in 2001, while senior designers earned a median of $50,000 annually. Salaried designers who advance to the position of creative/design director earned a median of $80,000 a year. The owner of a consulting firm can make $90,000 or more.

Graphic designers who work for large corporations receive full benefits, including health insurance, paid vacation, and sick leave.

WORK ENVIRONMENT

Most graphic designers work regular hours in clean, comfortable, pleasant offices or studios. Conditions vary depending on the design specialty. Some graphic designers work in small establishments with few employees; others work in large organizations with large design departments. Some deal mostly with their co-workers, while others may have a lot of public contact. Freelance designers are paid by the assignment. To maintain a steady income, they must constantly strive to please their clients and to find new ones. Computer graphic designers may have to work long, irregular hours in order to complete an especially ambitious project.

OUTLOOK

Chances for employment look very good for qualified graphic designers over the next several years, especially for those involved with computer graphics. The design field in general is expected to grow at a faster than average rate. As computer graphic technology continues to advance, there will be a need for well-trained computer graphic designers. Companies that have always used graphic designers will expect their designers to perform work on computers. Companies for which graphic design was once too time-consuming or costly are now sprucing up company newsletters and magazines, among other things, requiring the skills of design professionals.

Because the design field appeals to many talented individuals, competition is expected to be strong in all areas. Beginners and designers with only average talent or without formal education and technical skills may encounter some difficulty in finding a job.

FOR MORE INFORMATION

For more information about careers in graphic design, contact the following organizations:

American Institute of Graphic Arts
National Design Center
164 Fifth Avenue
New York, NY 10010
Tel: 212-807-1990
Email: comments@aiga.org
http://www.aiga.org

National Association of Schools of Art and Design
11250 Roger Bacon Drive, Suite 21
Reston, VA 20190
Tel: 703-437-0700
Email: info@arts-accredit.org
http://www.arts-accredit.org/nasad

Society for Environmental Graphic Design
1000 Vermont Avenue, Suite 400
Washington, DC 20005
Tel: 202-638-5555
Email: segd@segd.org
http://www.segd.org

HEALTH CARE MANAGERS

QUICK FACTS

School Subjects Biology Business	**Certification or Licensing** Required for certain positions
Personal Skills Helping/teaching Leadership/management	**Outlook** Faster than the average
Work Environment Primarily indoors One location with some travel	**DOT** 187 **GOE** 11.07.02
Minimum Education Level Bachelor's degree	**NOC** 0014
Salary Range $36,560 to $59,220 to $104,350+	**O*NET-SOC** 11-9111.00

OVERVIEW

Health care managers, also known as *health services managers* and *health services administrators,* direct the operation of hospitals, nursing homes, and other health care organizations. They are responsible for facilities, services, programs, staff, budgets, and relations with other organizations. There are more than 250,000 health care managers employed in the United States.

HISTORY

Health care institutions have changed considerably since Benjamin Franklin and Dr. Thomas Bond founded the Pennsylvania Hospital in Philadelphia in the mid-1700s. Rapid advances in medical science, highly specialized physicians, an increasing number of technical assistants, and expensive and elaborate medical equipment all require the structure of a well-organized health care facility in order to be effective. Thus, the ever-increasing complexity of this field created the need for the growing profession of hospital and health services managers.

In the past, physicians, nurses, or workers in other fields were appointed to the position of hospital administrator with little or no special training. The earliest recognition of hospital administration as a separate profession came in the 1890s, when the Association of Hospital Superintendents was organized. This group, whose membership includes nearly all of the hospitals in the United States, is today known as the American Hospital Association. In the 1930s, the American College of Hospital Administrators (now the American College of Healthcare Executives) was founded to increase the standards of practice and education in the field.

The broad range of today's health care institutions includes general hospitals, medical group practices, extended care facilities, nursing homes, rehabilitation institutions, psychiatric hospitals, health maintenance organizations (HMOs), and outpatient clinics. The field of long-term care is one of the fastest growing parts of the industry; today there are over 15,000 nursing homes throughout the United States. Health care managers currently hold over 250,000 jobs, more than half of which are in hospitals.

THE JOB

Health care managers, or *chief executive officers (CEOs)* of hospitals and health care facilities, organize and manage personnel, equipment, and auxiliary services. They hire and supervise personnel, handle budgets and fee schedules charged to patients, and establish billing procedures. In addition, they help plan space needs, purchase supplies and equipment, oversee building and equipment maintenance, and provide for mail, phones, laundry, and other services for patients and staff. In some health care institutions, many of these duties are delegated to assistants or to various department heads. These assistants may supervise operations in such clinical areas as surgery, nursing, dietary, or therapy and in such administrative areas as purchasing, finance, housekeeping, and maintenance.

The health services administrator works closely with the institution's governing board in the development of plans and policies. Following the board's directions, the administrator may carry out large projects that expand and develop hospital services. Such projects include organizing fund-raising campaigns and planning new research projects.

Health services managers meet regularly with their staffs to discuss achievements and address new problems. Managers may organize training programs for nurses, interns, and others in cooperation with the medical staff and department heads. Health care executives also represent the health care facility at community or professional meetings.

REQUIREMENTS
High School

If you are interested in a career in health management, you should start preparing in high school by taking college preparatory classes. Because communication skills are important, take as many speech and writing classes as possible. Courses in health, business, mathematics, and computer science are also excellent choices to help you prepare for this career.

Postsecondary Training

The training required to qualify for this work depends, to a large extent, on the qualifications established by the individual employer or a facility's governing board. Most employers prefer candidates with a graduate degree in health services administration. A few require that their chief executives be physicians, while others look for people with formal training in law or general business administration as well as experience in the health care field. The future health care administrator may have a liberal arts foundation with a strong background in the social sciences or business economics.

Specialized training in health services administration is offered at both graduate and undergraduate levels. The graduate program generally takes two years to complete. Graduate students split their time between studying in the classroom and working as an administrative resident in a program-approved health care facility. Successful completion of the course work, the residency, and perhaps a thesis is required to earn the master's degree. An optional third-year fellowship provides additional work experience supervised by a mentor. During this period, the individual may work in various hospital departments as an assistant to department heads.

Certification or Licensing

Licensure is not a requirement for health care services executives employed in hospitals. However, all states require nursing home administrators to be licensed. Most states use the licensing exam prepared by the National Association of Boards and Examiners for Nursing Home Administrators. Because requirements vary from state to state, those considering careers in nursing home administration should contact their state's licensing body for specific licensure requirements. Also, it should be noted that continuing education is now a condition of licensure in most states.

Other Requirements

Much of the work of health services managers consists of dealing with people—the hospital's governing board, the medical staff, the department heads and other employees, the patients and their families, and community leaders and businesses. Therefore, health care managers must be tactful and sympathetic.

In addition, administrators must be able to coordinate the health care facility's many related functions. They need to understand, for instance, financial operations, purchasing, organizational development, and public relations. They must also have the ability to make some decisions with speed and others only after considerable study. And, of course, health services executives should have a deep interest in the care of sick and injured patients.

Special hospitals, such as mental hospitals, often employ administrators who are physicians in the facility's specialty. Usually, facilities that are operated by religious groups employ administrators of the same faith as those of the group operating the hospital.

EXPLORING

If you are considering a career as a health services manager, you should take advantage of opportunities in high school to develop some of the skills required in this line of work. Because administrators and other health care executives should be leaders and talented speakers, participation in clubs as a leader or active member and in debate and speech clubs is helpful. Working in the school's health center is also useful. Hospitals, nursing homes, and other health service facilities offer part-time work after school, on weekends, and during the summer. Health services executives are often willing to speak to interested students, but it is suggested that you make an appointment first.

EMPLOYERS

Health care managers can find employment in facilities such as HMOs, group medical practices, and centers for urgent care, cardiac rehabilitation, and diagnostic imaging. Opportunities are also plentiful in long-term care facilities, such as nursing homes, home health care agencies, adult day care programs, life care communities, and other residential facilities.

STARTING OUT

A student in training as an administrative resident or postgraduate fellow may be offered a job as an administrative assistant or department head by the hospital or health care facility where the residency is served. The hospital's administrator at the place of training also may assist the student in locating a job.

Job openings can also be found by contacting the university's placement bureau or through bulletins of state and national associations. Large professional society meetings may offer on-site notices of job openings. Positions in federal- and state-operated health care institutions are filled by the civil service or by political appointment. Appointments to military hospitals are handled by the various branches of the armed services.

Although the majority of students prepare for this career with a four-year college program followed by graduate study, it is still possible to secure a health administration position through experience and training in subordinate jobs and working up the administrative ladder.

ADVANCEMENT

It is unusual to finish college and step into a position as an upper level health services executive. Most new graduates first gain experience in a more specialized clinical or administrative area of a health care facility. There they can become accustomed to working with health care personnel, patients, information systems, budgets, and finances. This experience and/or graduate work often leads to promotion to department head. Those with graduate training can expect to achieve higher level positions. Assistant administrator or vice president is often the next step and may lead to appointment as the hospital's chief executive.

EARNINGS

Salaries of health services executives depend on the type of facility, geographic location, the size of the administrative staff, the budget, and the policy of the governing board. The Bureau of Labor Statistics reports that the median annual earnings of medical and health services managers were $59,220 in 2001. Salaries ranged from less than $36,560 to more than $104,350. The *Occupational Outlook Handbook* reports that the median salary of health care managers who worked in hospitals was $60,360 and of those who worked in nursing and personal care facilities was $51,240 in 2000.

A *Modern Healthcare* survey reports the following median annual salaries for department managers in 2001: respiratory therapy, $67,200; home health care, $69,900; physical therapy, $71,400; radiology, $76,500; clinical laboratory, $77,100; rehabilitation services $79,700; outpatient services, $85,200; and nursing services, $113,800.

Health service administrators managing a small group practice, consisting of seven or fewer physicians, averaged $65,125 annually in 2000, as reported by the Medical Group Management Association. Administrators responsible for practices with seven to 25 physicians earned an average of $83,022, and in practices with more than 26 physicians, they earned $96,402.

Some administrators receive free meals, housing, and laundry service, depending on the facility in which they are employed. They usually receive paid vacations and holidays, sick leave, hospitalization and insurance benefits, and pension programs. The executive benefits package nowadays often includes management incentive bonuses based on job performance ranging from $25,000 to $225,000.

WORK ENVIRONMENT

To perform efficiently as an executive, health services administrators usually work out of a large office. They must maintain good communication with the staff and members of various departments.

Most administrators work five and a half days a week, averaging about 55–60 hours. However, hours can be irregular because hospitals and other health care facilities operate around the clock; emergencies may require the manager's supervision any time of the day or night.

OUTLOOK

Because every hospital and numerous other health care facilities employ administrators, employment opportunities in health care will be excellent over the next several years as the industry continues to diversify and deal with the problems of financing health care for everyone. The U.S. Department of Labor predicts that employment will grow at a rate faster than the average.

Not all areas will grow at the same rate, however. Changes in the health care system are taking place because of the need to control escalating costs. This will have the greatest impact on hospitals, traditionally the largest employer of health services executives. The number of hospitals is declining as separate companies are set up to provide services such as ambulatory surgery, alcohol and drug rehabilitation, or home health care. So, while hospitals may offer fewer jobs, many new openings are expected to be available in other health care settings. Employment will grow the fastest in residential care facilities and practitioners' offices and clinics. There will also be more opportunities with health care management companies who provide management services to hospitals and other organizations, as well as specific departments such as emergency, information management systems, managed care contract negotiations, and physician recruiting.

Many colleges and universities are reporting more graduates in health services administration than hospitals and other health care facilities can employ. As a result, there will be stiff competition for administrative jobs. However, many starting executives can find jobs working in health care settings other than hospitals, or they may be offered jobs at the department head or staff levels.

With hospitals adopting a more business-like approach aimed at lowering costs and increasing earnings, demand for M.B.A. graduates should remain steady. Individuals who have strong people skills and business or management knowledge will find excellent opportunities as administrators in nursing homes and other long-term facilities.

FOR MORE INFORMATION

For information on publications, networking opportunities, and student resources, contact:

American College of Health Care Administrators
300 North Lee Street, Suite 301
Alexandria, VA 22314-2807
Tel: 888-88-ACHCA
http://www.achca.org

Visit the ACHE website for information on accredited educational institutions and to read the online pamphlet, Your Career as a Healthcare Executive.

American College of Healthcare Executives (ACHE)
One North Franklin Street, Suite 1700
Chicago, IL 60606-4425
Tel: 312-424-2800

Email: GenInfo@ache.org
http://www.ache.org

For information on health care administration careers, scholarships, and accredited programs, contact:
Association of University Programs in Health Administration
730 11th Street, NW, 4th Floor
Washington, DC 20001-4510
Tel: 202-638-1448
http://www.aupha.org

For publications, news releases, and information from recent health care conferences, contact:
National Health Council
1730 M Street, NW
Washington, DC 20036
Tel: 202-785-3910
Email: info@nhcouncil.org
http://www.nationalhealthcouncil.org

MANAGEMENT ANALYSTS AND CONSULTANTS

QUICK FACTS

School Subjects Business Computer science Speech	**Certification or Licensing** Voluntary
Personal Skills Communication/ideas Leadership/management	**Outlook** Faster than the average
	DOT 161
Work Environment Primarily indoors Primarily multiple locations	**GOE** 05.01.06
Minimum Education Level Bachelor's degree	**NOC** 1122
Salary Range $35,020 to $57,970 to $250,000+	**O*NET-SOC** 13-1111.00

OVERVIEW

Management analysts and consultants analyze business or operating procedures to devise the most efficient methods of accomplishing work. They gather and organize information about operating problems and procedures and prepare recommendations for implementing new systems or changes. They may update manuals outlining established methods of performing work and train personnel in new applications. There are approximately 501,000 management analysts and consultants employed in the United States.

HISTORY

A number of people in business began experimenting with accepted management practices after the Industrial Revolution. For example, in the 1700s Josiah Wedgwood (1730–1795) applied new labor- and work-saving methods to his pottery business and was the first to formulate the concept of mass-producing articles of uniform quality. He believed the manufacturing process could be organized into a system that would use, and not abuse, the people harnessed to it. He organized the interrelationships between people, material, and events in his factory and took the time to reflect upon them. In short, he did in the 18th century what management analysts and consultants do today.

Frederick W. Taylor (1856–1915) was the creator of the "efficiency cult" in American business. Taylor invented the world-famous "differential piecework" plan, in which a productive worker could significantly increase take-home pay by stepping up the pace of work. Taylor's well-publicized study of the Midvale Steel plant in Pennsylvania was the first time-and-motion study. This study broke down elements of each part of each job and timed it; the study was therefore able to quantify maximum efficiency. Taylor earned many assignments and inspired James O. McKinsey, in 1910, to found a firm dealing with management and accounting problems.

Today, management analysts and consultants are thriving. As technological advances lead to the possibility of dramatic loss or gain in the business world, many executives feel more secure relying on all the specialized expertise they can find.

THE JOB

Management analysts and consultants are called in to solve any of a vast array of organizational problems. They are often needed when a rapidly growing small company needs a better system of control over inventories and expenses.

The role of the consultant is to come into a situation in which a client is unsure or inexpert and to recommend actions or provide assessments. There are many different types of management analysts and consultants, all of whom require knowledge of general management, operations, marketing, logistics, materials management and physical distribution, finance and accounting, human resources, electronic data processing and systems, and management science.

Management analysts and consultants may be called in when a major manufacturer must reorganize its corporate structure when acquiring a new division. For example, they assist when a company relocates to another state by coordinating the move, planning the new facility, and training new workers.

The work of management analysts and consultants is quite flexible and varies from job to job. In general, management analysts and consultants collect, review, and analyze data, make recommendations, and assist in the implementation of their proposals. Some projects require that several consultants work together, each specializing in a different area. Other jobs require the analysts to work independently.

Public and private organizations use management analysts for a variety of reasons. Some organizations lack the resources necessary to handle a project. Other organizations, before they pursue a particular course of action, will consult an analyst to determine what resources will be required or what problems will be encountered. Some companies seek outside advice on how to resolve organizational problems that have already been identified or to avoid troublesome problems that could arise.

Firms providing consulting practitioners range in size from solo practitioners to large international companies employing hundreds of people. The services are generally provided on a contract basis. A company will choose a consulting firm that specializes in the area that needs assistance, and then the two firms negotiate the conditions of the contract. Contract variables include the proposed cost of the project, staffing requirements, and the deadline.

After getting a contract, the analyst's first job is to define the nature and extent of the project. He or she analyzes statistics, such as annual revenues, employment, or expenditures. He or she may also interview employees and observe the operations of the organization on a day-to-day basis.

The next step for the analyst is to use his or her knowledge of management systems to develop solutions. While preparing recommendations, he or she must take into account the general nature of the business, the relationship of the firm to others in its industry, the firm's internal organization, and the information gained through data collection and analysis.

Once they have decided on a course of action, management analysts and consultants usually write reports of their findings and recommendations and present them to the client. They often make formal oral presentations about their findings as well. Some projects require only reports; others require assistance in implementing the suggestions.

REQUIREMENTS
High School

High school courses that will give you a general preparation for this field include business, mathematics, and computer science.

Management analysts and consultants must pass on their findings through written or oral presentations, so be sure to take English and speech classes, too.

Postsecondary Training

Employers generally prefer to hire management analysts and consultants with a master's degree in business or public administration, or at least a bachelor's degree and several years of appropriate work experience. Many fields of study provide a suitable formal educational background for this occupation because of the diversity of problem areas addressed by management analysts and consultants. These include many areas in the computer and information sciences, engineering, business and management, education, communications, marketing and distribution, and architecture and environmental design.

When hired directly from school, management analysts and consultants often participate in formal company training programs. These programs may include instruction on policies and procedures, computer systems and software, and management practices and principles. Regardless of their background, most management analysts and consultants routinely attend conferences to keep abreast of current developments in the field.

Certification and Licensing

The Institute of Management Consultants offers the Certified Management Consultant designation to those who pass an examination and meet minimum educational and experience criteria. Certification is voluntary but may provide an additional advantage to job seekers.

Other Requirements

Management analysts and consultants are often responsible for recommending layoffs of staff, so it is important that they learn to deal with people diplomatically. Their job requires a great deal of tact, enlisting cooperation while exerting leadership, debating their points, and pointing out errors. Consultants must be quick thinkers, able to refute objections with finality. They also must be able to make excellent presentations.

A management analyst must also be unbiased and analytical, with a disposition toward the intellectual side of business and a natural curiosity about the way things work best.

EXPLORING

The reference departments of most libraries include business areas that will have valuable research tools such as encyclopedias of business consultants and "who's who" of business consultants. These books should list management analysis and consulting firms across the country, describing their annual sales and area of specialization, like industrial, high tech, small business, and retail. After doing some research, you can call or write to these firms and ask for more information.

For more general business exploration, see if your school has a business or young leaders club. If there is nothing of the sort, you may want to explore Junior Achievement, a nationwide association that connects young business-minded students with professionals in the field for mentoring and career advice. Visit http://www.ja.org for more information.

EMPLOYERS

About a third of all management analysts and consultants are self-employed. Federal, state, and local governments employ many of the others. The Department of Defense employs the majority of those working for the federal government. The remainder work in the private sector for companies providing consulting services. Although management analysts and consultants are found throughout the country, the majority are concentrated in major metropolitan areas.

STARTING OUT

Most government agencies offer entry-level analyst and consultant positions to people with bachelor's degrees and no work experience. Many entrants are also career changers who were formerly mid- and upper-level managers. With one-third of the practicing management consultants self-employed, career changing is a common route into the field.

Anyone with some degree of business expertise or an expert field can begin to work as an independent consultant. The number of one- and two-person consulting firms in this country is well over 100,000. Establishing a wide range of appropriate personal contacts is by far the most effective way to get started in this field. Consultants have to sell themselves and their expertise, a task far tougher than selling a tangible product the customer can see and handle. Many consultants get their first clients by advertising in newspapers, magazines, and trade or professional periodicals. After some time in the field, word-of-mouth advertising is often the primary force.

ADVANCEMENT

A new consultant in a large firm may be referred to as an *associate* for the first couple of years. The next progression is to *senior associate,* a title that indicates three to five years' experience and the ability to supervise others and do more complex and independent work. After about five years, the analyst who is progressing well may become an *engagement manager* with the responsibility to lead a consulting team on a particular client project. The best managers become *senior engagement managers,* leading several study teams or a very large project team. After about seven years, those who excel will be considered for appointment as *junior partners* or *principals.* Partnership involves responsibility for marketing the firm and leading client projects. Some may be promoted to senior partnership or *director,* but few people successfully run this full course. Management analysts and consultants with entrepreneurial ambition may open their own firms.

EARNINGS

In 2001, management analysts and consultants had median annual earnings of $57,970, according to the Bureau of Labor Statistics. The lowest 10 percent earned less than $35,020, and the highest 10 percent earned more than $109,620.

Salaries and hourly rates for management analysts and consultants vary widely, according to experience, specialization, education, and employer. The *Occupational Outlook Handbook* reports that analysts and consultants working in the management and public relations industries earned median annual earnings of $61,290 in 2000, while those employed in the computer and data processing services industry earned $56,070. Management analysts and consultants employed by state government earned a median of $43,470.

Many consultants can demand between $400 and $1,000 per day. Their fees are often well over $40 per hour. Self-employed management consultants receive no fringe benefits and generally have to maintain their own office, but their pay is usually much higher than salaried consultants. They can make more than $2,000 per day or $250,000 in one year from consulting just two days per week.

Typical benefits for salaried analysts and consultants include health and life insurance, retirement plans, vacation and sick leave, profit sharing, and bonuses for outstanding work. All travel expenses are generally reimbursed by the employer.

WORK ENVIRONMENT

Management analysts and consultants generally divide their time between their own offices and the client's office or production facility. They can spend a great deal of time on the road.

Most management analysts and consultants work at least 40 hours per week plus overtime depending on the project. The nature of consulting projects—working on location with a single client toward a specific goal—allows these professionals to immerse themselves totally in their work. They sometimes work 14–16-hour days, and six- or seven-day workweeks can be fairly common.

While self-employed, consultants may enjoy the luxury of setting their own hours and doing a great deal of their work at home; the tradeoff is sacrificing the benefits provided by the large firms. Their livelihood depends on the additional responsibility of maintaining and expanding their clientele on their own.

Although those in this career usually avoid much of the potential tedium of working for one company all day, every day, they face many pressures resulting from deadlines and client expectations. Because the clients are generally paying generous fees, they want to see dramatic results, and the management analyst can feel the weight of this.

OUTLOOK

Employment of management analysts is expected to grow faster than the average for all occupations through the next decade, according to the U.S. Department of Labor. Industry and government agencies are expected to rely more and more on the expertise of these professionals to improve and streamline the performance of their organizations. Many job openings will result from the need to replace personnel who transfer to other fields or leave the labor force.

Competition for management consulting jobs will be strong. Employers can choose from a large pool of applicants who have a wide variety of educational backgrounds and experience. The challenging nature of this job, coupled with high salary potential, attracts many. A graduate degree, experience and expertise in the industry, as well as a knack for public relations, are needed to stay competitive.

Trends that have increased the growth of employment in this field include advancements in information technology and e-commerce, the growth of international business, and fluctuations in the economy that have forced businesses to streamline and downsize.

FOR MORE INFORMATION

For industry information, contact the following organizations:

American Institute of Certified Public Accountants
1211 Avenue of the Americas
New York, NY 10036
Tel: 212-596-6200
http://www.aicpa.org

American Management Association
1601 Broadway
New York, NY 10019
Tel: 800-262-9699
http://www.amanet.org

Association of Management Consulting Firms
380 Lexington Avenue, Suite 1700
New York, NY 10168
Tel: 212-551-7887
Email: info@amcf.org
http://www.amcf.org

For information on certification, contact:

Association of Internal Management Consultants, Inc.
19 Harrison Street
Framingham, MA 01702
Tel: 508-820-3434
Email: info@aimc.org
http://aimc.org

For information on certification, contact:

Institute of Management Consultants
2025 M Street, NW, Suite 800
Washington, DC 20036-3309
Tel: 800-221-2557
http://www.imcusa.org

MEDICAL RECORD TECHNICIANS

QUICK FACTS

School Subjects
Biology
English

Personal Skills
Following instructions
Technical/scientific

Work Environment
Primarily indoors
Primarily one location

Minimum Education Level
Associate's degree

Salary Range
$16,220 to $23,530 to
$50,000+

Certification or Licensing
Recommended

Outlook
Much faster than the
average

DOT
079

GOE
07.05.03

NOC
1413

O*NET-SOC
29-2071.00

OVERVIEW

In any hospital, clinic, or other health care facility, permanent records are created and maintained for all the patients treated by the staff. Each patient's medical record describes in detail his or her condition over time. Entries include illness and injuries, operations, treatments, outpatient visits, and the progress of hospital stays. *Medical record technicians* compile, code, and maintain these records. They also tabulate and analyze data from groups of records to assemble reports. They review records for completeness and accuracy; assign codes to the diseases, operations, diagnoses, and treatments according to detailed standardized classification systems; and post the codes on the medical record. They transcribe medical reports; maintain indices of patients, diseases, operations, and other categories of information; compile patient census data; and file records. In addition, they may direct the day-to-day operations of the medical records department. They maintain the flow of records and reports to and from other departments and sometimes assist medical staff in special studies or research that draws on information in the records. There are approximately 136,000 medical record technicians employed in the United States.

HISTORY

Medical practitioners have been recording information about their patients' illnesses and treatments for hundreds of years. Before the 20th and 21st centuries, such records were kept mostly to help the practitioners retain and learn as much as possible from their own experience. Because there was little centralization or standardization of this information, it was difficult to organize and share the knowledge that resulted from studying many instances of similar cases.

By the early 1900s, medical record-keeping was changing, along with many other aspects of health care. Medicine was more sophisticated, scientific, and successful in helping patients. Hospitals were increasingly becoming accepted as the conventional place for middle-class patients to go for care, and as a result, hospitals became more numerous and better organized. As hospitals grew larger and served more patients, the volume of patient records increased proportionately. With medical record-keeping becoming more important and time consuming, it was most efficient and sensible to centralize it within the hospital. Distinguished committees representing the medical profession also encouraged standardized record-keeping procedures.

By the 1920s, many hospitals in the United States had central libraries of patient information, with employees specifically hired to keep these records in good order. As time passed, their tasks became more complicated. The employees responsible for this work, who used to be called medical record librarians, eventually became differentiated into two basic professional categories: medical record administrators and medical record technicians. In 1953, the first formal training programs for medical record technicians started in hospital schools and junior colleges.

In recent years, the computerization of records, the growing importance of privacy and freedom of information issues, and the changing requirements of insurance carriers have all had major impacts on the field of medical records technology. These areas will undoubtedly continue to reshape the field in future years.

THE JOB

A patient's medical record consists of all relevant information and observations of any health care workers who have dealt with the patient. It may contain, for example, several diagnoses, X-ray and laboratory reports, electrocardiogram tracings, test results, and drugs prescribed. This summary of the patient's medical history is very important to the physician in making speedy and correct decisions about care. Later, information from the record is often needed in authenticating legal forms and insurance claims. The medical record documents the adequacy and appropriateness of the care received by the patient and is the basis of any investigation when the care is questioned in any way.

Patterns and trends can be traced when data from many records are considered together. Many different groups use these types of statistical reports. Hospital administrators, scientists, public health agencies, accrediting and licensing bodies, people who evaluate the effectiveness of current programs or plan future ones, and medical reimbursement organizations are examples of some groups that rely on health care statistics. Medical records can provide the data to show whether a new treatment or medication really works, the relative effectiveness of alternative treatments or medications, or patterns that yield clues about the causes or methods of preventing certain kinds of disease.

Medical record technicians are involved in the routine preparation, handling, and safeguarding of individual records as well as the statistical information extracted from groups of records. Their specific tasks and the scope of their responsibilities depend a great deal on the size and type of the employing institution. In large organizations, there may be a number of technicians and other employees working with medical records. The technicians may serve as assistants to the medical record administrator as needed, or they may regularly specialize in some particular phase of the work done by the department. In small facilities, however, technicians often carry out the whole range of activities and may function fairly independently, perhaps bearing the full responsibility for all day-to-day operations of the department. A technician in a small facility may even be a department director. Sometimes technicians handle medical records and also spend part of their time helping out in the business or admitting office.

Whether they work in hospitals or other settings, medical record technicians must organize, transfer, analyze, preserve, and locate vast quantities of detailed information when needed. The sources of this information include physicians, nurses, laboratory workers, and other members of the health care team.

In a hospital, a patient's cumulative record goes to the medical record department at the end of the hospital stay. A technician checks over the information in the file to be sure that all the essential reports and data are included and appear accurate. Certain specific items must be supplied in any record: signatures, dates, the patient's physical and social history, the results of physical examinations, provisional and final diagnoses, periodic progress notes on the patient's condition during the hospital stay, medications prescribed and administered, therapeutic treatments, surgical procedures, and an assessment of the outcome or the condition at the time of discharge. If any item is missing, the technician sends the record to the person who is responsible for supplying the information. After all necessary information has been received and the record has passed the review, it is considered the official document describing the patient's case.

The record is then passed to a *medical record coder*. Coders are responsible for assigning a numeric code to every diagnosis and procedure listed in a patient's file. Most hospitals in the United States use a nationally accepted system for coding. The lists of diseases, procedures, and conditions are published in classification manuals that medical records personnel refer to frequently. By reducing information in different forms to a single consistent coding system, the data contained in the record is rendered much easier to handle, tabulate, and analyze. It can be indexed under any suitable heading, such as by patient, disease, type of surgery, physician attending the case, and so forth. Cross-indexing is likely to be an important part of the medical record technician's job. Because the same coding systems are used nearly everywhere in the United States, the data may be used not only by people working inside the hospital, but may also be submitted to one of the various programs that pool information obtained from many institutions.

After the information on the medical record has been coded, technicians may use a packaged computer program to assign the patient to one of several hundred diagnosis-related groupings (DRGs). The DRG for the patient's stay determines the amount of money the hospital will receive if the patient is covered by Medicare or one of the other insurance programs that base their reimbursement on DRGs.

Because information in medical records is used to determine how much hospitals are paid for caring for patients, the accuracy of the work done by medical records personnel is vital. A coding error could cause the hospital or patient to lose money.

Another vital part of the job is filing. Regardless of how accurately and completely information is gathered and stored, it is worthless unless it can be retrieved promptly. If paper records are kept, technicians are usually responsible for preparing records for storage, filing them, and getting them out of storage when needed. In some organizations, technicians supervise other personnel who carry out these tasks.

In many health care facilities, computers, rather than paper, are used for nearly all the medical record-keeping. In such cases, medical and nursing staff make notes on an electronic chart. They enter patient-care information into computer files, and medical record technicians access the information using their own terminals. Computers have greatly simplified many traditional routine tasks of the medical records department, such as generating daily hospital census figures, tabulating data for research purposes, and updating special registries of certain types of health problems, such as cancer and stroke.

In the past, some medical records that were originally on paper were later photographed and stored on microfilm, particularly after they were a year or two old. Medical record technicians may be responsible for retrieving and maintaining those films. It is not unusual for a health care institution to have a combination of paper and microfilm files as well as computerized record storage, reflecting the evolution of technology for storing information.

Confidentiality and privacy laws have a major bearing on the medical records field. The laws vary in different states for different types of data, but in all cases, maintaining the confidentiality of individual records is of major concern to medical records workers. All individual records must be in secure storage but also be available for retrieval and specified kinds of properly authorized use. Technicians may be responsible for retrieving and releasing this information. They may prepare records to be released in response to a patient's written authorization, a subpoena, or a court order. This requires special knowledge of legal statutes and often requires consultation with attorneys, judges, insurance agents, and other parties with legitimate rights to access information about a person's health and medical treatment.

Medical record technicians may participate in the quality assurance, risk management, and utilization review activities of a health care facility. In these cases, they may serve as *data abstractors* and *data analysts*, reviewing records against established standards to ensure quality of care. They may also prepare statistical reports for the medical or administrative staff that reviews appropriateness of care.

With more specialized training, medical record technicians may participate in medical research activities by maintaining special records, called registries, related to such areas as cancer, heart disease, transplants, or adverse outcomes of pregnancies. In some cases, they are required to abstract and code information from records of patients with certain medical conditions. These technicians also may prepare statistical reports and trend analyses for the use of medical researchers.

REQUIREMENTS
High School

If you are contemplating a career in medical records, you should take as many high school English classes as possible, because technicians need both written and verbal communication skills to prepare reports and communicate with other health care personnel. Basic math or business math is very desirable because statistical skills are important in some job functions. Biology courses will help to familiarize yourself with the terminology that medical record technicians use. Other science courses, computer training, typing, and office procedures are also helpful.

Postsecondary Training

Most employers prefer to hire medical record technicians who have completed a two-year associate's degree program accredited by the American Medical Association's Commission on Accreditation of Allied Health Professions and the American Health Information Management Association (AHIMA). There are 177 of these accredited programs available throughout the United States, mostly offered in junior and community colleges. They usually include classroom instruction in such subjects as anatomy, physiology, medical terminology, medical record science, word processing, medical aspects of record-keeping, statistics, computers in health care, personnel supervision, business management, English, and office skills.

In addition to classroom instruction, the student is given supervised clinical experience in the medical records departments of local health care facilities. This provides students with practical experience in performing many of the functions learned in the classroom and the opportunity to interact with health care professionals.

An alternative educational method is open to individuals with experience in certain related activities. It requires completion of an independent study program offered by the AHIMA. Students in this program must successfully complete a lesson series and clinical experience internship in a health care institution. They must also earn 30 semester hours of credit in prescribed subjects at a college or university.

Certification or Licensing

Medical record technicians who have completed an accredited training program are eligible to take a national qualifying examination to earn the credential of Registered Health Information Technician (RHIT). Most health care institutions prefer to hire individuals with an RHIT credential as it signifies that they have met the standards established by the AHIMA as the mark of a qualified health professional.

Other Requirements

Medical records are extremely detailed and precise. Sloppy work could have serious consequences in terms of payment to the hospital or physician, validity of the patient records for later use, and validity of research based on data from medical records. Therefore, a prospective technician must have the capacity to do consistently reliable and accurate routine work. Records must be completed and maintained with care and attention to detail. You may be the only person who checks the entire record, and you must understand the responsibility that accompanies this task.

The technician needs to be able to work rapidly as well as accurately. In many medical record departments, the workload is very heavy, and you must be well organized and efficient in order to stay on top of the job. You must be able to complete your work accurately, in spite of interruptions, such as phone calls and requests for assistance. You also need to be discreet, as you will deal with records that are private and sometimes sensitive.

Computer skills also are essential, and some experience in transcribing dictated reports may be useful.

EXPLORING

To learn more about this and other medical careers, you may be able to find summer, part-time, or volunteer work in a hospital or other health care facility. Sometimes such jobs are available in the medical records area of an organization. You may also be able to arrange to talk with someone working as a medical record technician or administrator. Faculty and counselors at schools that offer medical record technician training programs may also be good sources of information. You also can learn more about this profession by reading journals and other literature available at a public library.

EMPLOYERS

Although most medical record technicians work in hospitals, many work in other health care settings, including health maintenance organizations (HMOs), industrial clinics, skilled nursing facilities, rehabilitation centers, large group medical practices, ambulatory care centers, and state and local government health agencies. Technicians also work for computer firms, consulting firms, and government agencies. Records are maintained in all these facilities, although record-keeping procedures vary.

Not all medical record technicians are employed in a single health care facility; some serve as consultants to several small facilities. Other technicians do not work in health care settings at all. They may be employed by health and property liability insurance companies to collect and review information on medical claims. A few are self-employed, providing medical transcription services.

STARTING OUT

Most successful medical record technicians are graduates of two-year accredited programs. Graduates of these programs should check with their schools' placement offices for job leads. Those who have taken the accrediting exam and have become certified can use the AHIMA's resume referral service.

You may also apply directly to the personnel departments of hospitals, nursing homes, outpatient clinics, and surgery centers. Many job openings are also listed in the classified advertising sections of local newspapers and with private and public employment agencies.

ADVANCEMENT

Medical record technicians may be able to achieve some advancement and salary increase without additional training by simply taking on greater responsibility in their job function. With experience, you may move to supervisory or department head positions, depending on the type and structure of the employing organization. Another means of advancing is through specialization in a certain area of the job. Some technicians specialize in coding, particularly Medicare coding or tumor registry. With a broad range of experience, you may be able to become an independent consultant. Generally, technicians with an associate's degree and the RHIT designation are most likely to advance.

More assured job advancement and salary increases come with the completion of a bachelor's degree in medical record administration. The bachelor's degree, along with AHIMA accreditation, makes the technician eligible for a supervisory position, such as department director. Because of a general shortage of medical record administrators, hospitals often assist technicians who are working toward a bachelor's degree by providing flexible scheduling and financial aid or tuition reimbursement.

EARNINGS

The salaries of medical record technicians are greatly influenced by the location, size, and type of employing institution, as well as the technician's training and experience. According to the AHIMA, beginning technicians with an associate's degree can earn between $20,000 and $30,000 annually. Those who have earned a bachelor's degree can expect to earn between $30,000 and $50,000 a year.

The AHIMA's 2001 membership profile reports that the majority of its members designated coding professionals earned between $30,000 and $40,000. However, with higher educational achievement come higher salaries. According to the same membership profile, 27 percent of those with a baccalaureate degree and 59 percent of those with master's degrees earn $50,000 or more annually.

According to the Bureau of Labor Statistics, the median annual earnings of medical records and health information technicians were $23,530 in 2001. Salaries ranged from less than $16,220 to more than $37,030.

In general, medical record technicians working in large urban hospitals make the most money, and those in rural areas make the least. Like most hospital employees, medical record technicians usually receive paid vacations and holidays, life and health insurance, and retirement benefits.

WORK ENVIRONMENT

Medical records departments are usually pleasantly clean, well-lit, and air-conditioned areas. Sometimes, however, paper or microfilm records are kept in cramped, out-of-the-way quarters. Although the work requires thorough and careful attention to detail, there may be a constant bustle of activity in the technician's work area, which can be disruptive. The job is likely to involve frequent routine contact with nurses, physicians, hospital administrators, other health care professionals, attorneys, and insurance agents. On occasion, individuals with whom the technicians may interact with are demanding or difficult. In such cases, technicians may find that the job carries a high level of frustration.

A 40-hour workweek is the norm, but because hospitals operate on a 24-hour basis, the job may regularly include night or weekend hours. Part-time work is sometimes available.

The work is extremely detailed and may be tedious. Some technicians spend the majority of their day sitting at a desk, working on a computer. Others may spend hours filing paper records or retrieving them from storage.

In many hospital settings, the medical record technician experiences pressure caused by a heavy workload. As the demands for health care cost containment and productivity increase, medical record technicians may be required to produce a significantly greater volume of high-quality work in shorter periods of time. Nevertheless, the knowledge that their work is significant for both patients and medical research can be very satisfying for medical record technicians.

OUTLOOK

Employment prospects over the next several years are excellent. The U.S. Department of Labor predicts that employment in this field will grow by 54.1 percent between 2000 and 2010. The demand for well-trained medical record technicians will grow rapidly and will continue to exceed the supply. This expectation is related to the health-care needs of a population that is both growing and aging and the trend toward more technologically sophisticated medicine and greater use of diagnostic procedures. It is also related to the increased requirements of regulatory bodies that scrutinize both costs and quality of care of health care providers. Because of the fear of medical malpractice lawsuits, doctors and other health care providers are documenting their diagnoses and treatments in greater detail. Also, because of the high cost of health care, insurance companies, government agencies, and courts are examining medical records with a more critical eye. These factors combine to ensure a healthy job outlook for medical record technicians.

Technicians with associate's degrees and RHIT status will have the best prospects, and the importance of such qualifications is likely to increase.

FOR MORE INFORMATION

For information on earnings, careers in health information management, and accreditation, contact:

**American Health Information Management
  Association**
233 North Michigan Avenue, Suite 2150
Chicago, IL 60601-5800
Tel: 312-233-1100
Email: info@ahima.org
http://www.ahima.org

For a list of schools offering accredited programs in health information management, contact:

**Commission on Accreditation of Allied Health
  Education Programs**
35 East Wacker Drive, Suite 1970
Chicago, IL 60601-2208
Tel: 312-553-9355
Email: caahep@caahep.org
http://www.caahep.org

OCCUPATIONAL THERAPISTS

QUICK FACTS

School Subjects
Biology
Health

Personal Skills
Helping/teaching
Mechanical/manipulative

Work Environment
Primarily indoors
Primarily one location

Minimum Education Level
Bachelor's degree

Salary Range
$33,780 to $51,370 to
$73,240+

Certification or Licensing
Required

Outlook
Faster than the
average

DOT
076

GOE
10.02.02

NOC
3143

O*NET-SOC
29-1122.00

OVERVIEW

Occupational therapists (OTs) select and direct therapeutic activities designed to develop or restore maximum function to individuals with disabilities. Approximately 78,000 occupational therapists are employed in the United States.

HISTORY

Since the 14th century, physicians have recognized the therapeutic value of developing constructive and rehabilitative activities for their patients. Providing mental patients with tasks and duties such as agriculture, weaving, working with animals, and sewing often hastened their recovery. Over time, this practice became quite common, and the conditions of many patients were improved.

Occupational therapy as we know it today had its beginning after World War I. The need to help disabled veterans of that war, and years later the veterans of World War II, stimulated the growth of this field. Even though its inception was in the psychiatric field, occupational therapy has become equally important other medical fields, including rehabilitation of physically disabled patients.

Traditionally, occupational therapists taught creative arts such as weaving, clay-modeling, leather work, jewelry-making, and other crafts to promote their patients' functional skills. Today's occupational therapists focus more on activities that promote skills for daily living, including self-care, employment education and job skills,(such as typing, computer proficiency, or the use of power tools), and community and social skills.

The difference between occupational therapists and physical therapists is an important one. Physical therapy is chiefly concerned with helping people with physical disabilities or injuries to regain functions or adapt to or overcome their physical limitations. Occupational therapists work with physical factors but also the psychological and social elements of their clients' disabilities, helping them become as independent as possible in the home, school, and workplace. Occupational therapists work not only with the physically challenged, but with people who have mental and emotional disabilities as well.

THE JOB

Occupational therapists use a wide variety of activities to help clients attain their goals for productive, independent living. These goals include developing maximum self-sufficiency in activities of daily living, such as eating, dressing, writing, using a telephone and other communication resources, as well as functioning in the community and the workplace.

When developing a therapeutic program for a client, the occupational therapist often works as a member of a team that can include physicians, nurses, psychiatrists, physical therapists, speech therapists, rehabilitation counselors, social workers, and other specialists. OTs use creative, educational, and recreational activities, as well as human ingenuity, to help people achieve their full potential, regardless of their disabilities. Each therapy program is designed specifically for the individual client.

Occupational therapists help clients explore their likes and dislikes, their abilities, and their creative, educational, and recreational experiences. Therapists assist people in choosing activities that have the most appeal and value for them. For example, an activity may be designed to promote greater dexterity for someone with arthritic fingers. Learning to use an adapted computer might help a young person with a spinal cord injury to succeed in school and career goals. The therapist works with the clients' interests and helps them develop practical skills and functional independence.

The occupational therapist may work with a wide range of clients. They may assist one client in learning to use an artificial limb and aid another in redeveloping motor functions after a suffering a stroke or other neurological disability. Therapists may assist in the growth and development of premature infants, or they may work with disabled children, helping them learn motor skills or develop skills and exercises that will aid them in their education and social interaction.

Some therapists also conduct research to develop new types of therapies and activities and to measure the effectiveness of a therapy program. They may also design and make special equipment or splints to help clients perform their activities.

Other duties may include supervision of volunteer workers, student therapists, and occupational therapy assistants who give instruction in a particular skill. Therapists must prepare reports to keep members of the professional team informed.

Chief occupational therapists in a hospital may teach medical and nursing students the principles of occupational therapy. Many occupational therapists have administrative duties such as directing different kinds of occupational therapy programs, coordinating patient activities, and acting as consultants or advisors to local and state health departments, mental health authorities, and the Division of Vocational Rehabilitation.

REQUIREMENTS
High School

Since you will need to get a college degree, taking college preparatory classes in high school is a must. Courses such as biology, chemistry, and health will expose you to the science fields. Other courses, such as art and social sciences, will help give you an understanding of other aspects of your future work. A strong background in English is also important. Remember, occupational therapy is about helping people. To be able to work with many different people with different needs, you will need excellent communication skills. Also keep in mind that college admission officers will look favorably at any experience you have had working in the health care field, either in volunteer or paid positions.

Postsecondary Training

To become an occupational therapist, you will need to complete an accredited program in occupational therapy. Accreditation is granted by the Accreditation Council for Occupational Therapy Education (ACOTE), which is a part of the American Occupational Therapy Association (AOTA). Currently, the ACOTE accredits bachelor's degree programs, certificate programs for those who already have a bachelor's degree in another field, and graduate (both master's and doctoral) programs. As of 2007, however, anyone wishing to receive the professional credential Occupational Therapist, Registered (OTR) from the National Board for Certification in Occupational Therapy (NBCOT) must have completed at least a master's degree in the field. Because of this change, the ACOTE will no longer accredit bachelor's degree programs after 2007. As of October 2002, more than 155 schools offering bachelor's degree programs or combined bachelor's and master's degree programs had ACOTE accreditation. Due to the change in requirements for the professional credential, however, many schools are closing their undergraduate-level programs and creating graduate-level programs.

As an undergraduate, you will need to take courses emphasizing biological and behavioral sciences. Your studies should include classes on anatomy, physiology, neurology, psychology, human growth and development, and sociology. Clinical subjects cover general medical and surgical conditions and interpretation of the principles and practice of occupational therapy in pediatrics, psychiatry, orthopedics, general medicine, and surgery. Many bachelor's degree programs require students to fulfill two years of general study before specializing in occupational therapy during the last two years. Graduate-level programs cover many of the same subject areas but in greater depth. In addition, emphasis is put on research and critical thinking. Management and administration are also areas covered more thoroughly in graduate programs.

In addition to classroom work, you must complete fieldwork requirements. According to the AOTA, students need to complete the equivalent of 24 weeks of supervised experience working with clients. This may be done on a full-time basis or a part-time (but not less than half-time) schedule. This training must be completed in order to qualify for professional certification.

Those working on bachelor's degrees are now advised to continue their education to at least the master's level. Doctoral programs in occupational therapy are also available. While those holding master's degrees will probably not see much difference in their starting salary as opposed to those with bachelor's degrees, they will likely find, as their career develops, that it is easier to move into higher level positions offering more responsibilities and higher pay. Those who want careers in teaching, administration, and research should certainly obtain graduate education.

In addition to these full-time study options, there are a limited number of part-time and evening programs that allow prospective occupational therapists to work in another field while completing their requirements in occupational therapy.

Certification or Licensing

All states and the District of Columbia regulate the practice of occupational therapy through certification and licensing. National certification is granted by the NBCOT. In order to take the NBCOT exam, you must graduate from an accredited program and complete the clinical practice period. Those who pass this written test are given the designation Occupational Therapist, Registered, and may use the initials OTR after their names. Initial certification is good for five years and must be renewed every five years after that. Many hospitals and other employers require that their occupational therapists have the OTR designation. In addition, the AOTA offers several specialty certifications, such as Board Certified in Pediatrics. To receive a specialty certification, you must fulfill education and experience requirements and pass an exam.

License requirements generally include graduation from an accredited program, passing the NBCOT certification exam, payment of license fees, and, in some cases, passing an exam covering state statutes and regulations. License renewal requirements vary by state.

Other Requirements

A successful occupational therapist enjoys working with people. To do this job you should have a patient, calm, and compassionate temperament and the ability to encourage and inspire your clients. Like your clients, you may encounter frustrating situations as a therapist. For example, it can be difficult and stressful when a client does not respond to treatment as you had hoped. In such situations, occupational therapists need to be persistent and not give up on the client. Imagination and creativity are also important at such times, because you may need to think of new ways to address the client's problem and create new methods or tools for the client to use.

EXPLORING

While in high school, you should meet with occupational therapists, visit the facilities where they work, and gain an understanding
of the types of equipment and skills they use. Many hospitals and
occupational therapy facilities and departments also have volunteer
opportunities, which will give you strong insight into this career.

EMPLOYERS

There are approximately 78,000 occupational therapists at work in
hospitals, schools, nursing homes, home health agencies, mental
health centers, adult day care programs, outpatient clinics, and residential care facilities. A growing number of occupational therapists are
self-employed in either solo or group practice or in consulting firms.
According to the American Occupational Therapy Association's 2000
salary survey, 20 percent of respondents classified themselves as self-
employed, either on a full-time or part-time basis.

STARTING OUT

Your school's placement office is usually the best place to start your
job search as a newly graduated occupational therapist. You may
also apply directly to government agencies (such as the U.S. Public
Health Service), private hospitals, and clinics. In addition, the AOTA
can provide job seekers with assistance through its employment
bulletins.

ADVANCEMENT

Newly graduated occupational therapists usually begin as staff therapists and may qualify as senior therapists after several years on the
job. The army, navy, air force, and the U.S. Public Health Service
commission occupational therapists; other branches of the federal
service give civil service ratings. Experienced therapists may become
directors of occupational therapy programs in large hospitals, clinics, or workshops, or they may become teachers. Positions such as
program coordinators and consultants are available with large institutions and agencies.

A few colleges and health agencies offer advanced courses in the
treatment of special disabilities, such as those resulting from cerebral
palsy. Some institutions provide in-service programs for therapists.

EARNINGS

According to the U.S. Department of Labor's *2001 National Occupational Employment and Wage Estimates,* salaries for occupational

therapists averaged about $51,370 in 2001. The lowest 10 percent earned $33,780 a year in 2001, and the top 10 percent earned more than $73,240.

Salaries for occupational therapists often vary according to where they work. In areas where the cost of living is higher, occupational therapists generally receive higher pay. Occupational therapists employed in public schools earn salaries that vary by school district. In some states, they are classified as teachers and are paid accordingly.

Therapists employed at hospitals and government and public agencies generally receive full benefit packages that include vacation and sick pay, health insurance, and retirement benefits. Self-employed therapists and those who run their own businesses must provide their own benefits.

WORK ENVIRONMENT
Occupational therapists work in occupational therapy workshops or clinics. As mentioned earlier, these workshops or clinics can be found at a variety of locations, such as hospitals, long-term care facilities, schools, and adult day care centers. No matter what the location, though, these workshops and clinics are well-lighted, pleasant settings. Generally, therapists work eight-hour days and 40-hour weeks, with some evening work required in a few organizations.

OUTLOOK
Opportunities for occupational therapists are expected to be highly favorable over the next several years and will grow faster than the average for all other careers, according to the *Occupational Outlook Handbook*. This growth will occur as a result of the increasing number of middle-aged and elderly people that require therapeutic services. The demand for occupational therapists is also increasing because of growing public interest in and government support for people with disabilities and for occupational therapy programs helping people attain the fullest possible functional status. The demand for rehabilitative and long-term care services is expected to grow strongly over the next decade. There will be numerous opportunities for work with mental health clients, children, and the elderly, as well as with those with disabling conditions.

As the health care industry continues to be restructured, there should be many more opportunities for occupational therapists in nontraditional settings. This factor and proposed changes in the laws should create an excellent climate for therapists wishing to enter private practice. Home health care may experience the greatest growth in the next decade.

FOR MORE INFORMATION

Visit AOTA's website to find out about accredited occupational therapy programs, career information, and news related to the field.

American Occupational Therapy Association (AOTA)
4720 Montgomery Lane
PO Box 31220
Bethesda, MD 20824-1220
Tel: 301-652-2682
Email: educate@aota.org
http://www.aota.org

For information on certification requirements, contact:

National Board for Certification in Occupational Therapy
Eugene B. Casey Building
800 South Frederick Avenue, Suite 200
Gaithersburg, MD 20877-4150
Tel: 301-990-7979
http://www.nbcot.org

PARALEGALS

QUICK FACTS

<table>
<tr><td>

School Subjects
  Computer science
  English
  Government

Personal Skills
  Communication/ideas
  Following instructions

Work Environment
  Primarily indoors
  Primarily multiple locations

Minimum Education Level
  Some postsecondary
  training

Salary Range
  $23,720 to $46,074 to
  $57,150+

</td><td>

Certification or Licensing
  Voluntary

Outlook
  Faster than the
  average

DOT
  119

GOE
  11.04.02

NOC
  4211

O*NET-SOC
  23-2011.00

</td></tr>
</table>

OVERVIEW

Paralegals, also known as *legal assistants*, assist in trial preparations, investigate facts, prepare documents such as affidavits and pleadings, and, in general, do much of work customarily performed by lawyers. Approximately 188,000 paralegals work in law firms, businesses, and government agencies all over the United States; the majority work with lawyers and legislators.

HISTORY

The U.S. legal system has undergone many changes over the past few decades as more people turn to lawyers for help in settling disputes. This increase in litigation has placed greater demands on lawyers and other legal professionals. To help meet these demands, lawyers have hired legal assistants to help provide legal services to more people at a lower cost.

The first paralegals were given a limited number of routine duties. Many started as legal secretaries who were gradually given more responsibilities. Today the work of the paralegal has expanded and formal training programs have been established.

Since this occupation first developed in the late 1960s, paralegals have taken on much of the routine work that lawyers once did themselves, such as researching, investigating, and preparing legal briefs. Their work enables lawyers to concentrate on the more technical aspects of legal services. The paralegal profession continues to grow as paralegals gain wider acceptance as legal professionals.

THE JOB

A paralegal's main duty is to do everything a lawyer needs to do but doesn't have time to do. Although the lawyer assumes responsibility for the paralegal's work, the paralegal may take on all the duties of the lawyer except for setting fees, appearing in court, accepting cases, and giving legal advice.

Paralegals spend much of their time in law libraries, researching laws and previous cases and compiling facts to help lawyers prepare for trial. Paralegals often interview witnesses as part of their research as well. After analyzing the laws and facts that have been compiled for a particular client, the paralegal often writes a report that the lawyer may use to determine how to proceed with the case. If a case is brought to trial, the paralegal helps prepare legal arguments and draft pleadings to be filed in court. They also organize and store files and correspondence related to cases.

Not all paralegal work centers on trials. Many paralegals work for corporations, agencies, schools, and financial institutions. *Corporate paralegals* create and maintain contracts, mortgages, affidavits, and other documents. They assist with corporate matters, such as shareholder agreements, contracts, and employee benefit plans. Paralegals must also stay on top of new laws and regulations to make sure the company is operating within those parameters.

Some paralegals work for the government. They may prepare complaints or talk to employers to find out why health or safety standards are not being met. They often analyze legal documents, collect evidence for hearings, and prepare explanatory material on various laws for use by the public. For example, a *court administrator paralegal* is in charge of keeping the courthouse functioning; tasks include monitoring personnel, handling the caseload for the court, and general administration.

Other paralegals are involved in community or public-service work. They may help specific groups (such as poor or elderly members of the community) by filing forms, researching laws, and preparing documents. They may also represent clients at hearings, although they may not appear in court on behalf of a client.

Many paralegals work for large law firms, agencies, and corporations and specialize in a particular area of law. Some work for smaller firms and have a general knowledge of many areas of law. Paralegals have varied duties, and an increasing number use computers in their work to conduct research and create reports.

INTERVIEW: Paralegal

Amy Inlander is a paralegal at Shefsky & Froelich, Ltd., a law firm in Chicago. She spoke with the editors of 25 Jobs That Have It All *about her career.*

Q. Where are you employed? What are your primary and secondary job duties?

A. I work for Shefsky & Froelich, Ltd., a mid-sized law firm that has approximately 60 attorneys and 10 paralegals. My primary job duties are to serve the law firm as a corporate paralegal. I organize corporate entities (corporations, partnerships, limited liability companies, etc.); draft corporate minutes, state filing documents, employment agreements, stock certificates, and stock transfer documents; meet with clients, attorneys, outside service companies, and state agency representatives; research corporate entities; prepare and file Uniform Commercial Code filings; and just about anything else a corporate attorney would do with the exception of giving legal advice. My secondary duty is to manage all the other paralegals in this firm. I have over 25 years of experience and know enough about many different practice areas, giving me the necessary skills to hire paralegals, monitor their workloads, and participate in their annual evaluations.

I rarely travel for my job and if I do it is usually a day trip by car. I have had corporate paralegal positions in the past that required multi-state travel.

Q. How did you train for this position?

A. My training consists of years of on-the-job training. My double major in college was political science and legal studies (an experimental paralegal program). Now it is very important for a person entering this field to have a postgraduate degree from an American Bar Association (ABA)-accredited paralegal program.

Q. How/where did you get your first job in this field? What did you do?

A. My first job was with a large law firm in Chicago, where I was carefully trained by a senior paralegal in my practice area, Estate Planning. Timing and networking count for everything when it comes to finding a job. I was referred to the law firm by a family friend for a courtesy interview. It just so happened that there was a paralegal opening in the estate planning department and apparently the people interviewing me thought I was intelligent enough to be trained for the position—not to mention I was right out of college and would be willing to work for a lower salary.

Q. How can aspiring paralegals find jobs in this field?

A. Available sources include professional associations (National Paralegal Association and National Legal Assistants Association), a multitude of employment agencies that specialize in placing permanent and temporary paralegals, ABA-approved/accredited paralegal programs, and of course people like me that have been doing this forever and are willing to share information with new folks.

Q. What are the most important qualities for someone who is interested in this career?

A. It is extremely important to be organized, analytical, and have a sense of urgency. People in this profession have to be able to move at a fast pace but never lose sight of getting the details of every project perfect. You must always be professional not only with the external clients but also with the internal clients (the attorneys you work with).

Q. What are the pros and cons of being a paralegal?

A. Pros:

- Independent work assignments while working as a member of a team
- Satisfactory compensation
- Intellectually stimulating work atmosphere

Cons:

- Understanding that a paralegal will never be promoted to attorney
- Sometimes being required to work with difficult personalities (although this is true for almost any job)
- Retirement benefits are often lacking in the private sector/law firms

Q. What is the most important piece of advice that you have to offer students as they graduate and look for jobs in this field?

A. Be professional in your actions as well as appearances. Exhibit an elevated energy level, yet provide a calming factor to your office work partners. Don't ever be afraid to ask questions. Always be willing to learn, and develop and polish your skills. Never say never, and enjoy your work.

REQUIREMENTS
High School

While in high school, take a broad range of subjects, including English, social studies or government, computer science, and languages, especially Spanish and Latin. Because legal terminology is used constantly in this profession, word origins and vocabulary should be a main focus.

Postsecondary Training

Requirements for paralegals vary by employer. Some paralegals start out as legal secretaries or clerical workers and gradually are given more training and responsibility. The majority, however, choose formal training and education programs.

Formal training programs usually range from one to three years and are offered in a variety of educational settings, such as four-year colleges and universities, law schools, community and junior colleges, business schools, proprietary schools, and paralegal associations. Admission requirements vary, but good grades in high school and college are always an asset. There are more than 1,000 paralegal programs, about 254 of which have been approved by the American Bar Association. The National Federation of Paralegal Associations reports that 84 percent of all paralegals receive formal paralegal education.

Some paralegal programs require a bachelor's degree for admission; others do not require any college education. In either case, those who have a college degree usually have an advantage over those who do not.

Certification or Licensing

Paralegals are not required to be licensed or certified. Instead, when lawyers employ paralegals, they often follow guidelines designed to protect the public from the practice of law by unqualified persons.

However, paralegal certification is available. To obtain certification paralegals may take and pass an extensive two-day test conducted by the National Association of Legal Assistants (NALA) Certifying Board. Paralegals who pass the test may use the title Certified Legal Assistant (CLA) after their names. According to NALA, as of January 2003, there were 11,678 CLAs in the United States.

In 1994, the National Federation of Paralegal Associations established the Paralegal Advanced Competency Exam (PACE) as a means for paralegals who fill education and experience requirements to acquire professional recognition. Paralegals who pass this exam and maintain the continuing education requirement may use the designation Registered Paralegal (RP).

Other Requirements

Communication skills, both verbal and written, are vital to working as a paralegal. You must be able to turn research into reports that a lawyer or corporate executive can use. You must also be able to think logically and learn new laws and regulations quickly. Research skills, computer skills, and people skills are other necessities.

EXPLORING

If you're interested in a career as a paralegal, colleges, universities, and technical schools have a wealth of paralegal career information available for the asking. Elizabeth Houser, a practicing paralegal, recommends contacting schools that have paralegal programs directly. "Ask questions. They are helpful and will give you a lot of information about being a paralegal," she says.

Look for summer or part-time employment as a secretary or in the mailroom of a law firm to get an idea of the nature of the work. If paid positions aren't available, offer to volunteer at law offices in your area. Ask your guidance counselor to help you set up a volunteer/internship agreement with a lawyer.

Talk to your history or government teacher about organizing a trip to a lawyer's office and a courthouse. Ask your teacher to set aside time for you to talk to paralegals working there and to their supervising attorneys.

If you have access to a computer, search the World Wide Web for information on student organizations that are affiliated with the legal profession. You can also contact the organizations listed at the end of this article for general information.

EMPLOYERS

Paralegals and legal assistants hold approximately 188,000 jobs. The majority works for lawyers in law offices or in law firms. Other paralegals work for the government, namely for the Federal Trade Commission, Justice Department, Treasury Department, Internal Revenue Service, Department of the Interior, and many other agencies and offices. Paralegals also work in the business community in any context where legal matters are part of the day-to-day work. Paralegals fit in well in business because many smaller corporations must deal with legal regulations but don't necessarily need an attorney or a team of lawyers.

Jobs in the paralegal field can be found all over the country. Larger cities employ more paralegals who focus on the legal side of the profession, and government paralegals will find the most opportunities in state capitals and Washington, D.C.

STARTING OUT

Although some law firms promote legal secretaries to paralegal status, most employers prefer to hire individuals who have completed paralegal programs. To have the best opportunity at getting a quality job in the paralegal field, you should attend a paralegal school. In addition to providing a solid background in paralegal studies, most schools help graduates find jobs. Even though the job market for paralegals is expected to grow rapidly over the next 10 years, those with the best credentials will get the best jobs.

For Elizabeth Houser, the internship program was the springboard to her first paralegal position. "The paralegal program of study I took required an internship. I was hired directly from that internship experience."

The National Federation of Paralegal Associations recommends using job banks that are sponsored by paralegal associations across the country. For paralegal associations that may be able to help, see the addresses listed at the end of this article. Many jobs for paralegals are posted on the Internet, as well.

ADVANCEMENT

There are no formal advancement paths for paralegals. There are, however, some possibilities for advancement, as large firms are beginning to establish career programs for paralegals.

For example, a person may be promoted from a paralegal to a head legal assistant who supervises others. In addition, a paralegal may specialize in one area of law, such as environmental, real estate, or medical malpractice. Many paralegals also advance by moving from small to large firms.

Expert paralegals who specialize in one area of law may go into business for themselves. Rather than work for one firm, these freelance paralegals often contract their services to many lawyers. Some paralegals with bachelor's degrees enroll in law school to train to become lawyers.

Paralegals can also move horizontally by taking their specialized knowledge of the law into another field, such as insurance, occupational health, or law enforcement.

EARNINGS

Salaries vary greatly for paralegals. The size and location of the firm and the education and experience of the employee are some factors that determine the annual earnings of paralegals.

According to the *2002 National Utilization and Compensation Survey Report* conducted by the National Association of Legal Assistants, the average total compensation earned by legal assistants was $46,074.

The U.S. Bureau of Labor Statistics reports that paralegals earned median annual earnings of $36,670 in 2001. The highest 10 percent earned more than $57,150, while the lowest 10 percent earned less than $23,720.

WORK ENVIRONMENT

Paralegals often work in pleasant and comfortable offices. Much of their work is performed in a law library. Some paralegals work out of their homes in special employment situations. When investigation is called for, paralegals may travel to gather information. Most paralegals work a 40-hour week, although long hours are sometimes required to meet court-imposed deadlines. Longer hours—sometimes as much as 90 hours per week—are usually the normal routine for paralegals starting out in law offices and firms.

Many of the paralegal's duties involve routine tasks, so they must have a great deal of patience. However, paralegals may be given increasingly difficult assignments over time. Paralegals are often unsupervised, especially as they gain experience and a reputation for quality work. Elizabeth Houser does much of her work unsupervised. "You get to put a lot of yourself into what you do and that provides a high level of job satisfaction," she says.

OUTLOOK

The employment outlook for paralegals through 2010 is very good; growth of 33 percent is expected during this time period. One reason for the expected rapid growth in the profession is the financial benefits of employing paralegals. The paralegal, whose duties fall between those of the legal secretary and those of the attorney, helps make the delivery of legal services more cost effective to clients. The growing need for legal services among the general population and the increasing popularity of prepaid legal plans is creating a tremendous demand for paralegals in private law firms. In the private sector, paralegals can work in banks, insurance companies, real estate firms, and corporate legal departments. In the public sector, there is a growing need for paralegals in the courts and community legal service programs, government agencies, and consumer organizations.

The growth of this occupation, to some extent, is dependent on the economy. Businesses are less likely to pursue litigation cases when profit margins are down, thus curbing the need for new hires.

FOR MORE INFORMATION

For information regarding accredited educational facilities, contact:
American Association for Paralegal Education
407 Wekiva Springs Road, Suite 241
Longwood, FL 32779
Tel: 407-834-6688
Email: info@aafpe.org
http://www.aafpe.org

For general information about careers in the law field, contact:
American Bar Association
541 North Fairbanks Court
Chicago, IL 60611
Tel: 312-988-5522
http://www.abanet.org

For career information, contact:
Association of Legal Administrators
175 East Hawthorn Parkway, Suite 325
Vernon Hills, IL 60061-1428
Tel: 847-816-1212
http://www.alanet.org

For information about educational and licensing programs, certification, and paralegal careers, contact:
National Association of Legal Assistants
1516 South Boston Avenue, Suite 200
Tulsa, OK 74119
Tel: 918-587-6828
Email: nalanet@nala.org
http://www.nala.org

For brochures about almost every aspect of becoming a paralegal, contact:
National Federation of Paralegal Associations
PO Box 33108
Kansas City, MO 64114-0108
Tel: 816-941-4000
Email: info@paralegals.org
http://www.paralegals.org

For information about employment networks and school listings, contact:
National Paralegal Association
PO Box 406
Solebury, PA 18963
Tel: 215-297-8333
Email: admin@nationalparalegal.org
http://www.nationalparalegal.org

PHARMACY TECHNICIANS

QUICK FACTS

School Subjects
Biology
Chemistry
Computer science

Personal Skills
Following instructions
Technical/scientific

Work Environment
Primarily indoors
Primarily one location

Minimum Education Level
Some postsecondary
training

Salary Range
$15,140 to $21,630 to
$31,760+

Certification or Licensing
Required by certain states

Outlook
Much faster than the
average

DOT
074

GOE
05.09.01

NOC
3414

O*NET-SOC
29-2052.00

OVERVIEW

Pharmacy technicians provide technical assistance for registered pharmacists and work under their direct supervision. They usually work in chain or independent drug stores, hospitals, community ambulatory care centers, home health care agencies, nursing homes, and the pharmaceutical industry. They perform a wide range of technical support functions and tasks related to the pharmacy profession. They maintain patient records; count, package, and label medication doses; prepare and distribute sterile products; and fill and dispense routine orders for stock supplies such as over-the-counter products. There are approximately 190,000 pharmacy technicians employed in the United States.

HISTORY

Professionally trained pharmacy technicians have assisted pharmacists since the 1950s. In recent years, the role of the pharmacist has shifted and evolved away from standard dispensing to consultation, restricting the time actually spent dispensing medication. Pharmacy technicians have filled this gap, enjoying a significant increase in duties and responsibilities, and becoming an even more integral part of the pharmaceutical health care team.

THE JOB

The roles of the pharmacist and pharmacy technician expanded greatly in the 1990s. The pharmacist's primary responsibility is to ensure that medications are used safely and effectively through clinical patient counseling and monitoring. In order to provide the highest quality of pharmaceutical care, pharmacists now focus on providing clinical services. As a result, pharmacy technicians' duties have evolved into a more specialized role known as pharmacy technology. Pharmacy technicians perform more of the manipulative functions associated with dispensing prescriptions. Their primary duties are drug-product preparation and distribution, but they are also concerned with the control of drug products. Technicians assemble, prepare, and deliver requested medication. Technicians are responsible for record-keeping, and they record drug-related information on specified forms, frequently doing this part of the work on computers. Depending on a technician's experience, he or she may order pharmaceuticals and take inventory of controlled substances, such as Valium and Ritalin.

Technicians who work in hospitals have the most varied responsibilities of all pharmacy technicians. In a hospital, technicians fill total parenteral nutrition preparations and standard and chemotherapy IVs (intravenous solutions) for patients under doctors' orders. Other duties that a hospital pharmacy technician may be required to do include filling "stat," or immediate, orders and delivering them; preparing special emergency carts stocked with medications; and monitoring defibrillators and resuscitation equipment. In an emergency, pharmacy technicians respond with doctors and nurses, rushing the cart and other equipment to the emergency site. They also keep legal records of the events that occur during an emergency. Technicians work in the hospital's outpatient pharmacy, which is similar to a commercial drugstore, and assist the pharmacist in dispensing medication.

Tamara Britton works as a technician in a hospital. Because the hospital pharmacy is open 24 hours a day, Tamara has worked all three shifts. Her work involves using a computer to create labels for large IV bags and "piggybacks" (small-volume IV bags). She stacks the IVs on carts, then delivers them to the appropriate nurse stations. She also delivers medications through a process known as "tubing and shagging." Two "tubes," or lines, (similar to those at a bank's drive-through) run through the entire hospital to every nurse unit. "Shagging" is the process of placing the nurse unit's medications in baggies; the meds are then shot through the tubes to the proper units. Tamara also prepares drug carts with the aid of a RxOBOT; this robotic arm is in a glassed-off room and fills the drawers of the carts with the correct medication for individual patients. Britton places coded labels on the drawers of the carts. She explains, "I put the drawers with labels facing Robota (we named her) and a conveyor belt takes them in the room for Robota to fill with all of the patients' existing meds for the day. The tray, after filling, drops down to a lower conveyor belt that brings the drawer back to me, which I replace in the cart."

As their roles increase, trained technicians have become more specialized. Some specialized types of pharmacy technicians include narcotics control pharmacy technicians, operating room pharmacy technicians, emergency room pharmacy technicians, nuclear pharmacy technicians, and home health care pharmacy technicians. Specially trained pharmacy technicians are also employed as data entry technicians, lead technicians, supervisors, and technician managers.

REQUIREMENTS
High School

You should take courses in mathematics and science (especially chemistry and biology), because you'll be dealing with patient records and drug dosages. Health classes can help you get a basic understanding of the health care industry and various medical treatments. Take English and speech classes to help you develop your writing and communication skills. You'll be using a computer a lot to maintain records and prepare labels, so take courses in computer fundamentals.

Postsecondary Training

In the past, pharmacy technicians received most of their training on the job in hospital and community pharmacy-training programs. Since technician functions and duties have changed greatly in recent years, most pharmacy technicians today receive their education through formal training programs offered through community colleges, vocational/technical schools, hospital community pharmacies, and government programs throughout the United States. Program length usually ranges from six months to two years, and leads to a certificate, diploma, or associate's degree in pharmacy technology. A high school diploma usually is required for entry into a training program. The American Society of Health-System Pharmacists (ASHP) is the national accrediting organization for pharmacy technician training programs. ASHP can provide you with information on approved programs across the country (see address at end of this article).

In a pharmacy technician training program, you'll receive classroom instruction and participate in supervised clinical apprenticeships in health institutions and community pharmacies. Courses include introduction to pharmacy and health care systems, pharmacy laws and ethics, medical terminology, chemistry and microbiology. Most pharmacy technicians continue their education even after their formal training ends by reading professional journals and attending training or informational seminars, lectures, review sessions, and audiovisual presentations.

Certification or Licensing

At least three states license pharmacy technicians and all 50 states have adopted a written, standardized test for voluntary certification of technicians. Some states, including Texas and Louisiana, require certification of pharmacy technicians. To receive certification from the Pharmacy Technician Certification Board, you'll be tested on such subjects as the top 200 drugs in use by the medical profession. After receiving certification, you'll be required to complete 20 hours of continuing education every two years as part of the qualifications for recertification. Even though it is not required in every state, certification is recommended to enhance your credentials, demonstrate to employers your commitment to the profession, and possibly qualify you for higher pay.

Other Requirements

As a pharmacy technician you must be precision-minded, honest, and mature as you are depended on for accuracy and high levels of quality control, especially in hospitals. "I pay attention to details," Tamara Britton says, "and try to catch all my own mistakes before a pharmacist checks my work." You need good communications skills to interact successfully with pharmacists, supervisors, and other technicians. You must be able to follow written and oral instructions precisely because a wide variety of people, including physicians, nurses, pharmacists, and patients, rely on your actions. You also need some computer aptitude to effectively record pharmaceutical data.

EXPLORING

Ask your school's guidance or career counselor to help you arrange for a trained pharmacy technician to talk to a group of students interested in this career. Your counselor may also be able to help you arrange for an informational interview with a pharmacy technician. During such an interview you will meet one-on-one with the technician and ask him or her about the work. Volunteer work at a local hospital or nursing home will provide you with an excellent opportunity to be in an environment similar to the one in which many professional technicians work. As a volunteer, you can hone your communication skills and learn about medical settings by interacting with both patients and medical staff. You may even have the opportunity to meet and talk with pharmacy technicians. Finally, look for a part-time or summer job at a local retail pharmacy. Although your duties may be limited to stocking the shelves, working the cash register, or making deliveries, you will still gain valuable experience by working in this environment and interacting with trained pharmacists and technicians. By doing this, you may even be able to find a mentor who is willing to give you advice about education and the pharmacy technician career.

EMPLOYERS

Approximately 190,000 pharmacy technicians are employed in the United States. Most opportunities for pharmacy technicians are in retail. According to the National Association of Chain Drug Stores, there are more than 34,000 pharmacies operated by traditional chain pharmacy companies and supermarkets, as well as nearly 21,000 independent pharmacies. Technicians also work in hospitals and long-term care facilities, as well as in clinics at military bases, prisons, and colleges. Technicians are also finding work with home health care agencies.

STARTING OUT

In some cases you may be able to pursue education and certification while employed as a pharmacy technician. Some chain drugstores pay the certification fees for their techs and rewarding certified techs with higher hourly pay. This practice will probably increase—industry experts predict a need for pharmacists and technicians as more chain drugstores open across the country, and more pharmacies offer 24-hour service.

Pharmacy technicians often are hired by the hospital or agency where they interned. If you don't find employment this way, you can use employment agencies or newspaper ads to help locate job openings. Tamara Britton found her hospital job in the classifieds. "There was an ad that said 'use your data entry skills and become a pharmacy technician.' They tested me on data entry and then interviewed me and gave me the job. They trained me on all I needed to know to do the job."

ADVANCEMENT

Depending on where they are employed, technicians may direct or instruct newer pharmacy technicians, make schedules, or move to purchasing or computer work. Some hospitals have a variety of tech designations, based on experience and responsibility, with a corresponding increase in pay. Some pharmacy techs return to school to pursue a degree in pharmacy.

EARNINGS

According to the U.S. Department of Labor's *2001 National Occupational Employment and Wage Estimates,* pharmacy technicians had median annual earnings of $21,630, or $10.40 per hour. The lowest paid 10 percent of technicians earned $15,140 per year ($7.28 per hour), while the highest paid 10 percent made $31,760 ($15.27 per hour).

A number of factors can influence the wages of pharmacy technicians. A Fall 2000 salary survey conducted by Pharmacy OneSource and *Pharmacy Week* found that technicians working in hospitals, for example, generally earned more per hour than those working in retail. In addition, technicians with certification earned more per hour than those without. According to the survey, certified technicians had median hourly wages of $11.31 (which translates into a yearly income of approximately $23,525), while non-certified technicians had median hourly wages of $9.65 (or a yearly salary of $20,072). A technician's experience is also another factor that influences earnings.

Benefits that technicians receive depend on their employers but generally include medical and dental insurance, retirement savings plans, and paid sick, personal, and vacation days.

WORK ENVIRONMENT

Pharmacy technicians work in clean, well-lit, pleasant, and professional surroundings. They may wear scrubs or other uniforms in hospitals, especially in the IV room. In a retail drugstore, a technician may be allowed to wear casual clothing along with a smock. Most pharmacy settings are extremely busy, especially hospital and retail. Tamara Britton says, "I feel like I'm part of a system to help the sick get better and maybe keep people from dying." The job of pharmacy technician, like any other occupation that demands skill, speed, and accuracy, can be stressful. Because most hospitals, nursing homes, health care centers, and retail pharmacies are open between 16 and 24 hours a day, multiple shifts, weekend, and holiday hours usually are required.

OUTLOOK

The U.S. Department of Labor projects much faster than average employment growth for pharmacy technicians over the next several years. As the role of the pharmacist shifts to consultation, more technicians will be needed to assemble and dispense medications. Furthermore, new employment avenues and responsibilities will mirror that of the expanding and evolving role of the pharmacist. A strong demand is emerging for technicians with specialized training to work in specific areas, such as emergency room and nuclear pharmacy. An increasing number of pharmacy technicians will be needed as the number of older Americans (who, on average, require more prescription medication than younger generations) continues to rise.

Those who want to work as pharmacy technicians should be aware that in the future they may need more education to gain certification because of the growing number of complex medications and new drug therapies on the market. Mechanical advances in the pharmaceutical field, such as robot-picking devices and automatic counting equipment, may eradicate some of the duties pharmacy technicians previously performed, yet there will remain a need for skilled technicians to clean and maintain such devices. Traditionally, pharmacists have been required to check the work of technicians; however, in some states, hospitals are allowing techs to check the work of other techs.

FOR MORE INFORMATION

Contact AAPT for more information on membership and continuing education. Their website also has helpful links for those interested in this field.

American Association of Pharmacy Technicians (AAPT)
PO Box 1447
Greensboro, NC 27402
Tel: 877-368-4771
Email: aapt@pharmacytechnician.com
http://www.pharmacytechnician.com

For more information on accredited pharmacy technician training programs, contact:
American Society of Health-System Pharmacists
7272 Wisconsin Avenue
Bethesda, MD 20814
Tel: 301-657-3000
Email: mmucha@ashp.org
http://www.ashp.org

For industry information and employment opportunities in retail, contact:
National Association of Chain Drug Stores
413 North Lee Street
PO Box 1417-D49
Alexandria, VA 22313-1480
Tel: 703-549-3001
http://www.nacds.org

To learn more about certification and training, contact:
Pharmacy Technician Certification Board
2215 Constitution Avenue, NW
Washington, DC 20037-2985
Tel: 202-429-7576
http://www.ptcb.org

Pharmacy Week is a newsletter for professionals and pharmacy students. Check out the website for articles, industry news, job listings, and continuing education information.
Pharmacy Week
http://www.pharmacyweek.com

PHYSICIAN ASSISTANTS

QUICK FACTS

School Subjects
Biology
Health

Personal Skills
Helping/teaching
Technical/scientific

Work Environment
Primarily indoors
Primarily multiple locations

Minimum Education Level
Some postsecondary training

Salary Range
$32,600 to $69,567 to
$100,000

Certification or Licensing
Required by all states

Outlook
Much faster than the average

DOT
079

GOE
10.02.01

NOC
3123

O*NET-SOC
29-1071.00

OVERVIEW

Physician assistants (PAs) practice medicine under the supervision of licensed doctors of medicine or osteopathy and provide various health care services to patients. Much of the work they do was once performed only by physicians. There are approximately 56,200 physician assistants employed in the United States.

HISTORY

Physician assistants are fairly recent additions to the health care profession. The occupation originated in the 1960s when many medical corpsmen received additional education that enabled them to help physicians with various medical tasks. Since then, the work of the physician assistant has grown and expanded, and the number of physician assistants in the United States has greatly increased. Fewer than 100 PAs were practicing in 1970; today there are more than 56,000.

THE JOB

Physician assistants help physicians provide medical care to patients. They may be assigned a variety of tasks: they may take medical histories of patients, do complete routine physical examinations, order laboratory tests, draw blood samples, give injections, decide on diagnoses, choose treatments, and assist in surgery. Although the duties of PAs vary by state, they always work under the supervision and direction of a licensed physician. The extent of the PA's duties depends on the specific laws of the state and the practices of the supervising physician, as well as the PA's experience and abilities. PAs work in a variety of health care settings, including hospitals, clinics, physician's offices, and federal, state, and local agencies.

Approximately 44 percent of all PAs specialize in primary care medicine, such as family medicine, internal medicine, general pediatrics, and obstetrics and gynecology. Twenty-three percent of PAs are in general surgery/surgical subspecialties, 10 percent specialize in emergency medicine, and 9 percent are in internal medicine subspecialties.

Forty-seven states, the District of Columbia, and Guam allow PAs to prescribe medicine to patients; Indiana, Louisiana, and Ohio do not authorize PAs to prescribe medication. Physician assistants may be known by other occupational titles such as *child health associates, MEDEX, physician associates, anesthesiologist's assistants,* or *surgeon's assistants.*

PAs are skilled professionals who assume a great deal of responsibility in their work. By handling various medical tasks for their physician employers, PAs allow physicians more time to diagnose and treat more severely ill patients.

REQUIREMENTS
High School

Since a PA must be good with numbers and understand how the human body works, anyone interested in this job can begin preparing in high school by taking classes in math, science (especially biology and chemistry), and health. English and social science classes, such as psychology, will also help you improve your communication skills and give you an understanding of people.

Also, keep in mind that it's not too early to gain some experience in the health care field. Many postsecondary institutions take into consideration an applicant's hands-on experience when deciding whom to accept, so look for paid or volunteer positions in your community.

Postsecondary Training

Most states require that PAs complete an educational program approved by the Commission on Accreditation of Allied Health Education Programs. There are approximately 134 fully or provisionally accredited PA programs. Admissions requirements vary, but two years of college courses in science or health, and some health care experience, are usually the minimum requirements. The American Academy of Physician Assistants (AAPA) reports that approximately 72 percent of all students accepted, however, have their bachelor's or master's degrees. Most educational programs last 24 to 25 months, although some last only one year and others may last as many as three years.

The first six to 24 months of most programs involve classroom instruction in human anatomy, physiology, microbiology, clinical pharmacology, applied psychology, clinical medicine, and medical ethics. In the last nine to 15 months of most programs, students engage in supervised clinical work, usually including assignments, or rotations, in various branches of medicine, such as family practice, pediatrics, and emergency medicine.

Graduates of these programs may receive a certificate, an associate's degree, a bachelor's degree, or a master's degree; most programs, however, offer graduates a bachelor's degree. The one MEDEX program that presently exists (at the University of Washington, http://www.washington.edu/medical/som/depts/medex) lasts only 18 months. It is designed for medical corpsmen, registered nurses, and others who have had extensive patient-care experience. MEDEX students usually obtain most of their clinical experience by working with a physician who will hire them after graduation.

PA programs are offered in a variety of educational and health care settings, including colleges and universities, medical schools and centers, hospitals, and the armed forces. State laws and regulations dictate the scope of the PA's duties, and, in all but a few states, PAs must be graduates of an approved training program.

Certification or Licensing

Currently, all states require that PAs be certified by the National Commission on Certification of Physician Assistants (NCCPA). To become certified, applicants must be graduates of an accredited PA program and pass the Physician Assistants National Certifying Examination (PANCE). The examination consists of three parts: the first part tests general medical knowledge, the second part tests the PA's specialty, either primary care or surgery, and the third part tests practical clinical knowledge. After successfully completing the examination, physician assistants can use the credential, Physician Assistant-Certified (PA-C).

Once certified, PAs are required to complete 100 hours of continuing medical education courses every two years, and in addition must pass a recertification examination every six years. Besides NCCPA certification, most states also require that PAs register with the state medical board. State rules and regulations vary greatly concerning the work of PAs, and applicants are advised to study the laws of the state in which they wish to practice.

Licensing for physician assistants varies by state. New graduates should contact their state's licensing board to find out about specific requirements. Some states grant temporary licenses to physician assistants who have applied for the PANCE. For permanent licensure, most states require verification of certification or an official record of their exam scores.

Other Requirements

To be a successful physician assistant, you must be able to work well with many different kinds of people, from the physician who supervises you to the many different patients you see every day. In addition to being a caring individual, you should also have a strong desire to continue learning in order to keep up with the latest medical procedures and recertification requirements. Since ill individuals depend on a physician assistant's decisions, anyone interested in this job should have leadership skills and self-confidence as well as compassion.

EXPLORING

If you are interested in exploring the profession, talk with school guidance counselors, practicing PAs, PA students, and various health care employees at local hospitals and clinics. You can also obtain information by contacting one of the organizations listed at the end of this chapter. Working as a volunteer in a hospital, clinic, or nursing home is a good way to get exposure to the health care profession. In addition, while in college, you may be able to obtain summer jobs as a hospital orderly, nurse assistant, or medical clerk.

Such jobs can help you assess your interest in and suitability for work as a PA before you apply to a PA program.

EMPLOYERS

PAs work in a variety of health care settings. According to the AAPA, 55 percent of all PAs are employed by single physicians or group practices; about 17 percent are employed by hospitals. PAs also work in clinics and medical offices. They are employed by nursing homes, long-term care facilities, and prisons. Many areas lacking quality medical care personnel, such as remote rural areas and the inner city, are hiring PAs to meet their needs.

STARTING OUT

PAs must complete their formal training programs before entering the job market. Once they complete their studies, PA students can utilize their schools' placement services to locate jobs. PAs may also seek employment at hospitals, clinics, medical offices, or other health care settings. Information about jobs with the federal government can be obtained by contacting the Office of Personnel Management. According to the American Academy of Physician Assistants (AAPA), 80 percent of PA graduates find employment as a PA in less than a year.

ADVANCEMENT

Since the PA profession is still quite new, formal lines of advancement have not yet been established. There are still several ways to advance. Hospitals, for example, do not employ head PAs. Those with experience can assume more responsibility at higher pay, or they move on to employment at larger hospitals and clinics. Some PAs go back to school for additional education to practice in a specialty area, such as surgery, urology, or ophthalmology.

EARNINGS

Salaries of PAs vary according to experience, specialty, and employer. Physician assistants with less than one year of experience earned a median of $61,363, according to the AAPA 2002 Census Survey. The U.S. Department of Labor reports that the lowest 10 percent of all physician assistants earned less than $32,600 in 2001. The Department also reports that physician assistants employed in offices and clinics of medical doctors had median annual earnings of $64,430 in 2000, while those employed in hospitals averaged

$61,460. The median annual average for all PAs was $69,567 in 2002, according to the AAPA 2002 Census Survey. Experienced PAs have the potential to earn close to $100,000 a year. PAs are well compensated compared with other occupations that have similar training requirements. Most PAs receive health and life insurance among other benefits.

WORK ENVIRONMENT
Most work settings are comfortable and clean, although, like physicians, PAs spend a good part of their day standing or walking. The workweek varies according to the employment setting. A few emergency room PAs may work 24-hour shifts, twice a week; others work 12-hour shifts, three times a week. PAs who work in physicians' offices, hospitals, or clinics may have to work weekends, nights, and holidays. PAs employed in clinics, however, usually work five-day, 40-hour weeks.

OUTLOOK
Employment for physician assistants, according to the U.S. Department of Labor, is expected to increase much faster than the average for all occupations. A 53.5 percent increase in the number of new jobs is projected through 2010. Opportunities will be best in rural areas and inner city clinics—settings which often have trouble attracting the most qualified candidates.

The role of the PA in delivering health care has also expanded over the past decade. PAs have taken on new duties and responsibilities, and they now work in a variety of health care settings.

FOR MORE INFORMATION
Visit the "Become a PA" section of the AAPA website for more information on PA careers, educational programs, and scholarships.

American Academy of Physician Assistants (AAPA)
950 North Washington Street
Alexandria, VA 22314-1552
Tel: 703-836-2272
Email: aapa@aapa.org
http://www.aapa.org

For industry information and to subscribe ($35 fee) to the Physician Assistants Program Directory, contact:

Association of Physician Assistant Programs
950 North Washington Street
Alexandria, VA 22314-1552
Tel: 703-548-5538
Email: apap@aapa.org
http://www.apap.org

For information on certification, contact:

National Commission on Certification of Physician Assistants
157 Technology Parkway, Suite 800
Norcross, GA 30092-2913
Tel: 770-734-4500
Email: nccpa@nccpa.net
http://www.nccpa.net

POLICE OFFICERS

QUICK FACTS

School Subjects Physical education Psychology	**Certification or Licensing** None available
Personal Skills Communication/ideas Leadership/management	**Outlook** Faster than the average **DOT** 375
Work Environment Indoors and outdoors Primarily multiple locations	**GOE** 04.01.02
Minimum Education Level High school diploma	**NOC** 6261
Salary Range $24,490 to $40,970 to $86,060+	**O*NET-SOC** 33-3021.01, 33-3021.02, 33-3051.00, 33-3051.01

OVERVIEW

Police officers perform many duties relating to public safety. Their responsibilities include not only preserving the peace, preventing criminal acts, enforcing the law, investigating crimes, and arresting those who violate the law, but also directing traffic, community relations work, and controlling crowds at public events. Police officers are employed at the federal, state, county, and city levels.

State police officers patrol highways and enforce the laws and regulations that govern the use of those highways, in addition to performing general police work. Police officers are under oath to uphold the law 24 hours a day. There are approximately 834,000 police and detectives employed in the United States.

HISTORY

People have historically sought some form of protection for their lives and property and to help preserve their welfare. The true origins of police work, however, are virtually unknown. In medieval times, feudal lords employed retainers who made sure taxes were paid. These employees may have attempted to maintain some kind of law and order among the people, but they often merely enforced their employers' wishes.

Colonial America followed the British form of police organization. A sheriff, appointed by the governor of a colony, enforced laws, collected taxes, and maintained public property throughout the colony. Constables performed similar duties in the cities and towns. Night watchmen protected the cities from fires and crime. However, as cities grew rapidly during the 19th century, a larger, more organized police service was needed to control growing problems with crimes and public disturbances.

In 1829 in London, Sir Robert Peel established the first modern, nonmilitary police force. The British police became known as *bobbies* after Sir Robert's name. The police force in New York City was established in 1844. These new police forces wore uniforms, worked 24 hours a day, and often carried guns. They patrolled the streets and soon became a fixture in many cities. On the American frontier, however, laws were often enforced by volunteer police officers until regular police forces were established. Many areas of the western United States were guarded by a sheriff and the sheriff's deputies. An early effort to create a statewide police force resulted in the creation of the Texas Rangers in 1835. In 1905, Pennsylvania formed the first official state police departments. Soon, almost every state had a state police department as well as those police units that worked for individual cities or towns.

These early police efforts were often notoriously inadequate. Many police departments were seats of corruption and abuse of authority. Police officers were generally untrained and were often appointed as agents serving the political machine of their city rather than the people. Efforts to clean up the police departments began in the early decades of the 20th century. Police were expected to be professionals. Higher selection standards and special training programs were instituted, and efforts were made to eliminate the influence of politics on the police department. Command of the police department soon became more centralized, with a chief of police supervising the operations of the entire department. Other ranks were created, such as sergeant and detective. At the same time, scientists working with the police were developing scientific advances in crime detection and prevention, such as fingerprinting.

Today, every state has uniformed police. State police operations are customarily confined to unincorporated areas as a matter of policy, although a few states restrict them by statute. In addition, police operate at the federal level in such agencies as the Federal Bureau of Investigation, the Immigration and Naturalization Service, and the Drug Enforcement Agency. While the many types of police forces operate independently, they often cooperate to provide more effective law enforcement.

THE JOB

Depending on the orders they receive from their commanding officers, police may direct traffic during the rush-hour periods and at special events when traffic is unusually heavy. They may patrol public places such as parks, streets, and public gatherings to maintain law and order. Police are sometimes called upon to prevent or break up riots and to act as escorts at funerals, parades, and other public events. They may administer first aid in emergency situations, assist in rescue operations of various kinds, investigate crimes, issue tickets to violators of traffic or parking laws or other regulations, or arrest drunk drivers. Officers in small towns may have to perform all these duties and administrative work as well.

As officers patrol their assigned beats, either on foot, bicycle, horseback, or in cars, they must be alert for any situations that arise and be ready to take appropriate action. Many times they must be alert to identify stolen cars, identify and locate lost children, and identify and apprehend escaped criminals and others wanted by various law enforcement agencies. While on patrol, they keep in constant contact with headquarters and their fellow officers by calling in regularly on two-way radios. Although their profession may at times be dangerous, police officers are trained not to endanger their own lives or the lives of ordinary citizens. If they need assistance, they radio for additional officers.

In large city police departments, officers usually have more specific duties and specialized assignments. The police departments generally comprised special work divisions such as communications, criminal investigation, firearms identification, fingerprint identification and forensic science, accident prevention, and administrative services. In very large cities, police departments may have special work units such as the harbor patrol, canine corps, mounted police, vice squad, fraud or bunco squad, traffic control, records control, and rescue units. A few of the job titles for these specialties are identification and records commanders and officers, narcotics and vice detectives or investigators, homicide squad commanding officers, detective chiefs, traffic lieutenants, sergeants, parking enforcement officers, public safety officers, accident-prevention squad officers, safety instruction police officers, and community relations lieutenants.

In very large city police departments, officers may fill positions as police chiefs, precinct sergeants and captains, desk officers, booking officers, police inspectors, identification officers, complaint evaluation supervisors and officers, and crime prevention police officers. Some officers work as plainclothes detectives in criminal investigation divisions. *Internal affairs investigators* are employed to police the police. Other specialized police officers include *police commanding officers*, who act as supervisors in missing persons and fugitive investigations; and officers who investigate and pursue nonpayment and fraud fugitives. Many police departments employ *police clerks*, who perform administrative and community-oriented tasks.

A major responsibility for state police officers (sometimes known as *state troopers* or *highway patrol officers*) is to patrol the highways and enforce the laws and regulations of those traveling on them. Riding in patrol cars equipped with two-way radios, they monitor traffic for troublesome or dangerous situations. They write traffic tickets and issue warnings to drivers who are violating traffic laws or otherwise not observing safe driving practices. They radio for assistance for drivers who are stopped because of breakdowns, flat tires, illnesses, or other reasons. They direct traffic around congested areas caused by fires, road repairs, accidents, and other emergencies. They may check the weight of commercial vehicles to verify that they are within allowable limits, conduct driver examinations, or give safety information to the public.

In the case of a highway accident, officers take charge of the activities at the site by directing traffic, giving first aid to any injured parties, and calling for emergency equipment such as ambulances, fire trucks, or tow trucks. They write up a report to be used by investigating officers who attempt to determine the cause of the accident.

In addition to these responsibilities, state police officers in most states do some general police work. They are often the primary law-enforcement agency in communities or counties that have no police force or a large sheriff's department. In those areas, they may investigate such crimes as burglary and assault. They also may assist municipal or county police in capturing lawbreakers or controlling civil disturbances.

Most police officers carry guns and are trained in the use of firearms. Police in special divisions, such as chemical analysis and handwriting and fingerprint identification, have special training to perform their work. Police officers often testify in court regarding cases with which they have been involved. Police personnel are required to complete accurate and thorough records of their cases.

REQUIREMENTS
High School

The majority of police departments today require that applicants have a high school education. Although a high school diploma is not always required, related work experience is generally required.

If you are interested in pursuing this career, you will find the subjects of psychology, sociology, English, law, mathematics, U.S. government and history, chemistry, and physics most helpful. Because physical stamina is very important in this work, sports and physical education are also valuable. Knowledge of a foreign language is especially helpful, and bilingual officers are often in great demand. If specialized and advanced positions in law enforcement interest you, pursue studies leading to college programs in criminology, criminal law, criminal psychology, or related areas.

Postsecondary Training

The best chance for advancement is by getting some postsecondary education, and many police departments now require a two- or four-year degree, especially for more specialized areas of police work. There are more than 800 junior colleges and universities offering two- and four-year degree programs in law enforcement, police science, and administration of justice. Many police departments require a two-year degree to make lieutenant and a bachelor's degree to make captain. The armed forces also offer training and opportunities in law enforcement that can be applied to civilian police work.

Newly recruited police officers must pass a special training program. After training, they are usually placed on a probationary period lasting from three to six months. In small towns and communities, you may get your training on the job by working with an experienced officer. Inexperienced officers are never sent out on patrol alone but are always accompanied by veteran officers.

Large city police departments give classroom instruction in laws, accident investigation, city ordinances, and traffic control. These departments also give instruction in the handling of firearms, methods of apprehension and arrest, self-defense tactics, and first-aid techniques. Both state and municipal police officers are trained in safe driving procedures and maneuvering an automobile at high speeds.

Other Requirements

Police job appointments in most large cities and in many smaller cities and towns are governed by local civil service regulations. You'll be required to pass written tests designed to measure your intelligence and general aptitude for police work. You will also be required to pass physical examinations, which usually include tests of physical agility, dexterity, and strength. Your personal history, background, and character will undergo careful scrutiny because honesty and law-abiding characteristics are essential traits for law-enforcement officers. Another important requirement is that you have no arrest record.

To be a police officer, you must be at least 21 years of age (or older for some departments), and some municipalities stipulate an age limit of not more than 35 years. You must have, in some cases, 20/20 uncorrected vision, good hearing, and weight proportionate to your height. You'll also be required to meet locally prescribed weight and height rules for your gender. Most regulations require that you be a U.S. citizen, and many police departments have residency requirements.

If you hope to be a police officer, you should enjoy working with people and be able to cooperate with others. Because of the stressful nature of much police work, you must be able to think clearly and logically during emergency situations, have a strong degree of emotional control, and be capable of detaching yourself from incidents.

Physical fitness training is a mandatory, continuing activity in most police departments, as are routine physical examinations. Police officers can have no physical disabilities that would prevent them from carrying out their duties.

EXPLORING

A good way to explore police work is to talk with various law enforcement officers. Most departments have community outreach programs and many have recruiting programs as well. You may also wish to visit colleges offering programs in police work or write for information on their training programs.

In some cases, high school graduates can explore this occupation by seeking employment as police cadets in large city police departments. These cadets are paid employees who work part time in clerical and other duties. They attend training courses in police science on a part-time basis. When you reach the age of 21, you'll be eligible to apply for regular police work. Some police departments also hire college students as interns.

EMPLOYERS

Police officers hold approximately 834,000 jobs in the United States. According to the U.S. Department of Labor, approximately 80 percent of police officers are employed by local governments. State police agencies employ approximately 13 percent of officers, and about 6 percent of officers work for federal agencies.

STARTING OUT

If you are interested in police work, you should apply directly to local civil service offices or examining boards to qualify as a candidate for police officer. In some locations, written examinations may be given to groups at specified times. For positions in smaller communities that do not follow civil service methods, you should apply directly to the police department or city government offices in that community. If you are interested in becoming a state police officer, you can apply directly to the state civil service commission or the state police headquarters, which are usually located in the state capital.

ADVANCEMENT

Advancement in these occupations is determined by several factors. An officer's eligibility for promotion may depend on a specified length of service, job performance, formal education and training courses, and results of written examinations. Those who become eligible for promotion are listed on the promotional list along with other qualified candidates. Promotions generally become available from six months to three years after starting, depending on the department. As positions of different or higher rank become available, candidates are promoted to fill them according to their position on the list. Lines of promotion usually begin with officer third grade and progress to grade two and grade one. Other possible promotional opportunities include the ranks of detective, sergeant, lieutenant, or captain. Many promotions require additional training and testing. Advancement to the very top-ranking positions, such as division, bureau, or department director or chief, may be made by direct political appointment. Most of these top positions are held by officers who have come up through the ranks.

Large city police departments offer the greatest number of advancement opportunities. Most of the larger departments maintain separate divisions, which require administration workers, line officers, and more employees in general at each rank level. Officers may move into areas that they find challenging, such as criminal investigation or forensics.

Most city police departments offer various types of in-service study and training programs. These programs allow police departments to keep up-to-date on the latest police science techniques and are often required for those who want to be considered for promotion. Police academies, colleges, and other educational institutions offer training courses. Some of the subjects offered are civil defense, foreign languages, and forgery detection. Some municipal police departments share the cost with their officers or pay all educational expenses if the officers are willing to work toward a college degree in either police work or police administration. Independent study is also often required.

Intensive 12-week administrative training courses are offered by the National Academy of the Federal Bureau of Investigation in Washington, D.C. A limited number of officers are selected to participate in this training program.

Advancement opportunities on police forces in small communities are considerably more limited by the rank and number of police personnel needed. Other opportunities for advancement may be found in related police, protective, and security service work with private companies, state and county agencies, and other institutions.

EARNINGS

According to the U.S. Department of Labor, police officers in 2001 earned an annual average salary of $40,970; the lowest 10 percent earned less than $24,490 a year, while the highest 10 percent earned over $61,870 annually. Police officers in supervisory positions earned median salaries of $57,210 a year in 2000, with a low of $34,660 and a high of more than $86,060. Salaries for police officers range widely based on geographic location. Police departments in the western and northern states generally pay more than those in southern states.

Most police officers receive periodic and annual salary increases up to a limit set for their rank and length of service. Police departments generally pay special compensation to cover the cost of uniforms. They usually provide any equipment required, such as firearms and handcuffs. Overtime pay may be given for certain work shifts or emergency duty. In these instances, officers are usually paid straight or time-and-a-half pay, while extra time off is sometimes given as compensation.

Because most police officers are civil service employees, they receive generous benefits, including health insurance and paid vacation and sick leave, and enjoy increased job security. In addition, most police departments offer retirement plans and retirement after 20 or 25 years of service, usually at half pay.

WORK ENVIRONMENT

Police officers work under many different types of circumstances. Much of their work may be performed outdoors, as they ride in patrol cars or walk the beats assigned to them. In emergency situations, no consideration can be made for weather conditions, time of day or night, or day of the week. Police officers may be on call 24 hours a day; even when they are not on duty, they are usually required by law to respond to emergencies or criminal activity. Although they are assigned regular work hours, individuals in police work must be willing to live by an unpredictable and often erratic work schedule. The work demands constant mental and physical alertness as well as great physical strength and stamina.

Police work generally consists of an eight-hour day and a five-day week, but police officers may work night and weekend shifts and on holidays. Emergencies may add many extra hours to an officer's day or week. The occupation is considered dangerous. Some officers are killed or wounded while performing their duties. Their work can involve unpleasant duties and expose them to sordid, depressing, or dangerous situations. They may be called on to deal with all types of people under many types of circumstances. While the routine of some assigned duties may become boring, the dangers of police work are often stressful for the officers and their families. Police work in general holds the potential for the unknown and unexpected, and most people who pursue this work have a strong passion for and commitment to police work.

OUTLOOK

Employment of police officers is expected to increase faster than the average for all occupations over the next several years, according to the U.S. Department of Labor. Federal "tough-on-crime" legislation passed in the mid-1990s has created new jobs in police departments at the federal, state, and local levels.

The opportunities that become available, however, may be affected by technological, scientific, and other changes occurring today in police work. Automation in traffic control is limiting the number of officers needed in this area, while the increasing reliance on computers throughout society is creating demands for new kinds of police work. New approaches in social science and psychological research are also changing the methodology used in working with public offenders. These trends indicate a future demand for more educated, specialized personnel.

This occupation has a very low turnover rate. However, new positions will open as current officers retire, leave the force, or move into higher positions. Retirement ages are relatively low in police work compared to other occupations. Many officers retire while in their forties and then pursue a second career. In response to increasing crime rates and threats of terrorism, some police departments across the country are expanding the number of patrol officers; however, budget problems faced by many municipalities may limit growth.

In the past decade, private security firms have begun to take over some police activities, such as patrolling public places. Some private companies have even been contracted to provide police forces for some cities. Many companies and universities also operate their own police forces.

FOR MORE INFORMATION

Created by the American Federation of Police and Concerned Citizens and the National Association of Chiefs of Police, the American Police Hall of Fame and Museum offers summer camps, scholarships, and other information for young people interested in police work.

American Police Hall of Fame and Museum
3801 Biscayne Boulevard
Miami, FL 33137
Tel: 305-573-0070
Email: policeinfo@aphf.org
http://www.aphf.org

The National Association of Police Organizations is a coalition of police unions and associations that work to advance the interests of law enforcement officers through legislation, political action, and education.

National Association of Police Organizations
750 First Street, NE, Suite 920
Washington, DC 20002
Tel: 202-842-4420
Email: napo@erols.com
http://www.napo.org

PUBLIC RELATIONS SPECIALISTS

QUICK FACTS

School Subjects
Business
English
Journalism

Personal Skills
Communication/ideas
Leadership/management

Work Environment
Primarily indoors
One location with
some travel

Minimum Education Level
Bachelor's degree

Salary Range
$23,930 to $41,010 to
$72,910+

Certification or Licensing
Voluntary

Outlook
Much faster than the
average

DOT
165

GOE
11.09.03

NOC
5124

O*NET-SOC
11-2031.00,
27-3031.00

OVERVIEW

Public relations (PR) specialists develop and maintain programs that present a favorable public image for an individual or organization. They provide information to the target audience (generally, the public at large) about the client, its goals and accomplishments, and any further plans or projects that may be of public interest.

PR specialists may be employed by corporations, government agencies, nonprofit organizations—almost any type of organization. Many PR specialists hold positions in public relations consulting firms or work for advertising agencies. There are approximately 137,000 public relations specialists in the United States.

HISTORY

The first public relations counsel was a reporter named Ivy Ledbetter Lee, who in 1906 was named press representative for coal-mine operators. Labor disputes were becoming a large concern of the operators, and they had run into problems because of their continual refusal to talk to the press and the hired miners. Lee convinced the mine operators to start responding to press questions and supply the press with information on the mine activities.

During and after World War II, the rapid advancement of communications techniques prompted firms to realize they needed professional help to ensure their messages were given proper public attention. Manufacturing firms that had turned their production facilities over to the war effort returned to the manufacture of peacetime products and enlisted the aid of public relations professionals to forcefully bring products and the company name before the buying public.

Large business firms, labor unions, and service organizations, such as the American Red Cross, Boy Scouts of America, and the YMCA, began to recognize the value of establishing positive, healthy relationships with the public that they served and depended on for support. The need for effective public relations was often emphasized when circumstances beyond a company's or institution's control created unfavorable reaction from the public.

Public relations specialists must be experts at representing their clients before the media. The rapid growth of the public relations field since 1945 is a testament to an increased awareness by all industries of the power of professional media usage and PR campaigns to maintain good relationships with many different publics: customers, employees, stockholders, contributors, and competitors.

THE JOB

Public relations specialists do a wide variety of tasks. Some work primarily as writers, creating reports, news releases, and booklet texts. Others write speeches or create copy for radio, TV, or film sequences. These workers spend much of their time contacting the press, radio, TV, and magazines on behalf of their employers. Some PR specialists work more as editors than writers, fact-checking and rewriting employee publications, newsletters, shareholder reports, and other management communications.

Specialists may choose to concentrate in graphic design, using their background knowledge of art and layout for developing brochures, booklets, and photographic communications. Other PR workers handle special events, such as press parties, convention exhibits, open houses, or anniversary celebrations.

PR specialists must be alert to any and all company or institutional events that are newsworthy. They prepare news releases and direct them toward the proper media. Specialists working for manufacturers and retailers are concerned with efforts that will promote sales and create goodwill for the firm's products. They work closely with the marketing and sales departments to announce new products, prepare displays, and attend occasional dealers' conventions.

A large firm may have a *director of public relations,* who is a vice president of the company and in charge of a staff that includes writers, artists, researchers, and other specialists. Publicity for an individual or a small organization may involve many of the same areas of expertise but may be carried out by a few people or possibly even one person.

Many PR workers act as consultants (rather than staff) of a corporation, institution, or organization. These workers have the advantage of being able to operate independently, state opinions objectively, and work with more than one type of business or association.

PR specialists are called upon to work with the public-opinion aspects of almost every corporate or institutional problem. These can range from the opening of a new manufacturing plant to a college's dormitory dedication to a merger or sale of a company.

Public relations professionals can also specialize. *Lobbyists* try to persuade legislators and other office holders to pass laws favoring the interests of the firms or people they represent. *Fund-raising directors* develop and direct programs designed to raise funds for social welfare agencies and other nonprofit organizations.

Early in their careers, public relations specialists become accustomed to having others receive credit for their behind-the-scenes work. The speeches they draft will be delivered by company officers, the magazine articles they prepare may be credited to the president of the company, and they may be consulted to prepare the message to stockholders from the chairman of the board that appears in the annual report.

REQUIREMENTS
High School
While in high school, take courses in English, journalism, public speaking, humanities, and languages, because public relations is

based on effective communication with others. Courses such as these will develop your skills in written and oral communication as well as provide a better understanding of different fields and industries to be publicized.

Postsecondary Training

Most people employed in public relations service have a college degree. Major fields of study most beneficial to developing the proper skills are public relations, English, and journalism. Some employers feel that majoring in the area in which the public relations person will eventually work is the best training. A knowledge of business administration is most helpful, as is a native talent for selling. A graduate degree may be required for managerial positions. People with a bachelor's degree in public relations can find staff positions with either an organization or a public relations firm.

More than 200 colleges and about 100 graduate schools offer degree programs or special courses in public relations. In addition, many other colleges offer at least courses in the field. The journalism or communication departments of schools sometimes offer PR programs. In addition to courses in theory and techniques of public relations, PR students may study organization, management and administration, and practical applications; they often specialize in areas such as business, government, and nonprofit organizations. Other preparation includes courses in creative writing, psychology, communications, advertising, and journalism.

Certification or Licensing

The Public Relations Society of America, the International Association of Business Communicators, and the Canadian Public Relations Society, Inc., accredit public relations workers who have passed a comprehensive examination. Such accreditation is a sign of competence in this field, although it is not a requirement for employment.

Other Requirements

Today's public relations specialist must be a businessperson first, both to understand how to perform successfully in business and to comprehend the needs and goals of the organization or client. Additionally, the public relations specialist needs to be a strong writer and speaker with good interpersonal, leadership, and organizational skills.

EXPLORING

Almost any experience in working with other people will help you to develop strong interpersonal skills, which are crucial in public relations. The possibilities are almost endless. Summer work on a newspaper or trade paper or with a radio or television station may give insight into communications media. Working as a volunteer on a political campaign can help you to understand the ways in which people can be persuaded. Being selected as a page for the U.S. Congress or a state legislature will help you grasp the fundamentals of government processes. A job in retail will help you to understand some of the principles of product presentation. A teaching job will develop your organization and presentation skills.

EMPLOYERS

Public relations specialists hold about 137,000 jobs. Workers may be paid employees of the organization they represent or they may be part of a public relations firm that works for organizations on a contract basis. Others are involved in fund-raising or political campaigning. Public relations may be done for a corporation, retail business, service company, utility, association, nonprofit organization, or educational institution.

Most PR firms are located in large cities that are centers of communications. New York, Chicago, Los Angeles, and Washington, D.C. are good places to search for a public relations job. Nevertheless, there are many good opportunities in cities across the United States.

STARTING OUT

There is no clear-cut formula for getting a job in public relations. Individuals often enter the field after gaining preliminary experience in another occupation closely allied to the field, usually some segment of communications, frequently journalism. Coming into public relations from newspaper work is still a recommended route. Another good method is to gain initial employment as a public relations trainee or intern, or as a clerk, secretary, or research assistant in a public relations department or a counseling firm.

ADVANCEMENT

In some large companies, an entry-level public relations specialist may start as a trainee in a formal training program for new employees. In others, new employees may expect to receive work that has a minimum of responsibility. They may assemble clippings or do rewrites on material that has already been accepted. They may make posters or assist in conducting polls or surveys, or compile reports from data submitted by others.

As workers acquire experience, they are given more responsibility. They write news releases, direct polls or surveys, or advance to writing speeches for company officials. Progress may seem to be slow, because some skills take a long time to master.

Some lower level PR workers advance in responsibility and salary in the same firm in which they started. Others find that the path to advancement is to accept a more attractive position in another firm. The goal of many public relations specialists is to open an independent office or to join an established consulting firm. To start an independent office requires a large outlay of capital and an established reputation in the field. However, those who are successful in operating their own consulting firms probably attain the greatest financial success in the public relations field.

EARNINGS

The Bureau of Labor Statistics reports that public relations specialists had median annual earnings of $41,010 in 2001. Salaries ranged from less than $23,930 to more than $72,910.

The U.S. Department of Labor reports the following 2000 median salaries for public relations specialists by type of employer: management and public relations, $43,690; state government, $39,560; local government, $40,760; and colleges and universities, $35,080.

Many PR workers receive a range of fringe benefits from corporations and agencies employing them, including bonus/incentive compensation, stock options, profit sharing/pension plans/401-K programs, medical benefits, life insurance, financial planning, maternity/paternity leave, paid vacations, and family college tuition. Bonuses can range from 5 to 100 percent of base compensation and often are based on individual and/or company performance.

WORK ENVIRONMENT

Public relations specialists generally work in offices with adequate secretarial help, regular salary increases, and expense accounts. They are expected to make a good appearance in tasteful, conservative clothing. They must have social poise, and their conduct in their personal life is important to their firms or their clients. The public relations specialist may have to entertain business associates.

The PR specialist seldom works the conventional office hours for many weeks at a time; although the workweek may consist of 35 to 40 hours, these hours may be supplemented by evenings and even weekends when meetings must be attended and other special events covered. Time behind the desk may represent only a small part of the total working schedule. Travel is often an important and necessary part of the job.

The life of the PR worker is so greatly determined by the job that many consider this a disadvantage. Because the work is concerned with public opinion, it is often difficult to measure the results of performance and to sell the worth of a public relations program to an employer or client. Competition in the consulting field is keen, and if a firm loses an account, some of its personnel may be affected. The demands it makes for anonymity will be considered by some as one of the profession's less inviting aspects. Public relations involves much more hard work and a great deal less glamour than is popularly supposed.

OUTLOOK

Employment of public relations professionals is expected to grow much faster than average for all other occupations, according to the U.S. Department of Labor. Competition will be keen for beginning jobs in public relations because so many job seekers are enticed by the perceived glamour and appeal of the field; those with both education and experience will have an advantage.

Most large companies have some sort of public relations resource, either through their own staff or through the use of a firm of consultants. They are expected to expand their public relations activities and create many new jobs. More of the smaller companies are hiring public relations specialists, adding to the demand for these workers.

FOR MORE INFORMATION

To read Communication World Online and other information for professionals in public relations, employee communications, marketing communications, and public affairs, contact:

International Association of Business Communicators
One Hallidie Plaza, Suite 600
San Francisco, CA 94102-2818
Tel: 415-544-4700
http://www.iabc.com

For statistics, salary surveys, and other information about the profession, contact:

Public Relations Society of America
33 Irving Place
New York, NY 10003-2376
Tel: 212-995-2230
Email: hq@prsa.org
http://www.prsa.org

This professional association for public relations professionals offers an accreditation program and opportunities for professional development.

Canadian Public Relations Society, Inc.
4195 Dundas Street West, Suite 346
Toronto, ON M8X 1Y4 Canada
Tel: 416-239-7034
http://www.cprs.ca

REGISTERED NURSES

QUICK FACTS

School Subjects Biology Chemistry Health **Personal Skills** Helping/teaching Technical/scientific **Work Environment** Primarily indoors Primarily multiple locations **Minimum Education Level** Some postsecondary training **Salary Range** $33,110 to $46,670 to $91,745+	**Certification or Licensing** Required **Outlook** Faster than the average **DOT** 075 **GOE** 10.02.01 **NOC** 3152 **O*NET-SOC** 29-1111.00

OVERVIEW

Registered nurses (RNs) help individuals, families, and groups to achieve health and prevent disease. They care for the sick and injured in hospitals and other health care facilities, physicians' offices, private homes, public health agencies, schools, camps, and industry. Some registered nurses are employed in private practice. RNs hold about 2.2 million jobs in the United States.

HISTORY

Modern ideas about hospitals and nursing as a profession did not develop until the 19th century. The life and work of Florence Nightingale (1820–1910) were a strong influence on the profession's development. Nightingale, who came from a wealthy, upper-class British family, dedicated her life to improving conditions in hospitals, beginning in an army hospital during the Crimean War. In the United States, many of Nightingale's ideas were put into practice for the care of the wounded during the Civil War. But concerned individuals rather than trained nurses provided care. These individuals had not received the kind of training that is required for nurses today.

The first school of nursing in the United States was founded in Boston in 1873. In 1938, New York State passed the first state law to require that practical nurses be licensed. Even though the first school for the training of practical nurses was started almost 74 years prior, and the establishment of other schools followed, the training programs lacked uniformity.

After the 1938 law was passed, a movement began that promoted organized training programs that would assure new standards in the field. The role and training of nurses have undergone radical changes since the first schools were opened.

Education standards for nurses have been improving constantly since that time. Today's nurse is a highly educated, licensed health care professional. Extended programs of training are offered throughout the country, and all states have enacted laws to assure that training standards are maintained and to assure qualification for licensure. The field of nursing serves an important role as a part of the health care system.

THE JOB

Registered nurses work under the direct supervision of nursing departments and in collaboration with physicians. Two-thirds of all nurses work in hospitals, where they may be assigned to general, operating room, or maternity room duty. They may also care for sick children or be assigned to other hospital units, such as emergency rooms, intensive care units, or outpatient clinics. There are many different kinds of RNs.

General duty nurses work together with other members of the health care team to assess the patient's condition and to develop and implement a plan of health care. These nurses may perform such tasks as taking patients' vital signs, administering medication and injections, recording the symptoms and progress of patients, changing dressings, assisting patients with personal care, conferring with members of the medical staff, helping prepare a patient for surgery, and completing any number of duties that require skill and understanding of patients' needs.

Surgical nurses oversee the preparation of the operating room and the sterilization of instruments. They assist surgeons during operations and coordinate the flow of patient cases in operating rooms.

Maternity nurses, or *neonatal nurses,* help in the delivery room, take care of newborns in the nursery, and teach mothers how to feed and care for their babies.

The activities of staff nurses are directed and coordinated by *head nurses* and *charge nurses.* Heading up the entire nursing program in the hospital is the *nursing service director,* who administers the nursing program to maintain standards of patient care. The nursing service director advises the medical staff, department heads, and the hospital administrator in matters relating to nursing services and helps prepare the department budget.

Private duty nurses may work in hospitals or in a patient's home. They are employed by the patient they are caring for or by the patient's family. Their service is designed for the individual care of one person and is carried out in cooperation with the patient's physician.

Office nurses usually work in the office of a dentist, physician, or health maintenance organization (HMO). An office nurse may be one of several nurses on the staff or the only staff nurse. If a nurse is the only staff member, this person may have to combine some clerical duties with those of nursing, such as serving as receptionist, making appointments for the doctor, helping maintain patient records, sending out monthly statements, and attending to routine correspondence. If the physician's staff is a large one that includes secretaries and clerks, the office nurse will concentrate on screening patients, assisting with examinations, supervising the examining rooms, sterilizing equipment, providing patient education, and performing other nursing duties.

Occupational health nurses, or *industrial nurses,* are an important part of many large firms. They maintain a clinic at a plant or factory and are usually occupied in rendering preventive, remedial, and educational nursing services. They work under the direction of an industrial physician, nursing director, or nursing supervisor. They may advise on accident prevention, visit employees on the job to check the conditions under which they work, and advise management about the safety of such conditions. At the plant, they render treatment in emergencies.

School nurses may work in one school or in several, visiting each for a part of the day or week. They may supervise the student clinic, treat minor cuts or injuries, or give advice on good health practices. They may examine students to detect conditions of the eyes or teeth that require attention. They also assist the school physician.

Community health nurses, also called *public health nurses,* require specialized training for their duties. Their job usually requires them to spend part of the time traveling from one assignment to another. Their duties may differ greatly from one case to another. For instance, in one day they may have to instruct a class of expectant mothers, visit new parents to help them plan proper care for the baby, visit an aged patient requiring special care, and conduct a class in nutrition. They usually possess many and varied nursing skills and often are called upon to meet unexpected or unusual situations.

Administrators in the community health field include nursing directors, educational directors, and nursing supervisors. Some nurses go into nursing education and work with nursing students to instruct them on theories and skills they will need to enter the profession. *Nursing instructors* may give classroom instruction and demonstrations or supervise nursing students on hospital units. Some instructors eventually become nursing school directors, university faculty, or deans of a university degree program. Nurses also have the opportunity to direct staff development and continuing education programs for nursing personnel in hospitals.

Advanced practice nurses are nurses with training beyond what is required for the RN designation. There are four primary categories of nurses included in this category: *nurse-midwives, clinical nurse specialists, nurse anesthetists, and nurse practitioners.*

Some nurses are consultants to hospitals, nursing schools, industrial organizations, and public health agencies. They advise clients on such administrative matters as staff organization, nursing techniques, curricula, and education programs. Other administrative specialists include *educational directors for the state board of nursing,* who are concerned with maintaining well-defined educational standards, and *executive directors of professional nurses' associations,* who administer programs developed by the board of directors and the members of the association.

Some nurses choose to enter the armed forces. All types of nurses, except private duty nurses, are represented in the military services. They provide skilled nursing care to active-duty and retired members of the armed forces and their families. In addition to basic nursing skills, *military nurses* are trained to provide care in various environments, including field hospitals, on-air evacuation flights, and onboard ships. Military nurses actively influence the development of health care through nursing research. Advances influenced by military nurses include the development of the artificial kidney (dialysis unit) and the concept of the intensive care unit.

INTERVIEW: Registered Nurse

Vanessa Woroszylo has worked as a registered nurse for the past three years. She currently works at Northwestern Memorial Hospital in Chicago, Illinois. She spoke with the editors of 25 Jobs That Have It All *about her career.*

Q. What are your primary and secondary job duties as a registered nurse?

A. My primary job is overseeing three to five patients during my 12-hour shift. This includes a full assessment, medication administration, observation, assisting with activities of daily living, patient and family education, and patient advocacy.

Sometimes I am required to be the acting charge nurse. On these days I may or may not have my own patient assignments depending on staffing. Some of the charge nurse responsibilities are assigning newly admitted patients to a registered nurse (RN), making the staff assignment for the next shift, updating the staffing department on staffing needs, and being available for the other RNs in emergency situations or just helping out in general, whether it is medicating their patients or starting an IV line.

Q. How did you train for this job? What was your college major?

A. I received my Bachelor's of Science in Nursing from Loyola University in Chicago. Most nursing programs require a number of clinical hours to transition a novice nurse into their professional role.

Before I became a nurse, I was a Certified Nursing Assistant (CNA). Being a CNA allowed me to assist RNs. I learned not only the duties of an RN, but patient care and nursing in a hospital setting.

Q. Where do you get your first job as a registered nurse?

A. My first job was at the hospital where I worked as a CNA. Basically, my manager knew that I was about to graduate from nursing school. I submitted an internal transfer form, then interviewed with nursing management. From there I needed to take and pass the NCLEX examination, the test that is required to become a licensed registered nurse.

Q. How can nursing graduates find jobs?

A. Nursing graduates can find jobs through the Internet, newspaper want ads, and word of mouth. Nursing publications often list different positions available for RNs. New graduates should also call or visit the human resources departments of hospitals and other employers of nurses for job leads.

Q. What personal qualities do registered nurses need to be successful?

A. Professionally, you have to be diligent about patient symptoms (i.e., following up with your observations with physicians and other staff members). You also have to be a patient advocate and speak up on your patients' behalf to make sure that they receive the best possible care. Since registered nurses work as part of a team (with physicians, physical and occupational therapists, dietitians, pharmacists, nurse aides, and patient care technicians), you need to develop a good working relationship with your coworkers.

You must be the type of person that can provide care but not get too wrapped up in the emotional aspects of the job. Because of the emotional and physical requirements of nursing, it is important to participate in activities outside of your job that allow you to relieve stress.

Q. What are the pros and cons of being a registered nurse?

A. **Pros:** Working as a nurse really allows you to help people, whether it is your patients or their families, deal with disease, symptom management, surgery, and end-of-life issues. Also, nursing offers a lot of flexibility and opportunities. I currently work three 12-hour shifts a week, which gives me ample opportunity for my outside interests. There are great opportunities to work in related fields, such as travel nursing, sales, teaching, infomatics, management, and as a nurse practitioner.

Cons: Although the hours may be flexible, nurses are often required to work weekends and holidays. Also, the physical and emotional aspects of the job can be difficult. Nursing can provide a comfortable lifestyle. However, most of my peers believe nurses are underpaid for the job requirements.

Q. What advice do you have for high school students interested in nursing?

A. Immerse yourself in some way in nursing. In high school or college, I really think it is important to work as a CNA or a patient care technician. This experience will teach you how to become comfortable working with patients and other team members as well as understand what nursing is really about.

Q. What advice would you give students who are just about to graduate from nursing programs?

A. Remember, as a novice nurse you aren't going to know everything when you first get out of college. Be sure to ask a lot of questions during your job interview and when you get your first job. Important questions include: (1) What is your nurse-to-patient ratio on each shift? (2) What is the average years of work experience of your staff? (3) Will I have to work rotating shifts? and (4) What is the weekend requirement?

Keep in mind that your first job should be interesting to you and your knowledge and clinical skills will improve with time. Don't be discouraged if you don't find a job right away. There are many opportunities waiting for you.

REQUIREMENTS
High School

If you are interested in becoming a registered nurse, you should take high school mathematics and science courses, including biology, chemistry, and physics. Health courses will also be helpful. English and speech courses should not be neglected because you must be able to communicate well with patients.

Postsecondary Training

There are three basic kinds of training programs that you may choose from to become a registered nurse: associate's degree, diploma, and bachelor's degree. Which of the three training programs to choose depends on your career goals. A bachelor's degree in nursing is required for most supervisory or administrative positions, for jobs in public health agencies, and for admission to graduate nursing programs. A master's degree is usually necessary to prepare for a nursing specialty or to teach. For some specialties, such as nursing research, a Ph.D. is essential.

The bachelor's degree program is offered by colleges or universities. It requires four (in some cases, five) years to complete. The graduate of this program receives a Bachelor of Science in Nursing (BSN) degree. The Associate Degree in Nursing (ADN) is awarded after completion of a two-year study program that is usually offered in a junior or community college. You receive hospital training at cooperating hospitals in the general vicinity of the community college. The diploma program, which usually lasts three years, is conducted by hospitals and independent schools. At the conclusion of each of these programs, you become a graduate nurse, but not, however, a registered nurse. To obtain the RN designation you must pass a licensing examination required in all states.

According to the National League for Nursing Accrediting Commission, there were approximately 1,666 RN programs in 2000, including about 885 ADN programs, 695 BSN programs, and 86 diploma programs. In addition, there were 358 master's degree and 75 doctoral degree programs. Nurses can pursue postgraduate training that allows them to specialize in certain areas, such as emergency room, operating room, premature nursery, or psychiatric nursing. This training is sometimes offered through hospital on-the-job training programs.

Certification or Licensing

All states and the District of Columbia require a license to practice nursing. To obtain a license, graduates of approved nursing schools must pass a national examination. Nurses may be licensed by more than one state. In some states, continuing education is a condition for license renewal. Different titles require different education and training levels.

Other Requirements

You should enjoy working with people, especially those who may experience fear or anger because of an illness. Patience, compassion, and calmness are qualities needed by anyone working in this career. In addition, you must be able to give directions as well as follow instructions and work as part of a health care team. Anyone interested in becoming a registered nurse should also have a strong desire to continue learning because new tests, procedures, and technologies are constantly being developed for the medical world.

EXPLORING

You can explore your interest in nursing in a number of ways. Read books on careers in nursing and talk with high school guidance counselors, school nurses, and local public health nurses. Visit hospitals to observe the work and talk with hospital personnel to learn more about the daily activities of nursing staff.

Some hospitals now have extensive volunteer service programs in which high school students may work after school, on weekends, or during vacations in order to both render a valuable service and to explore their interests. There are other volunteer work experiences available with the Red Cross or community health services. Camp counseling jobs sometimes offer related experiences. Some schools offer participation in Future Nurses programs.

The Internet is full of resources about nursing. Check out Nursing Net (http://www.nursingnet.org), and the American Nursing Association's Nursing World (http://www.nursingworld.org).

EMPLOYERS
Approximately 2.2 million registered nurses are employed in the United States. Inpatient and outpatient hospital departments account for about 3 out of 5 jobs for registered nurses. Nurses are employed by hospitals, managed-care facilities, long-term care facilities, clinics, industry, private homes, schools, camps, and government agencies.

STARTING OUT
The only way to become a registered nurse is through completion of one of the three kinds of educational programs, plus passing the licensing examination. Registered nurses may apply for employment directly to hospitals, nursing homes, home care agencies, temporary nursing agencies, companies, and government agencies that hire nurses. Jobs can also be obtained through school placement offices, by signing up with employment agencies specializing in placement of nursing personnel, or through the state employment office. Other sources of jobs include nurses' associations, professional journals, and newspaper want ads.

ADVANCEMENT
Increasingly, administrative and supervisory positions in the nursing field go to nurses who have earned at least the bachelor of science degree in nursing. Nurses with many years of experience who are graduates of a diploma program may achieve supervisory positions, but requirements for such promotions have become more difficult in recent years and in many cases require at least the BSN degree.

Nurses with bachelor's degrees are usually those who are hired as public health nurses. Nurses with master's degrees are often employed as clinical nurse specialists, faculty, instructors, supervisors, or administrators.

RNs can pursue further education to become advanced practice nurses, who have greater responsibilities and command higher salaries.

EARNINGS

According to the U.S. Department of Labor's *2001 National Occupational Employment and Wage Estimates,* registered nurses had median annual earnings of $46,670. Salaries ranged from less than $33,110 to more than $67,180. Earnings of RNs vary according to employer. According to the *Occupational Outlook Handbook,* those who worked for personnel supply services earned $46,860; those who worked at hospitals earned $45,780, and RNs who worked at nursing and personal care facilities earned $41,330.

The National Sample Survey of Registered Nurses for 2000, conducted by the Health Resources and Services Administration, shows that the average annual salary of full-time RNs was $46,782. WageWeb.com reports RNs earn an average mean salary of $44,902, with an average low of $38,142 and an average high of $51,666 in 2000. Nurse managers earn from $49,478 to $64,999, with an average of $57,193. Nurse directors earn from $73,688 to $91,745, with an average of $82,690.

Salary is determined by several factors: setting, education, and work experience. Most full-time nurses are given flexible work schedules as well as health and life insurance; some are offered education reimbursement and year-end bonuses. A staff nurse's salary is limited only by the amount of work he or she is willing to take on. Many nurses take advantage of overtime work and shift differentials. About 10 percent of all nurses hold more than one job.

WORK ENVIRONMENT

Most nurses work in facilities that are clean and well lighted and where the temperature is controlled, although some work in run-down inner city hospitals in less-than-ideal conditions. Usually, nurses work eight-hour shifts. Those in hospitals generally work any of three shifts: 7:00 A.M. to 3:00 P.M.; 3:00 P.M. to 11:00 P.M.; or 11:00 P.M. to 7:00 A.M.

Nurses spend much of the day on their feet, either walking or standing. Handling patients who are ill or infirm can also be very exhausting. Nurses who come in contact with patients with infectious diseases must be especially careful about cleanliness and sterility. Although many nursing duties are routine, many responsibilities are unpredictable. Sick persons are often very demanding, or they may be depressed or irritable. Despite this, nurses must maintain their composure and should be cheerful to help the patient achieve emotional balance.

Community health nurses may be required to visit homes that are in poor condition or very dirty. They may also come in contact with social problems, such as family violence. The nurse is an important health care provider and in many communities the sole provider.

Both the office nurse and the industrial nurse work regular business hours and are seldom required to work overtime. In some jobs, such as where nurses are on duty in private homes, they may frequently travel from home to home and work with various cases.

OUTLOOK

There are approximately 2.2 million nurses employed in the United States—making this field the largest of all health care occupations. Employment prospects for nurses are excellent. The U.S. Department of Labor projects registered nurses to be one of the top 25 occupations with fastest growth, high pay, and low unemployment. It is at the top of the list of occupations with largest number of job openings available through 2010, including 561,000 new jobs. The total job openings available including new jobs and replacements is projected at 1 million.

There has been a serious shortage of nurses in recent years. A national survey prepared by the Federation of Nurses and Health Professionals in 2001 found that one in five nurses plans to leave the profession within five years because of unsatisfactory working conditions, including low pay, severe understaffing, high stress, physical demands, mandatory overtime, and irregular hours. The shortage will also be exacerbated by the increasing numbers of baby-boomer-aged nurses who are expected to retire.

A survey released in December 2001 by the American Association of Colleges of Nursing reports that enrollments in entry-level bachelor's degree nursing programs has increased, ending a six-year period of decline. The increase, however, is not going to be enough to meet the demand to fill one million positions in the next decade.

Approximately 60 percent of all nursing jobs are found in hospitals. However, because of administrative cost cutting, increased nurse's workload, and rapid growth of outpatient services, hospital nursing jobs will experience slower than average growth. Employment in home care and nursing homes is expected to grow rapidly. Though more people are living well into their eighties and nineties, many need the kind of long-term care available at a nursing home. Also, because of financial reasons, patients are being released from hospitals sooner and admitted into nursing homes. Many nursing homes have facilities and staff capable of caring for long-term rehabilitation patients, as well as those afflicted with Alzheimer's. Many nurses will also be needed to help staff the growing number of outpatient facilities, such as HMOs, group medical practices, and ambulatory surgery centers.

Nursing specialties will be in great demand. There are, in addition, many part-time employment possibilities—approximately 25 percent of all nurses work on a part-time basis.

FOR MORE INFORMATION

Visit the AACN website to access a list of member schools and to read the online pamphlet, Your Nursing Career: A Look at the Facts.

American Association of Colleges of Nursing (AACN)
One Dupont Circle, Suite 530
Washington, DC 20036
Tel: 202-463-6930
http://www.aacn.nche.edu

For information about opportunities as an RN, contact:
American Nurses Association
600 Maryland Avenue, SW, Suite 100 West
Washington, DC 20024-2571
Tel: 800-274-4262
http://www.nursingworld.org

For information about state-approved programs and information on nursing, contact the following organizations:
National League for Nursing
61 Broadway
New York, NY 10006
Tel: 800-669-1656
http://www.nln.org

National Organization for Associate Degree Nursing
PO Box 3188
Dublin, OH 43016-0088
Tel: 614-451-1515
http://www.noadn.org

Discover Nursing, sponsored by Johnson & Johnson Health Care Systems,
provides information on nursing careers, nursing schools, and scholarships:
Discover Nursing
http://www.discovernursing.com

SECONDARY SCHOOL TEACHERS

QUICK FACTS

School Subjects
English
Psychology

Personal Skills
Communication/ideas
Helping/teaching

Work Environment
Primarily indoors
Primarily one location

Minimum Education Level
Bachelor's degree

Salary Range
$27,980 to $43,280 to
$67,940+

Certification or Licensing
Required by all states

Outlook
About as fast as the average

DOT
091

GOE
11.02.01

NOC
4141

O*NET-SOC
25-2022.00, 25-2023.00,
25-2031.00, 25-2032.00

OVERVIEW

Secondary school teachers teach students in grades 7–12. Specializing in one subject area, such as English or math, these teachers work with five or more groups of students during the day. They lecture, direct discussions, and test students' knowledge with exams, essays, and homework assignments. There are close to 1 million secondary school teachers employed in the United States.

HISTORY

Early secondary education was typically based upon training students to enter the clergy. Benjamin Franklin pioneered the idea of a broader secondary education with the creation of the academy, which offered a flexible curriculum and a wide variety of academic subjects.

It was not until the 19th century, however, that children of different social classes commonly attended school into the secondary grades. The first English Classical School, which was to become the model for public high schools throughout the country, was established in 1821 in Boston. An adjunct to the high school, the junior high school was conceived by Dr. Charles W. Eliot, president of Harvard. In a speech before the National Education Association in 1888, he recommended that secondary studies be started two years earlier than was the custom. The first such school opened in 1908, in Columbus, Ohio. Another opened a year later in Berkeley, California. By the early 20th century, secondary school attendance was made mandatory in the United States.

THE JOB

Many successful people credit secondary school teachers with helping guide them into college, careers, and other endeavors. The teachers' primary responsibility is to educate students in a specific subject. But secondary teachers also inform students about colleges, occupations, and such varied subjects as the arts, health, and relationships.

Secondary school teachers may teach in a traditional area, such as science, English, history, and math, or they may teach more specialized classes, such as information technology, business, and theater. Many secondary schools are expanding their course offerings to better serve the individual interests of their students. "School-to-work" programs, which are vocational education programs designed for high school students and recent graduates, involve lab work and demonstrations to prepare students for highly technical jobs. Though secondary teachers are likely be assigned to one specific grade level, they may be required to teach students in surrounding grades. For example, a secondary school mathematics teacher may teach algebra to a class of ninth-graders one period and trigonometry to high school seniors the next.

In the classroom, secondary school teachers rely on a variety of teaching methods. They spend a great deal of time lecturing, but they also facilitate student discussion and develop projects and activities to interest the students in the subject. They show films and videos, use computers and the Internet, and bring in guest speakers. They assign essays, presentations, and other projects. Each individual subject calls upon particular approaches, and may involve laboratory experiments, role-playing exercises, shop work, and field trips.

Outside of the classroom, secondary school teachers prepare lectures, lesson plans, and exams. They evaluate student work and calculate grades. In the process of planning their class, secondary school teachers read textbooks, novels, and workbooks to determine reading assignments; photocopy notes, articles, and other handouts; and develop grading policies. They also continue to study alternative and traditional teaching methods to hone their skills. They prepare students for special events and conferences and submit student work to competitions. Many secondary school teachers also serve as sponsors to student organizations in their field. For example, a French teacher may sponsor the French club and a journalism teacher may advise the yearbook staff. Some secondary school teachers also have the opportunity for extracurricular work as athletic coaches or drama coaches. Teachers also monitor students during lunch or break times and sit in on study halls. They may also accompany student groups on field trips, competitions, and events. Some teachers also have the opportunity to escort students on educational vacations to foreign countries, to Washington, D.C., and to other major U.S. cities. Secondary school teachers attend faculty meetings, meetings with parents, and state and national teacher conferences.

Some teachers explore their subject area outside of the requirements of the job. *English* and *writing teachers* may publish in magazines and journals, *business* and *technology teachers* may have small businesses of their own, *music teachers* may perform and record their music, *art teachers* may show work in galleries, and *sign-language teachers* may do freelance interpreting.

REQUIREMENTS
High School
You should follow your guidance counselor's college preparatory program and take advanced classes in such subjects as English, science, math, and government. You should also explore an extracurricular activity, such as theater, sports, and debate, so that you can offer these additional skills to future employers. If you're already aware of which subject you'd like to teach, take all the available courses in that area. You should also take speech and composition courses to develop your communication skills.

Postsecondary Training
There are over 500 accredited teacher education programs in the United States. Most of these programs are designed to meet the certification requirements for the state in which they're located. Some states may require that you pass a test before being admitted to an education program. You may choose to major in your subject area while taking required education courses, or you may major in secondary education with a concentration in your subject area. You'll

probably have advisers (both in education and in your chosen specialty) to help you select courses.

In addition to a degree, a training period of student teaching in an actual classroom environment is usually required. Students are placed in schools to work with full-time teachers. During this period, undergraduate students observe the ways in which lessons are presented and the classroom is managed, learn how to keep records of such details as attendance and grades, and get actual experience in handling the class, both under supervision and alone.

Besides licensure and courses in education, prospective high school teachers usually need 24 to 36 hours of college work in the subject they wish to teach. Some states require a master's degree; teachers with master's degrees can earn higher salaries. Private schools generally do not require an education degree.

Certification or Licensing

Public school teachers must be licensed under regulations established by the department of education of the state in which they teach. Not all states require licensure for teachers in private or parochial schools. When you've received your teaching degree, you may request that a transcript of your college record be sent to the licensure section of the state department of education. If you have met licensure requirements, you will receive a certificate and thus be eligible to teach in the public schools of the state. In some states, you may have to take additional tests. If you move to another state, you will have to resubmit college transcripts, as well as comply with any other regulations in the new state to be able to teach there.

Other Requirements

Working as a secondary school teacher, you'll need to have respect for young people and a genuine interest in their success in life. You'll also need patience; adolescence can be a troubling time for children, and these troubles often affect behavior and classroom performance. Because you'll be working with students who are at very impressionable ages, you should serve as a good role model. You should also be well organized, as you'll have to keep track of the work and progress of many students.

EXPLORING

By going to high school, you've already gained a good sense of the daily work of a secondary school teacher. But the requirements of a teacher extend far beyond the classroom, so ask to spend some time with one of your teachers after school, and ask to look at lecture notes and record-keeping procedures. Interview your teachers about the amount of work that goes into preparing a class and directing an extracurricular activity. To get some firsthand teaching experience, volunteer for a peer tutoring program. Many other teaching opportunities may exist in your community. Look into coaching an athletic team at the YMCA, counseling at a summer camp, teaching an art course at a community center, or assisting with a community theater production.

EMPLOYERS

Secondary school teachers are needed at public and private schools, including parochial schools, juvenile detention centers, vocational schools, and schools of the arts. They work in middle schools, junior high schools, and high schools. Though some rural areas maintain schools, most secondary schools are in towns and cities of all sizes. Teachers are also finding opportunities in charter schools, which are smaller, deregulated schools that receive public funding.

STARTING OUT

After completing the teacher certification process, including your months of student teaching, you'll work with your college's placement office to find a full-time position. The departments of education of some states maintain listings of job openings. Many schools advertise teaching positions in the classifieds of the state's major newspapers. You may also directly contact the principals and superintendents of the schools in which you'd like to work. While waiting for full-time work, you can work as a substitute teacher. In urban areas with many schools, you may be able to substitute full time.

ADVANCEMENT

Most teachers advance simply by becoming more of an expert in the job that they have chosen. There is usually an increase in salary as teachers acquire experience. Additional training or study can also bring an increase in salary.

A few teachers with management ability and interest in administrative work may advance to the position of principal. Others may advance into supervisory positions, and some may become *helping teachers* who are charged with the responsibility of helping other teachers find appropriate instructional materials and develop certain phases of their courses of study. Others may go into teacher education at a college or university. For most of these positions, additional education is required. Some teachers also make lateral moves into other education-related positions such as guidance counselor or resource room teacher.

EARNINGS

Most teachers are contracted to work nine months out of the year, though some contracts are made for 10 or 12 months. (When regular school is not in session, teachers are expected to conduct summer teaching, planning, or other school-related work.) In most cases, teachers have the option of prorating their salary up to 52 weeks.

According to the Bureau of Labor Statistics, the median annual salary for secondary school teachers was $43,280 in 2001. The lowest 10 percent earned $27,980; the highest 10 percent earned $67,940 or more.

The American Federation of Teachers reports that the national average salary for all teachers was 43,250 during the 2000–2001 school year. Beginning teachers earned approximately $28,986 a year.

Teachers can also supplement their earnings through teaching summer classes, coaching sports, sponsoring a club, or other extracurricular work.

On behalf of the teachers, unions bargain with schools over contract conditions such as wages, hours, and benefits. A majority of teachers join the American Federation of Teachers or the National Education Association. Depending on the state, teachers usually receive a retirement plan, sick leave, and health and life insurance. Some systems grant teachers sabbatical leave.

WORK ENVIRONMENT

Although the job of the secondary school teacher is not overly strenuous, it can be tiring and trying. Secondary school teachers must stand for many hours each day, do a lot of talking, show energy and enthusiasm, and handle discipline problems. But they also have the reward of guiding their students as they make decisions about their lives and futures.

Secondary school teachers work under generally pleasant conditions, though some older schools may have poor heating and electrical systems. Though violence in schools has decreased in recent years, media coverage of the violence has increased, along with student fears. In most schools, students are prepared to learn and to perform the work that's required of them. But in some schools, students may be dealing with gangs, drugs, poverty, and other problems, so the environment can be tense and emotional.

School hours are generally 8 A.M. to 3 P.M., but teachers work more than 40 hours a week teaching, preparing for classes, grading papers, and directing extracurricular activities. As a coach, or as a music or drama director, teachers may have to work some evenings and weekends. Many teachers enroll in master's or doctoral programs and take evening and summer courses to continue their education.

OUTLOOK

The U.S. Department of Education predicts that employment for secondary teachers will grow by 16.6 percent through 2010 to meet rising enrollments and to replace the large number of retiring teachers. The National Education Association believes this will be a challenge because of the low salaries that are paid to secondary school teachers. Higher salaries will be necessary to attract new teachers and retain experienced ones, along with other changes such as smaller classroom sizes and safer schools. Other challenges for the profession involve attracting more men into teaching. The percentage of male teachers at this level continues to decline.

In order to improve education for all children, changes are being considered by some districts. Some private companies are managing public schools. Though it is believed that a private company can afford to provide better facilities, faculty, and equipment, this hasn't been proven. Teacher organizations are concerned about taking school management away from communities and turning it over to remote corporate headquarters. Charter schools and voucher programs are two other controversial alternatives to traditional public education. Charter schools, which are small schools that are publicly funded but not guided by the rules and regulations of traditional public schools, are viewed by some as places of innovation and improved educational methods; others see charter schools as ill-equipped and unfairly funded with money that could better benefit local school districts. Vouchers, which exist only in a few cities, allow students to attend private schools courtesy of tuition vouchers; these vouchers are paid for with public tax dollars. In theory, the vouchers allow for more choices in education for poor and minority students, but private schools still have the option of being highly selective in their admissions. Teacher organizations see some danger in giving public funds to unregulated private schools.

FOR MORE INFORMATION

For information about careers and current issues affecting teachers, contact or visit the websites of the following organizations:

American Federation of Teachers
555 New Jersey Avenue, NW
Washington, DC 20001
Tel: 202-879-4400
Email: online@aft.org
http://www.aft.org

National Education Association
1201 16th Street, NW
Washington, DC 20036
Tel: 202-833-4000
http://www.nea.org

For information on accredited teacher education programs, contact:

National Council for Accreditation of Teacher Education
2010 Massachusetts Avenue, NW, Suite 500
Washington, DC 20036-1023
Tel: 202-466-7496
Email: ncate@ncate.org
http://www.ncate.org

SOFTWARE DESIGNERS

QUICK FACTS

School Subjects Computer science Mathematics	**Certification or Licensing** Voluntary
	Outlook Much faster than the average
Personal Skills Communication/ideas Technical/scientific	
	DOT 030
Work Environment Primarily indoors Primarily one location	**GOE** 11.01.01
Minimum Education Level Bachelor's degree	**NOC** 2173
Salary Range $42,590 to $75,130 to $140,000+	**O*NET-SOC** 15-1011.00

OVERVIEW

Software designers are responsible for creating new ideas and designing prepackaged and customized computer software. Software designers devise applications such as word processors, front-end database programs, and spreadsheets that make it possible for computers to complete given tasks and to solve problems. Once a need in the market has been identified, software designers first conceive of the program on a global level by outlining what the program will do. Then they write the specifications from which programmers code computer commands to perform the given functions.

HISTORY

In "Events in the History of Computing," published by the Institute of Electrical and Electronics Engineers (IEEE) Computer Society, the birth of the software industry is described as follows: "In 1983, software development exploded with the introduction of the personal computer. Standard applications included not only spreadsheets and word processors, but graphics packages and communications systems."

With the improvements in computer speed, memory, and overall efficiency over the past two decades, in addition to ever-increasing levels of professional and personal computer use, computer software designers have created an abundance of user-friendly, high-performance software for a variety of uses. Business and industry rely heavily on the power of computers and use both prepackaged software and software that has been custom-designed for industry-specific uses. Also, with more people purchasing computer systems for home use, the retail market for prepackaged software has grown steadily. Given these conditions, computer software designing will be an important field in the industry for years to come.

The software industry has many facets: personal computer packaged applications (known as "shrink-wrapped software"); operating systems for standalone and networked systems; management tools for networks; enterprise software that enables efficient management of large corporations' production, sales, and information systems; software applications and operating systems for mainframe computers; and customized software for specific industry management.

Packaged software is written for mass distribution, not for the specific needs of a particular user. Broad categories include operating systems, utilities, applications, and programming languages. Operating systems control the basic functions of a computer or network. Utilities perform support functions, such as backup or virus protection. Programming software is used to develop the sets of instructions that build all other types of software. The software that most computer users are familiar with is called application software. This category includes the word processing, spreadsheets, and email packages commonly used in business, as well as games and reference software used in homes, and subject- or skill-based software used in schools.

THE JOB

Without software, computer hardware would be useless. Computers need to be told exactly what to do. Software is the set of codes that gives the computer those instructions. It comes in the form of the familiar prepackaged software that you find in a computer store, such as games, word processing programs, spreadsheets, and desktop publishing programs, and in a customized application designed to fit the specific need of a particular business. Software designers are the initiators of these complex programs. *Computer programmers* then create the software by writing the code that carries out the directives of the designer.

Software designers must envision every detail of what an application will do, how it will do it, and how it will look (the user interface). A simple example is how a home accounting program is created. The software designer first lays out the overall functionality of the program, specifying what it should be able to do, such as balancing a checkbook, keeping track of incoming and outgoing bills, and maintaining records of expenses. For each of these tasks, the software designer will outline the design detail for the specific functions that he or she has mandated, such as what menus and icons will be used, what each screen will look like, and whether there will be help or dialog boxes to assist the user.For example, the designer may specify that the expense record part of the program produce a pie chart that shows the percentage of each household expense in the overall household budget. The designer can specify that the program automatically display the pie chart each time a budget assessment is completed or only after the user clicks on the appropriate icon on the toolbar.

Some software companies specialize in building custom-designed software. This software is highly specialized for specific needs or problems of particular businesses. Some businesses are large enough that they employ in-house software designers who create software applications for their computer systems. A related field is software engineering, which involves writing customized complex software to solve a specific engineering or technical problem of a business or industry.

Whether the designer is working on a mass-market or a custom application, the first step is to define the overall goals for the application. This is typically done in consultation with management if working at a software supply company, or with the client if working on a custom-designed project. Then the software designer studies the goals and problems of the project. If working on custom-designed software, the designer must also take into consideration the existing computer system of the client. Next, the software designer works on the program strategy and specific design detail that he or she has envisioned. At this point, the designer may need to write a proposal outlining the design and estimating time and cost allocations. Based on this report, management or the client decides if the project should proceed.

Once approval is given, the software designer and the programmers begin working on writing the software program. Typically, the software designer writes the specifications for the program, and the *applications programmers* write the programming codes.

In addition to the design detail duties, a software designer may be responsible for writing a user's manual or at least writing a report for what should be included in the user's manual. After testing and debugging the program, the software designer will present it to management or to the client.

REQUIREMENTS
High School

If you are interested in computer science, you should take as many computer, math, and science courses as possible; they provide fundamental math and computer knowledge and teach analytical thinking skills. Classes that focus on schematic drawing and flowcharts are also very valuable. English and speech courses will help you improve your communication skills, which are very important to software designers who must make formal presentations to management and clients. Also, many technical/vocational schools offer programs in software programming and design. The qualities developed by these classes, plus imagination and an ability to work well under pressure, are key to success in software design.

Postsecondary Training

A bachelor's degree in computer science plus one year's experience with a programming language is required for most software designers.

In the past, the computer industry has tended to be pretty flexible about official credentials; demonstrated computer proficiency and work experience have often been enough to obtain a good position. However, as more people enter the field, competition has increased, and job requirements have become more stringent. Technical knowledge alone does not suffice in the field of software design anymore. In order to be a successful software designer, you should have at least a peripheral knowledge of the field for which you intend to design software, such as business, education, or science. Individuals with degrees in education and subsequent teaching experience are much sought after as designers for educational software. Those with bachelor's degrees in computer science with a minor in business or accounting have an excellent chance for employment in designing business or accounting software.

Certification or Licensing

Certification in software development is offered by companies such as Sun Microsystems, Hewlett-Packard, IBM, Novell, and Oracle. While certification is not required, it tells employers that your skills meet industry education and training standards.

Other Requirements

Software design is project- and detail-oriented, therefore you must be patient and diligent. You must also enjoy problem-solving challenges and be able to work under a deadline with minimal supervision. As a software designer, you should also possess good communication skills for consulting both with management and with clients who will have varying levels of technical expertise.

Software companies are looking for individuals with vision and imagination to help them create new and exciting programs to sell in the ever-competitive software market. Superior technical skills and knowledge combined with motivation, imagination, and exuberance will make you an attractive candidate.

EXPLORING

Spending a day with a professional software designer or applications programmer will allow you to experience firsthand what this work entails. School guidance counselors can often help you organize such a meeting.

If you are interested in computer industry careers in general, you should learn as much as possible about computers. Keep up with new technology by talking to other computer users and by reading related magazines, such as *Computer* (http://www.computer.org/computer). You will also find it helpful to join computer clubs and use online services and the Internet to find more information about this field.

Advanced students can put their design/programming knowledge to work by designing and programming their own applications, such as simple games and utility programs.

EMPLOYERS

Software designers are employed throughout the United States. Opportunities are best in large cities and suburbs where business and industry are active. Programmers who develop software systems work for software manufacturers, many of whom are in Silicon Valley, in northern California. There is also a concentration of software manufacturers in Boston, Chicago, and Atlanta, among other places. Designers who adapt and tailor the software to meet specific needs of end-users work for those end-user companies, many of which are scattered across the country.

STARTING OUT

Software design positions are regarded as some of the most interesting, and therefore the most competitive, in the computer industry. Some software designers are promoted from an entry-level programming position. Software design positions in software supply companies and large custom software companies will be difficult to secure straight out of college or technical/vocational school.

Entry-level programming and design jobs may be listed in the help wanted sections of newspapers. Employment agencies and online job banks are other good sources.

Students in technical schools or universities should take advantage of the campus placement office. They should check regularly for internship postings, job listings, and notices of on-campus recruitment. Placement offices are also valuable resources for resume tips and interviewing techniques. Internships and summer jobs with such corporations are always beneficial and provide experience that will give you the edge over your competition. General computer job fairs are also held throughout the year in larger cities.

There are many online career sites listed on the Web that post job openings, salary surveys, and current employment trends. The Web also has online publications that deal specifically with computer jobs. You can also obtain information from computer organizations such as the IEEE Computer Society (see information at the end of this article). Because this is such a competitive field, you will need to show initiative and creativity that will set you apart from other applicants.

ADVANCEMENT

In general, programmers work between one and five years before being promoted to software designer. A programmer can move up by demonstrating an ability to create new software ideas that translate well into marketable applications. Individuals with a knack for spotting trends in the software market are also likely to advance.

Those software designers who demonstrate leadership may be promoted to *project team leader*. Project team leaders are responsible for developing new software projects and overseeing the work done by software designers and applications programmers. With experience as a project team leader, a motivated software designer may be promoted to a position as a *software manager* who runs projects from an even higher level.

EARNINGS

Salaries for software designers vary with the size of the company and with location. Salaries may be slightly higher in areas where there is a large concentration of computer companies, such as the Silicon Valley in northern California and parts of Washington, Oregon, and the east coast.

The National Association of Colleges and Employers reports that average starting salaries for graduates with a master's degree in computer science were $61,453 in 2001. Graduates with a bachelor's degree in computer science averaged $52,723.

Median salaries for computer and information scientists (which include software designers) were $75,130 in 2001, according to the U.S. Department of Labor's *National Occupational Employment and Wage Estimates*. Salaries ranged from less than $42,590 to $119,150 or more annually. At the managerial level, salaries are even higher and can reach $140,000 or more.

Most designers work for large companies, which offer a full benefits package that includes health insurance, vacation and sick time, and a profit sharing or retirement plan.

WORK ENVIRONMENT

Software designers work in comfortable environments. Many computer companies are known for their casual work atmosphere; employees generally do not have to wear suits, except during client meetings. Overall, software designers work standard weeks. However, they may be required to work overtime near a deadline. It is common in software design to share office or cubicle space with two or three co-workers, which is typical of the team approach to working. As a software designer or applications programmer, much of the day is spent in front of the computer, although a software designer will have occasional team meetings or meetings with clients.

Software design can be stressful work for several reasons. First, the market for software is very competitive and companies are pushing to develop more innovative software and to get it on the market before competitors do. For this same reason, software design is also very exciting and creative work. Second, software designers are given a project and a deadline. It is up to the designer and team members to budget their time to finish in the allocated time. Finally, working with programming languages and so many details can be very frustrating, especially when the tiniest glitch means the program will not run. For this reason, software designers must be patient and diligent.

OUTLOOK

Jobs in software design are expected to grow much faster than the average over the next several years, according to the *Occupational Outlook Handbook.* Employment will increase as technology becomes more sophisticated and organizations continue to adopt and integrate these technologies, making for plentiful job openings. Hardware designers and systems programmers are constantly developing faster, more powerful, and more user-friendly hardware and operating systems. As long as these advancements continue, the industry will need software designers to create software to use these improvements.

Business may have less need to contract for custom software as more prepackaged software arrives on the market that allows users with minimal computer skills to "build" their own software using components that they customize. However, the growth in the retail software market is expected to make up for this loss in customized services.

The expanding integration of Internet technologies by businesses has resulted in a rising demand for a variety of skilled professionals who can develop and support a variety of Internet applications.

FOR MORE INFORMATION

For information on internships, student membership, and the student magazine, Crossroads, *contact:*

Association for Computing Machinery
1515 Broadway
New York, NY 10036
Tel: 800-342-6626
Email: SIGS@acm.org
http://www.acm.org

For information on scholarships, student membership, and the student newsletter, looking.forward, *contact:*

IEEE Computer Society
1730 Massachusetts Avenue, NW
Washington, DC 20036-1992
Tel: 202-371-0101
Email: membership@computer.org
http://www.computer.org

For industry information, contact the following organizations:

Software & Information Industry Association
1090 Vermont Ave, NW, Sixth Floor
Washington, DC 20005
Tel: 202-289-7442
http://www.siia.net

Software Testing Institute
http://www.softwaretestinginstitute.com

SOFTWARE ENGINEERS

QUICK FACTS

School Subjects
Computer science
Mathematics

Personal Skills
Mechanical/manipulative
Technical/scientific

Work Environment
Primarily indoors
Primarily one location

Minimum Education Level
Bachelor's degree

Salary Range
$44,380 to $70,210 to
$125,000+

Certification or Licensing
Recommended

Outlook
Much faster than the
average

DOT
030

GOE
11.01.01

NOC
2173

O*NET-SOC
15-1031.00, 15-1032.00

OVERVIEW

Software engineers are responsible for customizing existing software programs to meet the needs and desires of a particular business or industry. Initially they spend considerable time researching, defining, and analyzing the problem at hand. Then they develop software programs to resolve the problem on the computer. There are over 697,000 computer software engineers employed in the United States.

HISTORY

Prior to the introduction of semiconductors to computer technology, the sheer size of computers made them unsuitable for widespread use. Semiconductors, however, allowed for the creation of smaller and less expensive computers. Starting in the 1950s, computers went beyond their use in the government sphere as businesses began to use them on a limited basis.

Since that time, computers have revolutionized the way we conduct our lives. From businesses of all kinds, to government agencies, charitable organizations, and private homes, computers are everywhere. Over the past 50 years, technology has continued to shrink computer size and increase speed at an unprecedented rate.

Advances in computer technology have enabled professionals to put computers to work in a range of activities once thought impossible. Computer software engineers have been able to take advantage of computer hardware improvements in speed, memory capacity, reliability, and accuracy to create programs that do just about anything. After new performance levels were achieved, computer engineering blossomed into a distinct sub-field in the computer industry. The relative lateness of this development is due to the complexity of the programs that software engineers write, in addition to the large amount of computing power the programs require. Although many computer scientists will continue to focus their research on further developing hardware, the emphasis in the field has moved more squarely to software, and it is predicted that software engineers will be the fastest growing occupation in the United States through the next decade. Given this, computer engineering will be an important field in the industry for years to come.

THE JOB

Every day, businesses, scientists, and government agencies encounter difficult problems that they cannot solve manually, either because the problem is just too complicated or because it would take too much time to calculate the appropriate solutions. For example, astronomers receive thousands of pieces of data every hour from probes and satellites in space as well as telescopes here on earth. If they had to process the information themselves, compile careful comparisons with previous years' readings, look for patterns or cycles, and keep accurate records of the origin of the various data, it would be so cumbersome and lengthy a project as to make it next to impossible. They can, however, process the data with the extensive help of computers. Computer software engineers define and analyze specific problems in business or science and help develop computer software applications that solve them effectively. The software engineers who work in the field of astronomy are well versed in its concepts, but there are many other kinds of software engineers as well.

Software engineers fall into two basic categories. *Systems software engineers* build and maintain entire computer systems for a company. *Applications software engineers* design, create, and modify general computer applications software or specialized utility programs.

Engineers who work on computer systems research how a company's departments and their respective computer systems are organized. For example, there might be customer service, ordering, inventory, billing, shipping, and payroll record-keeping departments. Systems software engineers suggest ways to coordinate all these parts. They might set up intranets or networks that link computers within the organization and ease communication.

Some applications software engineers develop packaged software applications, such as word processing, graphic design, or database programs, for software development companies. Other applications engineers design customized software for individual businesses or organizations. For example, a software engineer might work with an insurance company to develop new ways to reduce paperwork, such as claim forms, applications, and bill-processing. Applications engineers write programs using programming languages like C++ and Java.

Software engineers sometimes specialize in a particular industry, such as the chemical industry, insurance, or medicine, which requires knowledge of that particular industry in addition to computer expertise. Some engineers work for consulting firms that complete software projects for different clients on an individual basis. Others work for large companies that hire full-time engineers to develop software customized to their needs.

Software engineering technicians assist engineers in completing projects. They are usually knowledgeable in analog, digital, and microprocessor electronics and programming techniques. Technicians know enough about program design and computer languages to fill in details left out by engineers or programmers, who conceive of the program from a large-scale perspective. Technicians might also test new software applications with special diagnostic equipment.

Both systems and applications software engineering involve extremely detail-oriented work. Since computers do only what they are programmed to do, engineers have to account for every bit of information with a programming command. Thus, software engineers are required to be very well organized and precise. To achieve this, they generally follow strict procedures in completing an assignment.

First, they interview clients and colleagues to determine exactly what they want the final program to accomplish. Defining the problem by outlining the goal can sometimes be difficult, especially when clients have little technical training. Engineers then evaluate the software applications already in use by the client to understand how and why they are failing to fulfill the needs of the operation. After this period of fact-gathering, the engineers use methods of scientific analysis and mathematical models to develop possible solutions to the problems. These analytical methods help them predict and measure the outcomes of different proposed designs.

When they have developed a clear idea of what type of program is required to fulfill the client's needs, they draw up a detailed proposal that includes estimates of time and cost allocations. Management must then decide if the project will meet their needs, is a good investment, and whether or not it will be undertaken.

Once a proposal is accepted, both software engineers and technicians begin work on the project. They verify with hardware engineers that the proposed software program can be completed with existing hardware systems. Typically, the engineer writes program specifications and the technician uses his or her knowledge of computer languages to write preliminary programming. Engineers focus most of their effort on program strategies, testing procedures, and reviewing technicians' work.

Software engineers are usually responsible for a significant amount of technical writing, including project proposals, progress reports, and user manuals. They are required to meet regularly with clients in order to keep project goals clear and learn about any changes as quickly as possible.

When the program is completed, the software engineer organizes a demonstration of the final product to the client. Supervisors, management, and users are generally present. Some software engineers may offer to install the program, train users on it, and make arrangements for ongoing technical support.

REQUIREMENTS

A high school diploma is the minimum requirement for software engineering technicians, but an associate's degree is required for most of these positions. A bachelor's or advanced degree in computer science or engineering is required for most software engineers.

High School

If you are interested in pursuing this career, take as many computer, math, and science courses as possible, because they provide fundamental math and computer skills and teach analytical thinking. Classes that rely on schematic drawing and flowcharts are also very valuable. English and speech courses will help you improve your communication skills, which are very important for software engineers.

Postsecondary Training

There are several ways to enter the field of software engineering, although it is becoming increasingly necessary to pursue formal postsecondary education. If you don't have an associate's degree, you may first be hired in the quality assurance or technical support departments of a company. Many individuals complete associate degrees while working and then are promoted into software engineering technician positions. As more and more well-educated professionals enter the industry, however, it is becoming more important for you to have at least an associate's degree in computer engineering or programming. Many technical and vocational schools offer a variety of programs that will prepare you for a job as a software engineering technician.

If you are interested in this career, you should consider carefully your long-range goals. Being promoted from a technician's job to that of software engineer often requires a bachelor's degree. In the past, the computer industry has tended to be fairly flexible about official credentials; demonstrated computer proficiency and work experience have often been enough to obtain a good position. This may hold true for some in the future. The majority of young computer professionals entering the field for the first time, however, will be college educated. Therefore, if you have no formal education or work experience you will have less chance of employment.

Obtaining a postsecondary degree in computer engineering is usually considered challenging and even difficult. In addition to natural ability, you should be hard-working and determined to succeed. If you plan to work in a specific technical field, such as medicine, law, or business, you should receive some formal training in that particular discipline.

Certification or Licensing

Another option if you're interested in software engineering is to pursue commercial certification. These programs are usually run by computer companies that wish to train professionals to work with their products. Classes are challenging and examinations can be rigorous. New programs are introduced every year.

Other Requirements

As a software engineer, you will need strong communications skills in order to be able to make formal business presentations and interact with people having different levels of computer expertise. You must also be detail oriented and work well under pressure.

EXPLORING

Try to spend a day with a working software engineer or technician in order to experience firsthand what their job is like. School guidance counselors can help you arrange such a visit. You can also talk to your high school computer teacher for more information.

In general, you should be intent on learning as much as possible about computers and computer software. You should learn about new developments by reading trade magazines and talking to other computer users. You also can join computer clubs and surf the Internet for information about working in this field.

EMPLOYERS

More than 697,000 computer software engineers are employed in the United States. Approximately 380,000 work with applications and 317,000 work with systems software. Software engineering is done in many fields, including medical, industrial, military, communications, aerospace, scientific, and other commercial businesses. The majority of software engineers, though, are employed by computer and data processing companies and by consulting firms.

STARTING OUT

If you have work experience and perhaps even an associate's degree, you may be promoted to a software engineering technician position from an entry-level job in quality assurance or technical support. Those already employed by computer companies or large corporations should read company job postings to learn about promotion opportunities. If you are already employed and would like to train in software engineering, either on the job or through formal education, you can investigate future career possibilities within your same company and advise management of your wish to change career tracks. Some companies offer tuition reimbursement for employees who train in areas applicable to business operations.

As a technical, vocational, or university student of software engineering, you should work closely with your schools' placement offices, as many professionals find their first position through on-campus recruiting. Placement office staff are well trained to provide tips on resume writing, interviewing techniques, and locating job leads.

Individuals not working with a school placement office can check the classified ads for job openings. They also can work with a local employment agency that places computer professionals in appropriate jobs. Many openings in the computer industry are publicized by word of mouth, so you should stay in touch with working computer professionals to learn who is hiring. In addition, these people may be willing to refer you directly to the person in charge of recruiting.

ADVANCEMENT

Software engineers who demonstrate leadership qualities and thorough technical know-how may become *project team leaders* who are responsible for full-scale software development projects. Project team leaders oversee the work of technicians and engineers. They determine the overall parameters of a project, calculate time schedules and financial budgets, divide the project into smaller tasks, and assign these tasks to engineers. Overall, they do both managerial and technical work.

Software engineers with experience as project team leaders may be promoted to a position as *software manager,* running a large research and development department. Managers oversee software projects with a more encompassing perspective; they help choose projects to be undertaken, select project team leaders and engineering teams, and assign individual projects. In some cases, they may be required to travel, solicit new business, and contribute to the general marketing strategy of the company.

Many computer professionals find that their interests change over time. As long as individuals are well qualified and keep up to date with the latest technology, they are usually able to find positions in other areas of the computer industry.

EARNINGS

Computer software engineers with a bachelor's degree in computer engineering earned starting salaries of $53,924 in 2001, according to the National Association of Colleges and Employers. New computer engineers with a master's degree averaged $58,026. Computer engineers specializing in applications earned median annual salaries of $70,210 in 2001, according to the U.S. Department of

Labor's *National Occupational Employment and Wage Estimates*. The lowest 10 percent averaged less than $44,380; the highest 10 percent earned $109,170 or more annually. Software engineers specializing in systems software earned median salaries of $73,280 in 2001. The lowest-paid 10 percent averaged $45,820 annually, and the highest-paid engineers made $110,750 per year. Experienced software engineers can earn over $125,000 a year. When software engineers are promoted to project team leader or software manager, they earn even more. Software engineers generally earn more in geographical areas where there are clusters of computer companies, such as the Silicon Valley in northern California.

Most software engineers work for companies that offer extensive benefits, including health insurance, sick leave, and paid vacation. In some smaller computer companies, however, benefits may be limited.

WORK ENVIRONMENT
Software engineers usually work in comfortable office environments. Overall, they usually work 40-hour weeks, but this depends on the nature of the employer and expertise of the engineer. In consulting firms, for example, it is typical for engineers to work long hours and frequently travel to out-of-town assignments.

Software engineers generally receive an assignment and a time frame within which to accomplish it; daily work details are often left up to the individuals. Some engineers work relatively lightly at the beginning of a project, but work a lot of overtime at the end in order to catch up. Most engineers are not compensated for overtime. Software engineering can be stressful, especially when engineers must work to meet deadlines. Working with programming languages and intense details is often frustrating. Therefore, software engineers should be patient, enjoy problem-solving challenges, and work well under pressure.

OUTLOOK
The field of software engineering is expected to be the fastest growing occupation over the next several years, according to the U.S. Department of Labor. Demands made on computers increase every day and from all industries. The development of one kind of software sparks ideas for many others. In addition, users rely on software programs that are increasingly user-friendly.

Since technology changes so rapidly, software engineers are advised to keep up on the latest developments. While the need for software engineers will remain high, computer languages will probably change every few years and software engineers will need to attend seminars and workshops to learn new computer languages and software design. They also should read trade magazines, surf the Internet, and talk with colleagues about the field. These kinds of continuing education techniques help ensure that software engineers are best equipped to meet the needs of the workplace.

FOR MORE INFORMATION

For information on internships, student membership, and the student magazine, Crossroads, *contact:*

Association for Computing Machinery
1515 Broadway
New York, NY 10036
Tel: 800-342-6626
Email: sigs@acm.org
http://www.acm.org

For certification information, contact:

Institute for Certification of Computing Professionals
2350 East Devon Avenue, Suite 115
Des Plaines, IL 60018-4610
Tel: 800-843-8227
http://www.iccp.org

For information on scholarships, student membership, and the student newsletter, looking.forward, *contact:*

IEEE Computer Society
1730 Massachusetts Avenue, NW
Washington, DC 20036-1992
Tel: 202-371-0101
Email: membership@computer.org
http://www.computer.org

For more information on careers in computer software, contact:

Software and Information Industry Association
1090 Vermont Ave, NW, Sixth Floor
Washington, DC 20005
Tel: 202-289-7442
http://www.siia.net

SPECIAL EDUCATION TEACHERS

QUICK FACTS

School Subjects English Speech	**Certification or Licensing** Required by all states
	Outlook Faster than the average
Personal Skills Communication/ideas Helping/teaching	**DOT** 094
Work Environment Primarily indoors Primarily one location	**GOE** 10.02.03
Minimum Education Level Bachelor's degree	**NOC** 4141, 4142
Salary Range $26,640 to $40,880 to $66,210+	**O*NET-SOC** 25-2041.00, 25-2042.00, 25-2043.00

OVERVIEW

Special education teachers teach students aged three through 21 who have a variety of disabilities. These teachers design individualized education plans and work with students one-on-one to help them learn academic subjects and life skills. Approximately 422,000 special education teachers are employed in the United States.

HISTORY

Modern special education traces its origins to 16th-century Spain, where Pedro Ponce de Leon and Juan Pablo Bonet taught deaf students to read and write. In the late 18th century in Paris Valentin Huay established the first institute for blind children. The first U.S. schools for the blind were founded in 1832 in Boston and New York.

By the early 19th century, attempts were made to educate the mentally handicapped. Edouard Sequin, a French psychiatrist, established the first school for the mentally handicapped in 1939 in Orange, New Jersey.

In the first half of the 20th century, special education became increasingly popular in the United States. By the 1960s and early 1970s, parents began to lobby state and local officials for improved special education programs for their children with disabilities. To address continuing inequities in the public education of special needs students, Congress passed the Education for All Handicapped Children Act (Public Law 94-142) in 1975. The Act required public schools to provide disabled students with a "free appropriate education" in the "least restrictive environment" possible. The Act was reauthorized in 1990 and 1997 and renamed the Individuals with Disabilities Education Act. This Act allows approximately 6 million children (roughly 10 percent of all school-aged children) to receive special education services from highly trained special education teachers.

THE JOB

Special education teachers instruct students who have a variety of disabilities. Their students may have physical disabilities, such as vision, hearing, or orthopedic impairment. They may also have learning disabilities or serious emotional disturbances. Although less common, special education teachers sometimes work with students who are gifted and talented, children who have limited proficiency in English, children who have communicable diseases, or children who are neglected and abused.

In order to teach special education students, these teachers design and modify instruction so that it is tailored to individual student needs. Teachers collaborate with school psychologists, social workers, parents, and occupational, physical, and speech-language therapists to develop a specially designed program called an Individualized Education Program (IEP) for each of their students. The IEP sets personalized goals for a student, based upon his or her learning style and ability, and outlines specific steps to prepare him or her for employment or postsecondary schooling.

Special education teachers teach at a pace that is dictated by the individual needs and abilities of their students. Unlike most regular classes, special education classes do not have an established curriculum that is taught to all students at the same time. Because student abilities vary widely, instruction is individualized and it is part of the teacher's responsibility to match specific techniques with a student's learning style and abilities. They may spend much time working with students one-on-one or in small groups.

Working with different types of students requires a variety of teaching methods. Some students may need to use special equipment or skills in the classroom in order to overcome their disabilities. For example, a teacher working with a student with a physical disability might use a computer that is operated by touching a screen or by voice commands. To work with hearing-impaired students, the teacher may need to use sign language. With visually impaired students, he or she may use teaching materials that have Braille characters or large, easy-to-see type. Gifted and talented students may need extra challenging assignments, a faster learning pace, or special attention in one curriculum area, such as art or music.

In addition to teaching academic subjects, special education teachers help students develop both emotionally and socially. They work to make students as independent as possible by teaching them functional skills for daily living. They may help young children learn basic grooming, hygiene, and table manners. Older students might be taught how to balance a checkbook, follow a recipe, or use the public transportation system.

Special education teachers meet regularly with their students' parents to inform them of their child's progress and offer suggestions of how to promote learning at home. They may also meet with school administrators, social workers, psychologists, various types of therapists, and students' general education teachers.

The current trend in education is to integrate students with disabilities into regular classrooms to the extent that it is possible and beneficial to them. This is often called "mainstreaming." As mainstreaming becomes increasingly common, special education teachers frequently work with general education teachers in general education classrooms. They may help adapt curriculum materials and teaching techniques to meet the needs of students with disabilities and offer guidance on dealing with students' emotional and behavioral problems.

In addition to working with students, special education teachers are responsible for a certain amount of paperwork. They document each student's progress and may fill out any forms that are required by the school system or the government.

REQUIREMENTS
High School

If you are considering a career as a special education teacher, you should focus on courses that will prepare you for college. These classes include natural and social sciences, mathematics, and English. Speech classes would also be a good choice for improving your communication skills. Finally, classes in psychology might be helpful both to help you understand the students you will eventually teach, and prepare you for college-level psychology course work.

Postsecondary Training

All states require that teachers have at least a bachelor's degree and that they complete a prescribed number of subject and education credits. It is increasingly common for special education teachers to complete an additional fifth year of training after they receive their bachelor's degree. Many states require special education teachers to get a master's degree in special education.

There are approximately 800 colleges and universities in the United States that offer programs in special education, including undergraduate, master's, and doctoral programs. These programs include general and specialized courses in special education, including educational psychology, legal issues of special education, child growth and development, and knowledge and skills needed for teaching students with disabilities. The student typically spends the last year of the program student-teaching in an actual classroom, under the supervision of a licensed teacher.

Certification or Licensing

All states require that special education teachers be licensed, although the particulars of licensing vary by state. In some states, these teachers must first be certified as elementary or secondary school teachers, then meet specific requirements to teach special education. Some states offer general special education licensure; others license several different subspecialties within special education. Some states allow special education teachers to transfer their license from one state to another, but many still require these teachers to pass licensing requirements for that state.

Other Requirements

To be successful in this field, you need to have many of the same personal characteristics as regular classroom teachers: the ability to communicate, a broad knowledge of the arts, sciences, and history, and a love of children. In addition, you will need a great deal of patience and persistence. You need to be creative, flexible, cooperative, and accepting of differences in others. Finally, you need to be emotionally stable and consistent in your dealings with students.

EXPLORING

There are a number of ways to explore the field of special education. One of the first and easiest is to approach a special education teacher at his or her school and ask to talk about the job. Perhaps the teacher could provide a tour of the special education classroom, or allow you to visit while a class is in session.

You might also want to become acquainted with special-needs students at your own school or become involved in a school or community mentoring program for these students. There may also be other opportunities for volunteer work or part-time jobs in schools, community agencies, camps, or residential facilities that will allow you to work with persons with disabilities.

EMPLOYERS

The majority of special education teachers teach in public and private schools. Others work in state education agencies, homebound or hospital environments, or residential facilities.

STARTING OUT

Because public school systems are by far the largest employers of special education teachers, this is where you should begin your job search.

You can also use your college's career placement center to locate job leads. This may prove a very effective place to begin. You may also write to your state's department of education for information on placement and regulations, or contact state employment offices to inquire about job openings. Applying directly to local school systems can sometimes be effective. Even if a school system does not have an immediate opening, it will usually keep your resume on file, should a vacancy occur.

ADVANCEMENT

Advancement opportunities for special education teachers, as for regular classroom teachers, are fairly limited. They may take the form of higher wages, better facilities, or more prestige. In some cases, these teachers advance to become supervisors or administrators, although this may require continued education on the teacher's part. Another option is for special education teachers to earn advanced degrees and become instructors at the college level.

EARNINGS

In some school districts, salaries for special education teachers follow the same scale as general education teachers. The average salary for special education teachers in 2000 was $40,880, according to the *Occupational Outlook Handbook*. The lowest 10 percent earned less than $26,640, while the highest 10 percent earned more than $66,210. Special education teachers employed by middle schools earned a median annual salary of $40,010 in 2001, according to the *2001 National Occupational and Employment and Wage Statistics* published by the U.S. Department of Labor. Special education teachers employed by secondary schools earned $42,780. Private school teachers usually earn less as compared with their public school counterparts. Teachers can supplement their annual salaries by becoming an activity sponsor, or by summer work.

Other school districts pay their special education teachers on a separate scale, which is usually higher than that of general education teachers.

Regardless of the salary scale, special education teachers usually receive a complete benefits package, which includes health and life insurance, paid holidays and vacations, and a pension plan.

WORK ENVIRONMENT

Special education teachers usually work from 7:30 or 8:00 A.M. to 3:00 or 3:30 P.M. Like most teachers, however, they typically spend several hours in the evening grading papers, completing paperwork, or preparing lessons for the next day. Altogether, most special education teachers work more than the standard 40 hours per week.

Although some schools offer year-round classes for students, the majority of special education teachers work the traditional 10-month school year, with a two-month vacation in the summer. Many teachers find this work schedule very appealing, as it gives them the opportunity to pursue personal interests or additional education during the summer break. Teachers typically also get a week off at Christmas and for spring break.

Special education teachers work in a variety of settings in schools, including both ordinary and specially equipped classrooms, resource rooms, and therapy rooms. Some schools have newer and better facilities for special education than others. Although it is less common, some teachers work in residential facilities or tutor students who are homebound or hospitalized.

Working with special education students can be very demanding, due to their physical and emotional needs. Teachers may fight a constant battle to keep certain students, particularly those with behavior disorders, under control. Other students, such as those with mental impairments or learning disabilities, learn so slowly that it may seem as if they are making no progress. The special education teacher must deal daily with frustration, setbacks, and classroom disturbances.

These teachers must also contend with heavy workloads, including a great deal of paperwork to document each student's progress. In addition, they may sometimes be faced with irate parents who feel that their child is not receiving proper treatment or an adequate education.

The positive side of this job is that special education teachers help students overcome their disabilities and learn to be as functional as possible. For a special education teacher, knowing that he or she is making a difference in a child's life can be very rewarding and emotionally fulfilling.

OUTLOOK

The field of special education is expected to grow faster than the average over the next several years, according to the U.S. Department of Labor. This demand is caused partly by the growth in the number of special education students needing services. Medical advances resulting in more survivors of illness and accidents, the rise in birth defects, especially in older pregnancies, as well as general population growth, are also significant factors for strong demand. Because of the rise in the number of youths with disabilities under the age of 21, the government has given approval for more federally funded programs. Growth of jobs in this field has also been influenced positively by legislation emphasizing training and employment for individuals with disabilities and a growing public awareness and interest in those with disabilities.

Finally, there is a fairly high turnover rate in this field, as special education teachers find the work too stressful and switch to mainstream teaching or change jobs altogether. Many job openings will arise out of a need to replace teachers who leave their positions. There is a shortage of qualified teachers in rural areas and in the inner city. Jobs will also be plentiful for teachers who specialize in speech and language impairments, learning disabilities, and early childhood intervention. Bilingual teachers with multicultural experience will be in high demand.

FOR MORE INFORMATION

For information on current issues, legal cases, and conferences, contact:

Council of Administrators of Special Education
Fort Valley State University
1005 State University Drive
Fort Valley, GA 31030
http://www.casecec.org

For information on accredited schools, teacher certification, financial aid, and careers in special education, contact:

**National Clearinghouse for Professions
in Special Education**
1110 North Glebe Road, Suite 300
Arlington, VA 22201-5704
Tel: 800-641-7824
Email: ncpse@cec.sped.org
http://www.special-ed-careers.org

For links to more information on special education, visit:

SPED Online
http://www.spedonline.com

SPEECH–LANGUAGE PATHOLOGISTS AND AUDIOLOGISTS

QUICK FACTS

School Subjects
Biology
Health
Speech

Personal Skills
Helping/teaching
Technical/scientific

Work Environment
Primarily indoors
Primarily one location

Minimum Education Level
Master's degree

Salary Range
$32,050 to $46,900 to
$71,960+

Certification or Licensing
Required for certain
positions

Outlook
Much faster than the
average

DOT
076

GOE
02.03.04

NOC
3141

O*NET-SOC
29-1121.00, 29-1127.00

OVERVIEW

Speech–language pathologists and *audiologists* help people who have speech and hearing defects. They identify the problem, then use tests to further evaluate it. Speech–language pathologists try to improve the speech and language skills of clients with communications disorders. Audiologists perform tests to measure the hearing ability of clients, who may range in age from the very young to the very old. Since it is not uncommon for clients to require assistance in both speech and hearing, pathologists and audiologists may frequently work together to help clients. Some professionals decide to combine these jobs into one, working as *speech–language pathologists/audiologists*. Audiologists and speech–language pathologists may work for school systems, in private practice, and at clinics and other medical facilities. Other employment possibilities for these professionals are teaching, for example, at universities, and conducting research on what causes certain speech and hearing defects. There are approximately 101,000 speech–language pathologists and audiologists employed in the United States.

HISTORY

The diagnosis and treatment of speech and hearing defects is a new part of medical science. In the past, physicians weren't able to help patients with these types of problems because there was usually nothing visibly wrong, and little was known about how speech and hearing were related. Until the middle of the 19th century, medical researchers didn't know whether speech defects were caused by lack of hearing, or whether the patient was the victim of two separate ailments. And even if they could figure out why something was wrong, doctors still couldn't communicate with the patient.

Alexander Graham Bell (1847–1922), the inventor of the telephone, provided some of the answers. His grandfather taught elocution (the art of public speaking), and Bell grew up interested in the problems of speech and hearing. It became his profession, and, by 1871, Bell was lecturing to a class of teachers of deaf people at Boston University. Soon afterward, Bell opened his own school, where he experimented with the idea of making speech visible to his pupils. If he could make them see the movements made by different human tones, they could speak by learning to produce similar vibrations. Bell's efforts not only helped deaf people of his day, but also led directly to the invention of the telephone in 1876. Probably the most famous deaf person was Helen Keller (1880–1968), whose teacher, Anne Sullivan (1866–1936), applied the discoveries of Bell to help Keller overcome her blindness and deafness.

THE JOB

Even though the two professions seem to blend together at times, speech–language pathology and audiology are very different from one another. However, because both speech and hearing are related to one another, a person competent in one discipline must have familiarity with the other.

The duties performed by speech–language pathologists and audiologists differ depending on education and experience and place of employment. Most speech–language pathologists provide direct clinical services to individuals and independently develop and carry out treatment programs. In medical facilities, they may work with physicians, social workers, psychologists, and other therapists to develop and execute treatment plans. In a school environment, they develop individual or group programs, counsel parents, and sometimes help teachers with classroom activities.

Clients of speech–language pathologists include: people who cannot make speech sounds or cannot make them clearly; those with speech rhythm and fluency problems, such as stuttering; people with voice quality problems, such as inappropriate pitch or harsh voice; those with problems understanding and producing language; and those with cognitive communication impairments, such as attention, memory, and problem-solving disorders. Speech–language pathologists may also work with people who have oral motor problems that cause eating and swallowing difficulties. Clients' problems may be congenital, developmental, or acquired and caused by hearing loss, brain injury or deterioration, cerebral palsy, stroke, cleft palate, voice pathology, mental retardation, or emotional problems.

Speech–language pathologists conduct written and oral tests and use special instruments to analyze and diagnose the nature and extent of impairment. They develop an individualized plan of care, which may include automated devices and sign language. They teach clients how to make sounds, improve their voices, or increase their language skills to communicate more effectively. Speech–language pathologists help clients develop, or recover, reliable communication skills.

People who have hearing, balance, and related problems consult audiologists, who use audiometers and other testing devices to discover the nature and extent of hearing loss. Audiologists interpret these results and may coordinate them with medical, educational, and psychological information to make a diagnosis and determine a course of treatment.

Hearing disorders can result from trauma at birth, viral infections, genetic disorders, or exposure to loud noise. Treatment may include examining and cleaning the ear canal, fitting and dispensing a hearing aid or other device, and audiologic rehabilitation (including auditory training or instruction in speech or lip reading). Audiologists provide fitting and tuning of cochlear implants and help those with implants adjust to the implant amplification systems. They also test noise levels in workplaces and conduct hearing protection programs in industry, as well as in schools and communities.

Audiologists provide direct clinical services to clients and sometimes develop and implement individual treatment programs. In some environments, however, they work as members of professional teams in planning and implementing treatment plans.

In a research environment, speech pathologists and audiologists investigate communicative disorders and their causes and ways to improve clinical services. Those teaching in colleges and universities instruct students on the principles and bases of communication, communication disorders, and clinical techniques used in speech and hearing.

Speech–language pathologists and audiologists keep records on the initial evaluation, progress, and discharge of clients to identify problems and track progress. They counsel individuals and their families on how to cope with the stress and misunderstanding that often accompany communication disorders.

REQUIREMENTS
High School
Since a college degree is a must for practicing this profession, make sure your high school classes are geared toward preparing you for higher education. Health and science classes, including biology, are important to take. Mathematics classes and English classes will help you develop research, writing, and math skills that you will need in college. Because speech pathologists and audiologists work so intensely with language, you may also find it beneficial to study a foreign language, paying special attention to how you learn to make sounds and remember words. Speech classes will also improve your awareness of sounds and language as well as improve your speaking and listening skills.

Postsecondary Training
Most states require a master's degree in speech–language pathology or audiology for a beginning job in either profession. Typical majors for those going into this field include communication sciences and disorders, speech and hearing, or education. Regardless of your career goal (speech–language pathologist or audiologist), your undergraduate course work should include classes in anatomy, biology, physiology, physics, and other related areas, such as linguistics, semantics, and phonetics. It's also helpful to have some exposure to child psychology.

To be eligible for certification, which most employers and states require, you must have at least a master's degree from a program accredited by the accreditation council of the American Speech-Language-Hearing Association (ASHA). According to the ASHA, as of 2012, audiologists will have to earn a doctorate in order to be certified. Currently there are more than 240 programs offering speech–language pathology and audiology degrees; however, not all of these programs are accredited. It is in your best interest to contact ASHA for a listing of accredited programs before you decide on a graduate school to attend. Some schools offer graduate degrees only in speech–language pathology or graduate degrees only in audiology. A number of schools offer degrees in both fields. Graduate-level course work in audiology includes such studies as hearing and language disorders, normal auditory and speech–language development, balance, and audiology instrumentation. Graduate-level work for those in speech–language pathologist includes studies in evaluating and treating speech and language disorders, stuttering, pronunciation, and voice modulation. Students of both disciplines are required to complete supervised clinical fieldwork or practicum.

If you plan to go into research, teaching, or administration, you will need to complete a doctorate degree.

Certification or Licensing

To work as a speech pathologist or audiologist in a public school, you will be required to be a certified teacher and you must meet special state requirements if treating children with disabilities. Fourteen states require audiologists and speech–language pathologists to be licensed, regardless of work setting (including school-based personnel). Forty-seven states regulate audiology and/or speech–language pathology through licensure or title registration, and all but six of those require continuing education for license renewal. Twenty-five states permit audiologists to dispense hearing aids under an audiology license. Education and experience requirements, type of regulation, and title use vary by state.

Forty-four states base their licensing laws on ASHA certification. ASHA offers speech–language pathologists the Certificate of Clinical Competence in Speech–Language Pathology and audiologists the Certificate of Clinical Competence in Audiology. To be eligible for these certifications, you must meet certain education requirements, such as the supervised clinical fieldwork experience, and have completed a postgraduate clinical fellowship. The fellowship must be no less than 36 weeks of full-time professional employment or its part-time equivalent. You must then pass an examination in the area in which you want certification.

Other Requirements

Naturally, speech–language pathologists and audiologists should have strong communication skills. Note, though, that "communication skills" means more than being able to speak clearly. You must be able to explain diagnostic test results and treatment plans in an easily understood way for a variety of clients who are already experiencing problems. As a speech–language pathologist and audiologist, you should enjoy working with people, both your clients and other professionals who may be involved in the client's treatment. In addition, you need patience and compassion. A client's progress may be slow, and you should be supportive and encouraging during these times.

EXPLORING

Although the specialized nature of this work makes it difficult for you to get an informal introduction to either profession, there are opportunities to be found. Official training must begin at the college or university level, but it is possible for you to volunteer in clinics and hospitals. As a prospective speech–language pathologist and audiologist, you may also find it helpful to learn sign language or volunteer your time in speech, language, and hearing centers.

EMPLOYERS

According to the *Occupational Outlook Handbook,* there are about 101,000 speech–language pathologists and audiologists employed in the United States, about one-half of whom are employed in education, from elementary school to the university level. Others work in speech, language, and hearing centers; hospitals; nursing homes; and physicians' offices. A small but growing number of speech–language pathologists and audiologists are in private practice, generally working with patients referred to them by physicians and other health practitioners.

Some speech–language pathologists and audiologists contract to provide services in schools, hospitals, or nursing homes, or work as consultants to industry. Audiologists are more likely to be employed in independent health care offices, while speech–language pathologists are more likely to work in school settings.

STARTING OUT

If you want to work in the public school systems, the college placement office can help you with interviewing skills. Professors sometimes know of job openings and may even post these openings on a centrally located bulletin board. It may be possible to find employment by contacting a hospital or rehabilitation center. To work in colleges and universities as a specialist in the classroom, clinic, or research center, it is almost mandatory to be working on a graduate degree. Many scholarships, fellowships, and grants for assistants are available in colleges and universities giving courses in speech–language pathology and audiology. Most of these and other assistance programs are offered at the graduate level. The U.S. Rehabilitation Services Administration, the Children's Bureau, the U.S. Department of Education, and the National Institutes of Health allocate funds for teaching and training grants to colleges and universities with graduate study programs. In addition, the Department of Veterans Affairs provides stipends (a fixed allowance) for predoctoral work.

ADVANCEMENT

Advancement in speech–language pathology and audiology is based chiefly on education. Individuals who have completed graduate study will have the best opportunities to enter research and administrative areas, supervising other speech–language pathologists or audiologists either in developmental work or in public school systems.

EARNINGS

The U.S. Department of Labor's *2001 National Occupational Employment and Wage Estimates* reports that speech–language pathologists earned a median annual salary of $48,510. Salaries ranged from to less than $32,090 to more than $71,960. Also in 2001, speech–language audiologists earned a median annual salary of $46,900. The lowest 10 percent of these workers earned less than $32,050, while the highest 10 percent earned $70,840 or more per year. Geographic location and type of facility are important salary variables. Almost all employment situations provide fringe benefits such as paid vacations, sick leave, and retirement programs.

WORK ENVIRONMENT

Most speech–language pathologists and audiologists work 40 hours a week at a desk or table in clean comfortable surroundings.

Speech–language pathologists and audiologists who focus on research, however, may work longer hours. The job is not physically demanding but does require attention to detail and intense concentration. The emotional needs of clients and their families may be demanding.

OUTLOOK

Population growth, lengthening life spans, and increased public awareness of the problems associated with communicative disorders indicate a highly favorable employment outlook for well-qualified personnel. The U.S. Department of Labor predicts that employment for speech–language pathologists and audiologists will grow much faster than the average over the next several years. Much depends on economic factors, further budget cutbacks by health care providers and third-party payers, and legal mandates requiring services for people with disabilities.

Nearly half of the new jobs emerging through the end of the decade are expected to be in speech and hearing clinics, physicians' offices, and outpatient care facilities. Speech–language pathologists and audiologists will be needed in these places, for example, to carry out the increasing number of rehabilitation programs for stroke victims and patients with head injuries.

Substantial job growth will continue to occur in elementary and secondary schools because of the Education for All Handicapped Children Act of 1975 and the Individuals with Disabilities Education Act in 1990 and 1997. Such laws guarantee special education and related services to minors with disabilities.

Many new jobs will be created in hospitals, nursing homes, rehabilitation centers, and home health agencies; most of these openings will probably be filled by private practitioners employed on a contract basis. Opportunities for speech–language pathologists and audiologists in private practice should increase in the future. There should be a greater demand for consultant audiologists in the area of industrial and environmental noise as manufacturing and other companies develop and carry out noise-control programs.

FOR MORE INFORMATION

The American Auditory Society is concerned with hearing disorders, how to prevent them, and the rehabilitation of individuals with hearing and balance dysfunction.

American Auditory Society
352 Sundial Ridge Circle
Dammeron Valley, UT 84783
Tel: 435-574-0062
http://www.amauditorysoc.org

This professional, scientific, and credentialing association offers infor-mation about communication disorders and career and membership information.

American Speech-Language-Hearing Association
10801 Rockville Pike
Rockville, MD 20852
Tel: 800-638-8255
Email: actioncenter@asha.org
http://www.asha.org

This association is for undergraduate and graduate students studying human communication. For news related to the field and to find out about regional chapters, contact:

National Student Speech, Language, and Hearing Association
10801 Rockville Pike
Rockville, MD 20852
Tel: 800-498-2071
Email: nsslha@asha.org
http://www.nsslha.org

TECHNICAL SUPPORT SPECIALISTS

OVERVIEW

Technical support specialists investigate and resolve computer problems. They listen to customer complaints, walk customers through possible solutions, and write technical reports based on these events. Technical support specialists have different duties depending on whom they assist and what they fix. Regardless of specialty, all technical support specialists must be very knowledgeable about the products they work with and be able to communicate effectively with users from different technical backgrounds. They must be patient with frustrated users and be able to perform well under stress. The cause of a computer malfunction is not always easy to discern, so support specialists should enjoy the challenge of problem solving and have strong analytical thinking skills. There are approximately 493,200 computer support specialists employed in the United States.

HISTORY

Today, computers are everywhere, from businesses of all kinds to government agencies, charitable organizations, and private homes. Over the years, technology has continued to shrink computer size and increase speed at an unprecedented rate.

Technical support has been around since the development of the first computers for the simple reason that, like all machines, computers always experience problems at one time or another. Several market phenomena explain the increase in demand for competent technical support specialists. First of all, as more and more companies enter the computer hardware, software, and peripheral market, the intense competition to win customers has resulted in many companies offering free or reasonably priced technical support as part of the purchase package. A company uses its reputation and the availability of a technical support department to differentiate its products from those of other companies, even though the tangible products like a hard drive, for example, may actually be physically identical. Second, personal computers have entered private homes in large numbers, and the sheer quantity of users has risen so dramatically that more technical support specialists are needed to field their complaints. Third, new processors and software applications are developed and released so quickly that quality assurance departments cannot possibly identify all the glitches in programming beforehand. Finally, given the great variety of computer equipment and software on the market, it is often difficult for users to reach a high proficiency level with each individual program. When they experience problems, often due to their own errors, users call on technical support to help them.

The goal of many computer companies is to release a product for sale that requires no technical support, so that the technical support department has nothing to do. Given the speed of development, however, this is not likely to occur anytime soon. Until it does, there will be a strong demand for technical support specialists.

THE JOB

It is relatively rare today to find a business that does not rely on computers in some way. Some use them heavily and in many areas: daily operations, such as employee time clocks; monthly projects, such as payroll and sales accounting; and major reengineering of fundamental business procedures, such as form automation in government agencies, insurance companies, and banks. Once employees get used to performing their work on computers, they soon can barely remember how they ever got along without them. As more companies become increasingly reliant on computers, it becomes increasingly critical that they function properly all the time. Any computer downtime can be extremely expensive, in terms of work left undone and sales not made, for example. When employees experience problems with their computer system, they call technical support for help. Technical support specialists investigate and resolve problems in computer functioning.

Technical support can generally be broken up into at least three distinct areas, although these distinctions vary greatly with the nature, size, and scope of the company: technical support, user support, and microcomputer support. Most technical support specialists perform some combination of the tasks explained below.

The jobs of technical support specialists vary according to whom they assist and what they fix. Some specialists help private users exclusively; others are on call to a major corporate buyer. Some work with computer hardware and software, while others help with printer, modem, and fax problems. *User support specialists,* also known as *help desk specialists,* work directly with users themselves, who call when they experience problems. The support specialist listens carefully to the user's explanation of the precise nature of the problem and the commands entered that seem to have caused it. Some companies have developed complex software that allows the support specialist to enter a description of the problem and wait for the computer to provide suggestions about what the user should do.

The initial goal is to isolate the source of the problem. If user error is the culprit, the technical support specialist explains procedures related to the program in question, whether it is a graphics, database, word processing, or printing program. If the problem seems to lie in the hardware or software, the specialist asks the user to enter certain commands in order to see if the computer makes the appropriate response. If it does not, the support specialist is closer to isolating the cause. The support specialist consults supervisors, programmers, and others in order to outline the cause and possible solutions.

Some technical support specialists who work for computer companies are mainly involved with solving problems whose cause has been determined to lie in the computer system's operating system, hardware, or software. They make exhaustive use of resources, such as colleagues or books, and try to solve the problem through a variety of methods, including program modifications and the replacement of certain hardware or software.

Technical support specialists employed in the information systems departments of large corporations do this kind of troubleshooting, as well. They also oversee the daily operations of the various computer systems in the company. Sometimes they compare the system's work capacity to the actual daily workload in order to determine if upgrades are needed. In addition, they might help out other computer professionals in the company with modifying commercial software for their company's particular needs.

Microcomputer support specialists are responsible for preparing computers for delivery to a client, including installing the operating system and desired software. After the unit is installed at the customer's location, the support specialists might help train users on appropriate procedures and answer any questions they have. They help diagnose problems that occur, transferring major concerns to other technical support specialists.

All technical support work must be well documented. Support specialists write detailed technical reports on every problem they work on. They try to tie together different problems on the same software, so programmers can make adjustments that address all of the issues. Record-keeping is crucial because designers, programmers, and engineers use technical support reports to revise current products and improve future ones. Some support specialists help write training manuals. They are often required to read trade magazines and company newsletters in order to keep up to date on their products and the field in general.

REQUIREMENTS
High School

A high school diploma is a minimum requirement for technical support specialists. Any technical courses you can take, such as computer science, schematic drawing, or electronics, can help you develop the logical and analytical thinking skills necessary to be successful in this field. Courses in math and science are also valuable for this reason. Since technical support specialists have to deal with both computer programmers on the one hand and computer users who may not know anything about computers on the other, you should take English and speech classes to improve your communications skills, both verbal and written.

Postsecondary Training

Technical support is a field as old as computer technology itself, so it might seem odd that postsecondary programs in this field are not more common or standardized. The reason behind this situation is relatively simple: formal education curricula cannot keep up with the changes, nor can they provide specific training on individual products. Some large corporations might consider educational background, both as a way to weed out applicants and to insure a certain level of proficiency. Most major computer companies, however, look for energetic individuals who demonstrate a willingness and ability to learn new things quickly and who have general computer knowledge. These employers count on training new support specialists themselves.

Individuals interested in pursuing a job in this field should first determine what area of technical support appeals to them the most and then honestly assess their level of experience and knowledge. Large corporations often prefer to hire people with an associate's degree and some experience. They may also be impressed with commercial certification in a computer field, such as networking. However, if they are hiring from within the company, they will probably weigh experience more heavily than education when making a final decision.

Employed individuals looking for a career change may want to commit themselves to a program of self-study in order to be qualified for technical support positions. Many computer professionals learn a lot of what they know by playing around on computers, reading trade magazines, and talking with colleagues. Self-taught individuals should learn how to effectively demonstrate knowledge and proficiency on the job or during an interview. Besides self-training, employed individuals should investigate the tuition reimbursement programs offered by their company.

High school students with no experience should seriously consider earning an associate's degree in a computer-related technology. The degree shows the prospective employer that the applicant has attained a certain level of proficiency with computers and has the intellectual ability to learn technical processes, a promising sign for success on the job.

There are many computer technology programs that lead to an associate's degree. A specialization in personal computer support and administration is certainly applicable to technical support. Most computer professionals eventually need to go back to school to earn a bachelor's degree in order to keep themselves competitive in the job market and prepare themselves for promotion to other computer fields.

Certification or Licensing

Though certification is not an industry requirement, it is highly recommended. According to the Help Desk Institute, most individuals wishing to qualify to work in a support/help desk environment will need to obtain certification within a month of being on the job. A number of organizations offer several different types of certification. The Computing Technology Industry Association, for example, offers the "A+" certification for entry-level computer service technicians. Help Desk Institute has training courses and offers a number of certifications for those working in support and help desk positions.

To become certified, you will need to pass a written test and in some cases may need a certain amount of work experience. Although going through the certification process is voluntary, becoming certified will most likely be to your advantage. It will show your commitment to the profession as well as your level of expertise. In addition, certification may qualify you for certain jobs and lead to new employment opportunities.

Other Requirements

To be a successful technical support specialist, you should be patient, enjoy challenges of problem solving, and think logically. You should work well under stress and demonstrate effective communication skills. Working in a field that changes rapidly, you should be naturally curious and enthusiastic about learning new technologies as they are developed.

EXPLORING

If you are interested in becoming a technical support specialist, you should try to organize a career day with an employed technical support specialist. Local computer repair shops that offer technical support service might be a good place to contact. Otherwise, you should contact major corporations, computer companies, and even the central office of your school system.

If you are interested in any computer field, you should start working and playing on computers as much as possible; many working computer professionals became computer hobbyists at a very young age. You can surf the Internet, read computer magazines, and join school or community computer clubs.

You might also attend a computer technology course at a local technical/vocational school. This would give you hands-on exposure to typical technical support training. In addition, if you experience problems with your own hardware or software, you should call technical support, paying close attention to how the support specialist handles the call and asking as many questions as the specialist has time to answer.

EMPLOYERS

Technical support specialists work for computer hardware and software companies, as well as in the information systems departments of large corporations and government agencies. There are approximately 493,240 technical support specialists employed in the United States.

STARTING OUT

Most technical support positions are considered entry-level. They are found mainly in computer companies and large corporations. Individuals interested in obtaining a job in this field should scan the classified ads for openings in local businesses and may want to work with an employment agency for help finding out about opportunities. Since many job openings are publicized by word of mouth, it is also very important to speak with as many working computer professionals as possible. They tend to be aware of job openings before anyone else and may be able to offer a recommendation to the hiring committee.

If students of computer technology are seeking a position in technical support, they should work closely with their school's placement office. Many employers inform placement offices at nearby schools of openings before ads are run in the newspaper. In addition, placement office staffs are generally very helpful with resume and interviewing techniques.

If an employee wants to make a career change into technical support, he or she should contact the human resources department of the company or speak directly with appropriate management. In companies that are expanding their computing systems, it is often helpful for management to know that current employees would be interested in growing in a computer-related direction. They may even be willing to finance additional education.

ADVANCEMENT

Technical support specialists who demonstrate leadership skills and a strong aptitude for the work may be promoted to supervisory positions within technical support departments. Supervisors are responsible for the more complicated problems that arise, as well as for some administrative duties such as scheduling, interviewing, and job assignments.

Further promotion requires additional education. Some technical support specialists may become commercially certified in computer networking so that they can install, maintain, and repair computer networks. Others may prefer to pursue a bachelor's degree in computer science, either full-time or part-time. The range of careers available to college graduates is widely varied. *Software engineers* analyze industrial, business, and scientific problems and develop software programs to handle them effectively. *Quality assurance engineers* design automated quality assurance tests for new software applications. *Internet quality assurance specialists* work specifically with testing and developing companies' websites. *Computer systems programmer/analysts* study the broad computing picture for a company or a group of companies in order to determine the best way to organize the computer systems.

There are limited opportunities for technical support specialists to be promoted into managerial positions. Doing so would require additional education in business but would probably also depend on the individual's advanced computer knowledge.

EARNINGS

Technical support specialist jobs are plentiful in areas where clusters of computer companies are located, such as northern California and Seattle, Washington. Median annual earnings for technical support specialists were $38,560 in 2001, according to the *2001 National Occupational Employment and Wage Estimates* compiled by the U.S. Department of Labor. The highest 10 percent earned more than $67,650, while the lowest 10 percent earned less than $22,710. Those who have more education, responsibility, and expertise have the potential to earn much more.

Technical support specialists earned the following median annual salaries by industry in 2000 (according to the U.S. Department of Labor): professional and commercial equipment, $42,970; computer and data processing services, $37,860; personnel supply services, $34,080; colleges and universities, $32,830; and miscellaneous business services, $21,070.

Most technical support specialists work for companies that offer a full range of benefits, including health insurance, paid vacation, and sick leave. Smaller service or start-up companies may hire support specialists on a contractual basis.

WORK ENVIRONMENT

Technical support specialists work in comfortable business environments. They generally work regular, 40-hour weeks. For certain products, however, they may be asked to work evenings or weekends or at least be on call during those times in case of emergencies. If they work for service companies, they may be required to travel to clients' sites and log overtime hours.

Technical support work can be stressful, since specialists often deal with frustrated users who may be difficult to work with. Communication problems with people who are less technically qualified may also be a source of frustration. Patience and understanding are essential for handling these problems.

Technical support specialists are expected to work quickly and efficiently and be able to perform under pressure. The ability to do this requires thorough technical expertise and keen analytical ability.

OUTLOOK

The U.S. Department of Labor predicts that the technical support specialist position will be one of the fastest growing of all occupations over the next several years. Each time a new computer product is released on the market or another system is installed, there will be problems ranging from user error or technical difficulty. Thus will always be a need for technical support specialists to solve the problems. Since technology changes so rapidly, it is very important for these professionals to keep up to date on advances. They should read trade magazines, surf the Internet, and talk with colleagues in order to know what is happening in the field.

Since some companies stop offering technical support on old products or applications after a designated time, the key is to be technically flexible. This is important for another reason as well. While the industry as a whole will require more technical support specialists in the future, it may be the case that certain computer companies go out of business. It can be a volatile industry for start-ups or young companies dedicated to the development of one product. Technical support specialists interested in working for computer companies should therefore consider living in areas in which many such companies are clustered.

FOR MORE INFORMATION

For information on internships, scholarships, student membership, and the student magazine, Crossroads, *contact:*

Association for Computing Machinery
1515 Broadway
New York, NY 10036
Tel: 800-342-6626
http://www.acm.org

For information on certification, contact:

Computing Technology Industry Association
1815 South Meyers Road, Suite 300
Oakbrook Terrace, IL 60181-5228
Tel: 630-678-8300
http://www.comptia.org

For more information on this organization's training courses and certification, contact:

Help Desk Institute
6385 Corporate Drive, Suite 301
Colorado Springs, CO 80919
Tel: 800-248-5667
Email: support@thinkhdi.com
http://www.thinkhdi.com

For information on careers, scholarships, student membership, and the student newsletter, looking.forward, *contact:*

IEEE Computer Society
1730 Massachusetts Avenue, NW
Washington, DC 20036-1992
Tel: 202-371-0101
http://www.computer.org

WRITERS AND EDITORS

QUICK FACTS

School Subjects English Journalism	**Certification or Licensing** None available
	Outlook Faster than the average
Personal Skills Communication/ideas Helping/teaching	
	DOT 131, 132
Work Environment Primarily indoors Primarily one location	**GOE** 01.01.01, 01.01.02
Minimum Education Level Bachelor's degree	**NOC** 5121, 5122
Salary Range $20,570 to $42,450 to $83,180+ (writers) $23,090 to $39,960 to $73,460+ (editors)	**O*NET-SOC** 27-3041.00, 27-3042.00, 27-3043.01, 27-3043.02, 27-3043.03, 27-3043.04

OVERVIEW

Writers express, edit, promote, and interpret ideas and facts in written form for books, magazines, trade journals, newspapers, technical studies and reports, company newsletters, radio and television broadcasts, and advertisements. They develop fiction and nonfiction ideas for plays, novels, poems, and other related works; report, analyze, and interpret facts, events, and personalities; review art, music, drama, and other artistic presentations; and persuade the general public to choose or favor certain goods, services, and personalities.

Editors perform a wide range of functions, but their primary responsibility is to ensure that text provided by writers is suitable in content, format, and style for the intended audiences. Readers are an editor's first priority.

HISTORY

The skill of writing has existed for thousands of years. Papyrus fragments with writing by ancient Egyptians date from about 3000 B.C., and archaeological findings show that the Chinese had developed books by about 1300 B.C. A number of technical obstacles had to be overcome before printing and the profession of writing evolved. Books of the Middle Ages were copied by hand on parchment. The ornate style that marked these books helped ensure their rarity. Also, few people were able to read. Religious fervor prohibited the reproduction of secular literature.

Two major historical events helped in the development of the publishing industry: the invention of the printing press by Johannes Gutenberg (ca. 1397–ca. 1468) in the middle of the 15th century and the liberalism of the Protestant Reformation, which helped encourage a wider range of publications, greater literacy, and the creation of a number of works of literary merit. The first authors worked directly with printers.

The modern publishing age began in the 18th century. Printing became mechanized, and the novel, magazine, and newspaper developed. The first newspaper in the American colonies appeared in the early 18th century, but it was Benjamin Franklin (1706–1790) who, as editor and writer, made the *Pennsylvania Gazette* one of the most influential in setting a high standard for his fellow American journalists. Franklin also published the first magazine in the colonies, *The American Magazine,* in 1741.

Advances in the printing trades, photoengraving, retailing, and the availability of capital produced a boom in newspapers and magazines in the 19th century. Further mechanization in the printing field, such as the use of the Linotype machine, high-speed rotary presses, and special color reproduction processes, set the stage for still further growth in the book, newspaper, and magazine industry.

In addition to the print media, the broadcasting industry has contributed to the development of the professional writer. Film, radio, and television are sources of entertainment, information, and education that provide employment for thousands of writers.

The history of book editing is tied closely to the history of the book and bookmaking and the history of the printing process. As mentioned earlier, in the early days of publishing, authors worked directly with the printer; the printer was often the publisher and seller of the author's work. Eventually, however, booksellers began to work directly with the authors and eventually took over the role of publisher. The publisher then became the middleman between author and printer.

The publisher worked closely with the author and sometimes acted as the editor; the word *editor,* in fact, derives from the Latin word *edere* or *editum* and means supervising or directing the preparation of text. Eventually, specialists were hired to perform the editing function. These editors, who were also called advisors or literary advisors in the 19th century, became an integral part of the publishing business.

The editor, also called the *sponsor* in some houses, sought out the best authors, worked with them, and became their advocate in the publishing house. So important did some editors become that their very presence in a publishing house could determine the quality of author that might be published there. Some author–editor collaborations have become legendary. The field has grown through the 20th and 21st centuries, with computers greatly speeding up the process by which editors move copy to the printer.

THE JOB

Writers work in the field of communications. Specifically, they deal with the written word, whether it is destined for the printed page, broadcast, computer screen, or live theater. The nature of their work is as varied as the materials they produce: books, magazines, trade journals, newspapers, technical reports, company newsletters and other publications, advertisements, speeches, scripts for motion picture and stage productions, and scripts for radio and television broadcast. Writers develop ideas and write for all media.

Because the field of writing is so broad, workers usually specialize in a particular type of writing. For example, those who prepare scripts for motion pictures or television are called *screenwriters* or *scriptwriters. Playwrights* do similar writing but for theater. Those who write copy for advertisements are called *copywriters.*

Newswriters prepare stories for newspapers, radio, and television. *Columnists* specialize in writing about matters from their personal viewpoints. *Critics* review and comment upon the work of other authors, musicians, artists, and performers. In addition to all of these types of writers, there are also technical writers, novelists, biographers, poets, essayists, comedy writers, and short story writers.

Good writers gather as much information as possible about a subject and then carefully check the accuracy of their sources. Usually, this involves extensive library research and interviews or long hours of observation and personal experience. Writers keep notes from which they prepare an outline. They often rewrite sections of the material, always searching for the best way to express an idea or opinion. A manuscript may be reviewed, corrected, and revised many times before a final copy is ready.

Writers can be employed either as in-house staff or as freelancers. Freelancers must provide their own office space and equipment, such as computers and fax machines. Freelance writers also are responsible for keeping tax records, sending out invoices, negotiating contracts, and providing their own health insurance.

Editors work for many kinds of publishers, publications, and corporations. Editors' titles vary widely, not only from one area of publishing to another but also within each area. *Book editors* prepare written material for publication. In small publishing houses, the same editor may guide the material through all the stages of the publishing process. They may work with typesetters, printers, designers, advertising agencies, and other members of the publishing industry. In larger publishing houses, editors tend to be more specialized, being involved in only a part of the publishing process.

Acquisitions editors are the editors who find new writers and sign on new projects. They are responsible for finding new ideas for books that will sell well and for finding writers who can create the books.

Production editors are responsible for taking the manuscript written by an author and polishing the work into a finished book. They correct grammar, spelling, and style, and check all the facts. They make sure the book reads well and suggest changes to the author if it does not. The production editor may be responsible for getting the cover designed and the art put into a book.

Copy editors assist the production editor in polishing the author's writing. Copy editors review each page and make all the changes required to give the book a good writing style. *Line editors* review the text to make sure specific style rules are obeyed. They make sure the same spelling is used for words where more than one spelling is correct (for example, grey and gray).

Fact checkers and *proofreaders* read the manuscript to make sure everything is spelled correctly and that all the facts in the text have been checked.

The basic functions performed by *magazine* and *newspaper editors* are much like those performed by book editors, but a significant amount of the writing that appears in magazines and newspapers, or periodicals, is done by staff writers. Periodicals often use editors who specialize in specific areas, such as *city editors*, who oversee the work of reporters who specialize in local news, and *department editors*. Department editors specialize in areas such as business, fashion, sports, and features, to name only a few. These departments are determined by the interests of the audience that the periodical intends to reach. Like book houses, periodicals use copy editors, researchers, and fact checkers, but at small periodicals, one or a few editors may be responsible for tasks that would be performed by many people at a larger publication.

INTERVIEW: Editor

David Hayes is the Editor in Chief of the New Standard Encyclopedia. *He spoke with the editors of* 25 Jobs That Have It All *about his career.*

Q. What are your primary and secondary job duties as the Editor in Chief of the Encyclopedia?

A. I am responsible for the overall content and revisions of a multi-volume general encyclopedia and I supervise a small editorial staff.

My job incorporates a great number of secondary duties. These duties could be classified as editorial, managerial, technological, creative, and administrative. A sampling (in no particular order): editing and writing manuscripts; making decisions about what will be revised; selecting appropriate photographs for revisions, providing instructions to artists and reviewing their artwork; keeping abreast of developments in various subject areas; monitoring and controlling costs and expenses; interviewing candidates for job openings; planning editorial and production schedules and workflow; meeting with staff personnel; evaluating and purchasing computer software and hardware; developing and maintaining a variety of databases for managing the work on the encyclopedia and its content; contacting and working with vendors and freelancers.

Q. What type of education did you pursue to work in this job?

A. I attended Cornell College, where I had a dual major—in physics and mathematics—for my Bachelor's of Arts degree. My liberal arts education served me well as preparation for my first editorial job, as subject editor for science and technology. My coursework included writing term papers for professors with very high writing standards.

I also worked on the college newspaper for several years, composing type at first and then eventually running the paper.

Q. How can aspiring editors get their first job in the field?

A. I learned of my first editorial job through an ad for the job that had been sent to the career center at my college. Newspaper classified ads are a good source of information about jobs in the field. Job-search agencies are a source of information for selected jobs. Professional organizations and word-of-mouth information are also good sources, especially for freelance work. Courses offered at some universities for certification in editorial skills can provide leads for jobs at various local publishers.

Q. What are the most important qualities for successful editors?

A. Important qualities for persons in a reference-work editorial job include having a desire to learn, a compunction for accuracy, and a tenacity for uncovering and resolving discrepancies and ambiguities. Clear, concise writing and the ability to work with deadlines are also very important, as are being able to organize ideas and having well-organized work habits.

Q. What are the pros and cons of being an editor?

A. Enjoyable things about this kind of work can include the accomplishment of crafting solutions to sometimes puzzling problems, the exercising of an active curiosity, and the satisfaction of helping readers learn about and understand a great variety of topics.

The work can be stressful, entailing long hours and relentless deadlines.

Q. What is an important piece of advice that you have to offer college students as they graduate and look for jobs in this field?

A. Develop proofreading skills and become proficient using word processing, spreadsheet, and database software. These skills will prove valuable at entry-level positions and beyond.

REQUIREMENTS
High School

If you are interested in becoming a writer or an editor, take English, literature, foreign languages, general science, social studies, computer science, and typing classes while in high school. The ability to type is almost a requisite for all positions in the communications field, as is familiarity with computers.

Editors and writers must be expert communicators, so you should excel in English if you wish to work in these careers. You must learn to write extremely well, since you will be correcting and even rewriting the work of others. If they are offered at your school, take elective classes in writing or editing, such as journalism and business communications.

Don't forget, however, that a successful writer or editor must have a wide range of knowledge. Don't hesitate to explore areas that you find interesting. Do everything you can to satisfy your intellectual curiosity. As far as most writers and editors are concerned, there is no useless information.

Postsecondary Training

Most writing and editing jobs require a college education. Many employers prefer that you have a broad liberal arts background or majors in English, literature, history, philosophy, or one of the social sciences. Other employers desire communications or journalism training in college. Occasionally a master's degree in a specialized writing or editing field may be required. Most schools offer courses in journalism and some have more specialized courses in book publishing, publication management, and newspaper and magazine writing.

In addition to formal course work, most employers look for practical writing and editing experience. If you have served on high school or college newspapers, yearbooks, or literary magazines, you will make a better candidate, as well as if you have worked for small community newspapers or radio stations, even in an unpaid position. Many book publishers, magazines, newspapers, and radio and television stations have summer internship programs that provide valuable training if you want to learn about the publishing and broadcasting businesses. Interns do many simple tasks, such as running errands and answering phones, but some may be asked to perform research, conduct interviews, or even write or edit some minor pieces.

Writers or editors who specialize in technical fields may need degrees, concentrated course work, or experience in specific subject areas. This applies frequently to engineering, business, or one of the sciences. Also, technical communications is a degree now offered at many universities and colleges.

If you wish to enter positions with the federal government, you will have to take a civil service examination and meet certain specified requirements, according to the type and level of position.

Other Requirements

Writers and editors should be creative and able to express ideas clearly, have a broad general knowledge, be skilled in research techniques, and be computer literate. Other assets include curiosity, persistence, initiative, resourcefulness, and an accurate memory. For some jobs—on a newspaper, for example, where the activity is hectic and deadlines short—the ability to concentrate and produce under pressure is essential.

You must be detail oriented to succeed as a writer or an editor. You must also be patient, since you may have to spend hours synthesizing information into the written word or turning a few pages of near-gibberish into powerful, elegant English. If you are the kind of person who can't sit still, you probably will not succeed in these careers. To be a good writer or editor, you must be a self-starter who is not afraid to make decisions. You must be good not only at identifying problems but also at solving them, so you must be creative.

EXPLORING

As a high school or college student, you can test your interest and aptitude in the fields of writing and editing by working as a reporter or writer on school newspapers, yearbooks, and literary magazines. If you cannot work for the school paper, try to land a part-time job on a local newspaper or newsletter. If that doesn't work, you might want to publish your own newsletter. There is nothing like trying to put together a small publication to help you understand how publishing works. You may try combining another interest with your interest in writing or editing. For example, if you are interested in environmental issues, you might want to start a newsletter that deals with environmental problems and solutions in your community. Use your imagination.

Small community newspapers and local radio stations often welcome contributions from outside sources, although they may not have the resources to pay for them. Jobs in bookstores, magazine shops, and even newsstands offer a chance to become familiar with the various publications.

Information on writing and editing as a career may also be obtained by visiting local newspapers, publishers, or radio and television stations and interviewing some of the people who work there. Career conferences and other guidance programs frequently include speakers on the entire field of communications from local or national organizations.

EMPLOYERS

Nearly one-fourth of salaried writers and editors work for newspapers, magazines, and book publishers, according to the *Occupational Outlook Handbook*. Writers and editors are also employed by advertising agencies, in radio and television broadcasting, public relations firms, Internet sites, and for journals and newsletters published by business and nonprofit organizations, such as professional associations, labor unions, and religious organizations. Other employers are government agencies and film production companies.

STARTING OUT

A fair amount of experience is required to gain a high-level position in the writing field. Most writers start out in entry-level positions. These jobs may be listed with college placement offices, or they may be obtained by applying directly to the employment departments of the individual publishers or broadcasting companies. Graduates who previously had internships with these companies often have the advantage of knowing someone who can give them a personal recommendation. Want ads in newspapers and trade journals are another source for jobs. Because of the competition for positions, however, few vacancies are listed with public or private employment agencies.

Employers in the communications field usually are interested in samples of your published writing. These are often assembled in an organized portfolio or scrapbook. Stories with bylines that show you have written the work are more impressive and convincing than stories whose source is not identified.

Beginning positions as a *junior writer* usually involve library research, preparation of rough drafts for part or all of a report, cataloging, and other related writing tasks. These are generally carried on under the supervision of a senior writer.

Some technical writers have entered the field after working in public relations departments or as technicians or research assistants, then transferring to technical writing as openings occur. Many firms now hire writers directly upon application or recommendation of college professors and placement offices.

There is tremendous competition for editorial jobs, so it is important for a beginner who wishes to break into the business to be as well prepared as possible. College students who have gained experience as interns, have worked for publications during summer vacations, or have attended special programs in publishing will be at an advantage. In addition, applicants for any editorial position must be extremely careful when preparing cover letters and resumes. Even a single error in spelling or usage will disqualify an applicant. Applicants for editorial or proofreading positions must also expect to take and pass tests that are designed to determine their language skills.

Many editors enter the field as editorial assistants or proofreaders. Some editorial assistants perform only clerical tasks, whereas others may also proofread or perform basic editorial tasks. Typically, an editorial assistant who performs well will be given the opportunity to take on more and more editorial duties as time passes. Proofreaders have the advantage of being able to look at the work of editors, so they can learn while they do their own work.

Good sources of information about job openings are school placement offices, classified ads in newspapers and trade journals, specialized publications such as *Publishers Weekly* (http://publishersweekly.com), and Internet sites. One way to proceed is to identify local publishers through the Yellow Pages. Many publishers have websites that list job openings, and large publishers often have telephone job lines that serve the same purpose.

ADVANCEMENT

Most writers find their first jobs as editorial or production assistants. Advancement may be more rapid in small companies, where beginners learn by doing a little bit of everything and may be given writing tasks immediately. In large firms, duties are usually more compartmentalized. Assistants in entry-level positions are assigned such tasks as research, fact checking, and copyrighting, but it generally takes much longer to advance to full-scale writing duties.

Promotion into more responsible positions may come with the assignment of more important articles and stories to write, or it may be the result of moving to another company. Freelance or self-employed writers earn advancement in the form of larger fees as they gain exposure and establish their reputations.

In book publishing houses, employees who start as editorial assistants or proofreaders and show promise generally become copy editors. After gaining skill in that position, they may be given a wider range of duties while retaining the same title. The next step may be a position as a *senior copy editor,* which involves overseeing the work of junior copy editors, or as a project editor. The *project editor* performs a wide variety of tasks, including copyediting, coordinating the work of in-house and freelance copy editors, and managing the schedule of a particular project. From this position, an editor may move up to become first assistant editor, then managing editor, then editor-in-chief. These positions involve more management and decision-making than is usually found in the positions described previously. The *editor in chief* works with the publisher to ensure that a suitable editorial policy is being followed, while the *managing editor* is responsible for all aspects of the editorial department. The *assistant editor* provides support to the managing editor.

Newspaper editors generally begin working on the copy desk, where they progress from less significant stories and projects to major news and feature stories. A common route to advancement is for copy editors to be promoted to a particular department, where they may move up the ranks to management positions. An editor who has achieved success in a department may become a city editor, who is responsible for news, or a managing editor, who runs the entire editorial operation of a newspaper.

The advancement path for magazine editors is similar to that of book editors. After they become copy editors, they work their way up to become senior editors, managing editors, and editors in chief. In many cases, magazine editors advance by moving from a position on one magazine to the same position with a larger or more prestigious magazine. Such moves often bring significant increases in both pay and status.

EARNINGS

In 2001, the median salary for writers was $42,450 a year, according to the U.S. Bureau of Labor Statistics (BLS). The lowest-paid 10 percent earned less than $20,570, while the highest-paid 10 percent earned $83,180. Earnings of those in technical writing jobs are somewhat higher. In 2001, technical writers earned a median salary of $49,370.

The BLS reports that the median annual earnings for editors were $39,960 in 2001. the lowest-paid 10 percent earned $23,090 or less, while the highest-paid 10 percent earned $73,460 or more.

In addition to their salaries, many writers and editors earn income from freelance work. Freelance earnings vary widely. Full-time established freelance writers and editors may earn up to $75,000 a year.

WORK ENVIRONMENT

Working conditions vary for writers. Although the workweek usually runs 35 to 40 hours, many writers work overtime. The work is especially hectic on newspapers and at broadcasting companies, which operate seven days a week. Writers often work nights and weekends to meet deadlines or to cover a late-developing story.

Most writers work independently, but they often must cooperate with artists, photographers, art directors, rewriters, and advertising people who may have widely differing ideas of how the materials should be prepared and presented.

Physical surroundings range from comfortable private offices to noisy, crowded newsrooms filled with other workers typing and talking on the telephone. Some writers must confine their research to the library or telephone interviews, but others may travel to other cities or countries or to local sites, such as theaters, ballparks, airports, factories, or other offices.

The work is arduous, but writers are seldom bored. Each day brings new and interesting problems. The jobs occasionally require travel. The most difficult element is the continual pressure of deadlines. People who are the most content as writers enjoy and work well with deadline pressure.

The environments in which editors work vary widely. For the most part, publishers of all kinds realize that a quiet atmosphere is conducive to work that requires tremendous concentration. It takes an unusual ability to focus to edit in a noisy place. Most editors work in private offices or cubicles. Book editors often work in quieter surroundings than do newspaper editors or quality-control people in advertising agencies, who sometimes work in rather loud and hectic situations.

Even in relatively quiet surroundings, however, editors often have many distractions. A project editor who is trying to do some copyediting or review the editing of others may, for example, have to deal with phone calls from authors, questions from junior editors, meetings with members of the editorial and production staff, and questions from freelancers, among many other distractions. In many cases, editors have computers that are exclusively for their own use, but in others, editors must share computers that are located in a common area.

Deadlines are an important issue for virtually all editors. Newspaper and magazine editors work in a much more pressurized atmosphere than book editors because they face daily or weekly deadlines, whereas book production usually takes place over several months.

In almost all cases, editors must work long hours during certain phases of the editing process. Some newspaper editors start work at 5 A.M., others work until 11 P.M. or even through the night. Feature editors, columnists, and editorial page editors usually can schedule their day in a more regular fashion, as can editors who work on weekly newspapers. Editors working on hard news, however, may receive an assignment that must be completed, even if work extends well into the next shift.

OUTLOOK

The employment of writers and editors is expected to increase faster than the average rate of all occupations over the next several years, according to the *Occupational Outlook Handbook*. There will be increasing job opportunities for writers and editors in Internet publishing as online publishing and services continue to grow. Advertising and public relations will also provide job opportunities.

The major book and magazine publishers, broadcasting companies, advertising agencies, public relations firms, and the federal government account for the concentration of writers and editors in large cities such as New York, Chicago, Los Angeles, Boston, Philadelphia, San Francisco, and Washington, D.C. Opportunities at small newspapers, corporations, and professional, religious, business, technical, and trade publications can be found throughout the country.

Individuals entering this field should realize that the competition for jobs is extremely keen. Students just out of college, especially, may have difficulty finding employment. Of the thousands who graduate each year with degrees in English, journalism, communications, and the liberal arts, intending to establish a career as writer or editor, many turn to other occupations when they find that applicants far outnumber the job openings available. College students would do well to keep this in mind and prepare for an alternate career in the event they are unable to obtain a position as writer or editor.

FOR MORE INFORMATION

The following organization is an excellent source of information about careers in copyediting. The ACES organizes educational seminars and maintains lists of internships.

American Copy Editors Society (ACES)
38309 Genesee Lake Road
Oconomowoc, WI 53066
Email: administrator@copydesk.org
http://www.copydesk.org

The AAP is an organization of book publishers. Its extensive website is a good place to begin learning about the book business.

Association of American Publishers (AAP)
71 Fifth Avenue
New York, NY 10010
Tel: 212-255-0200
http://www.publishers.org

The Fund provides information about internships and about the newspaper business in general.

Dow Jones Newspaper Fund
PO Box 300
Princeton, NJ 08543-0300
Tel: 609-452-2820
Email: newsfund@wsj.dowjones.com
http://www.dowjones.com/newsfund

The EFA is an organization for freelance editors. Members receive a newsletter and a free listing in their directory.

Editorial Freelancers Association (EFA)
71 West 23rd Street, Suite 1910
New York, NY 10010-4102
Tel: 866-929-5400
Email: info@the-efa.org
http://www.the-efa.org

The MPA is a good source of information about internships.

Magazine Publishers of America (MPA)
919 Third Avenue
New York, NY 10022
Tel: 212-872-3700
http://www.magazine.org

Information on writing and editing careers in the field of communications is available from:

National Association of Science Writers
PO Box 890
Hedgesville, WV 25427
Tel: 304-754-5077
http://www.nasw.org

This organization offers student memberships for those interested in opinion writing.

National Conference of Editorial Writers
3899 North Front Street
Harrisburg, PA 17110
Tel: 717-703-3015
Email: ncew@pa-news.org
http://www.ncew.org

FURTHER READING

The following books provide additional information on career fields mentioned in this book, as well as general advice on searching for a job.

Bly, Robert W. *Careers for Writers and Others Who Have a Way with Words*. 2nd ed. New York: McGraw Hill, 2003.

Feirsen, Robert, and Seth Wietzman. *How to Get the Teaching Job You Want: The Complete Guide for College Graduates, Returning Teachers, and Career Changers*. Sterling, Va.: Stylus, 2000.

Field, Shelly. *Career Opportunities in Advertising and Public Relations*. New York: Facts On File, 2002.

Field, Shelly, and Arthur E. Weintraub. *Career Opportunities in Health Care*. New York: Facts On File, 2002.

Fry, Ronald. *101 Great Answers to the Toughest Interview Questions*. Franklin Lakes, N.J.: Career Press, 2000.

Guide to College Majors: Everything You Need to Know to Choose the Right Major. New York: Princeton Review, 2002.

Johnston, Susan M. *The Career Adventure: Your Guide to Personal Assessment, Career Exploration, and Decision Making*. 3rd ed. Upper Saddle River, N.J.: Prentice Hall, 2001.

Mongan, John, and Noha Suojanen. *Programming Interviews Exposed: Secrets to Landing Your Next Job*. Hoboken, N.J.: Wiley, 2000.

Rosenberg, Arthur D., and David V. Hizer. *The Resume Handbook: How to Write Outstanding Resumes and Cover Letters for Every Situation*. 3rd ed. Adams Media Corp., 1996.

Rubinstein, Ellen. *Scoring a Great Internship (Students Helping Students)*. New York: Natavi Guides, 2002.

Ruhl, Janet. *Computer Job Survival Guide*. Technion Books, 2000.

Tullier, L. Michelle. *Networking for Everyone*. Indianapolis, Ind.: Jist Works, 1998.

Wendleton, Kate, and Wendy Alfus Rothman. *Targeting the Job You Want*. 3rd ed. Franklin Lakes, N.J.: Career Press, 2000.

INDEX

Entries in **bold** indicate major treatment of a topic.